Into New Territory

STUDIES IN AMERICAN THOUGHT AND CULTURE

Into New Territory

American Historians and the Concept of US Imperialism

James G. Morgan

THE UNIVERSITY OF WISCONSIN PRESS

Publication of this volume has been made possible, in part, through support from the **Anonymous Fund of the College of Letters and Sciences** at the University of Wisconsin–Madison.

The University of Wisconsin Press
1930 Monroe Street, 3rd Floor
Madison, Wisconsin 53711-2059
uwpress.wisc.edu

3 Henrietta Street
London WC2E 8LU, England
eurospanbookstore.com

Printed in the United States of America

Library of Congress Cataloging-in-Publication Data

Morgan, James G., author.
Into new territory: American historians and the concept of US imperialism / James G. Morgan.
pages cm — (Studies in American thought and culture)
Includes bibliographical references and index.
ISBN 978-0-299-30044-9 (pbk.: alk. paper)
ISBN 978-0-299-30043-2 (e-book)
1. Williams, William Appleman. 2. United States—Territorial expansion—Historiography.
3. United States—Foreign relations—Historiography.
4. United States—Foreign relations—Philosophy—Historiography.
5. Imperialism—Historiography. 6. Historians—United States. 7. Historians—Wisconsin.
I. Title. II. Series: Studies in American thought and culture.
E183.7.M74 2014
973.072—dc23
2013042703

To my family

Contents

Acknowledgments

Above all I must thank Professor Kendrick Oliver from the University of Southampton. It was Kendrick's undergraduate seminars on the Vietnam War that initially sparked my interest in American history; it was also Kendrick's tutelage, help, and advice through my graduate studies and beyond that made this book possible. I cannot thank him enough.

I would also like to thank Professor Campbell Craig (Aberystwyth University), Dr. Steven Casey (London School of Economics), and Professor Ian Talbot (University of Southampton) for their advice during my PhD work. The late Professor Paul S. Boyer, who was kind enough to meet me and discuss my project when I visited the University of Wisconsin–Madison in 2009, was also a great help.

A number of people also assisted me during my research trip to the University of Wisconsin. I would like to thank the staff at the Steenbock Library Archives, Professor Thomas McCormick, who agreed to be interviewed, and Professor Walter LaFeber, who provided several key insights via e-mail.

Finally, I would like to thank my family for all their support over the last few years—particularly my mother and father, Christobelle and Glyn, my wife, Lindsay, and her parents, Ted and Celia. Lindsay, in particular, has always been a huge support, as well as being a fantastic wife and a brilliant mother to our son, Dylan. Thanks for all your love and patience.

Into New Territory

Introduction

"We cannot end the war by protest or begging. We must begin to take apart the institutions which carry it on. Our fight to stop the war and democratize the university are the same."[1] These emotive words, taken from a protest flyer titled "The War Is Coming Home," were written by members of SDS (Students for a Democratic Society) in November 1968. Distributed at the University of Wisconsin (UW), the year after violent clashes between the police and student antiwar protestors, they became a clarion call for the New Left to fight US imperialism by attacking authority in all its guises. The radicals' immediate objective was to depose UW's administrators, who allegedly collaborated with corporate America by allowing Dow Chemical (the company that manufactured napalm) to recruit on campus, but the ultimate goal was the destruction of the US government; only revolution would enable the impassioned dissidents to "nail the war-makers against the wall" and reform the capitalist structures they believed made imperialism inevitable.[2]

This fervent Marxist rhetoric was typical of the radical New Left during the 1960s. As the Vietnam War escalated, the radical students moved away from the Port Huron Statement (which had initially positioned the New Left as a break from the past) and embraced critiques of US imperialism that were influenced by the Old Left. In particular they venerated scholars like William Appleman Williams, whose conception of US expansion had much in common with the progressive interpretations of the 1930s; they found Williams's critique particularly attractive because it contextualized the Cold War as part of a broader history of US imperialism. According to the New Left, protecting the ostensibly democratic South Vietnamese regime from communism was not US policymakers' primary aim; rather, the Vietnam War was designed to protect the United States' burgeoning empire from revolutionary nationalism in the developing world. The war was not a mistake, the student radicals cried, it was systemic: the culmination of Americans' longstanding penchant for economic expansion and a by-product of the United States' capitalist economy. As a result, the critical concept of US imperialism was disseminated for the very first time. This prompted a fierce intellectual debate that began in classrooms but soon spilled over onto the streets of America.

The assertion that the United States was an imperial nation was as contentious an assertion as it was possible to make. To be imperialist was un-American; to call the United States imperialist was especially un-American. The New Left, however, relished their dissidence. Many radical students and intellectuals came to see themselves as revolutionaries fighting capitalism and imperialism alongside fellow Marxists across the world. In an essay titled "Notes on a Decade Ready for the Dustbin," Carl Oglesby, the former president of SDS, argued that there was no solution short of social revolution for the New Left, because there was "no totalizing philosophy of revolution" other than Marxism-Leninism for student radicals to follow.[3] Having embraced this radical ideology, the radical New Left committed itself to a Marxist-Leninist view of imperialism too. They adopted the same narrow interpretation of US foreign policy as international revolutionaries like the talismanic Che Guevara, who argued that imperialism was an inevitable consequence of capitalism. In doing so they subscribed to economic determinism: the conviction that a country's economic structure determined its development. This was not a sophisticated perspective, nor was it original, but it possessed a powerful logic that complemented the radical New Left's political aspirations.

Because the radicals proposed a Marxist critique of US imperialism at the height of the Cold War, a time when orthodox scholars depicted the United States as a defensively minded nation fighting a malevolent Soviet imperialism, an association between radicalism and the concept of American imperialism became entrenched. Yet two decades after the fall of Saigon, it became increasingly common for orthodox historians to discuss the subject of American empire without prejudice. Whereas historians were once "frightened" of discussing US imperialism because the term was "so politicized and rife with pejorative connotations," there eventually appeared to be "appreciable common ground and at least some agreement on the existence of an American empire" among "historians trying to see the bigger picture." Indeed, at the start of the new millennium, Edward Crapol argued that "coming to terms with American empire and the nation's imperial history" was "the key to understanding the United States' role in the world." Claiming that US imperialism "appears to be the best analytical approach for reinvigorating diplomatic history," Crapol argued it was "fundamental" to the future of the craft.[4]

This dramatic change in attitude was one of the most fascinating and significant metamorphoses in the historiography of US foreign relations. But how did it come about? If critiques of American empire were the preserve of subversive New Left radicals who sought revolution on the streets, what prompted orthodox intellectuals to reappraise the merits of studying US imperialism? The short answer, and the simplest one, is that behind the raucous rhetoric of Marxist revolutionaries lay a far more sophisticated intellectual discussion concerning the origins of American expansion. Over time, as the intellectual conformity of the Cold War relaxed, many orthodox historians accepted that the serious scholars who promoted the concept of US imperialism had a point. The reality, however, is that not all critiques of American empire were persuasive. Only a handful of interpretations that used imperialism as an analytical framework for the study of US foreign relations, rather than as a political stick to beat the establishment, convinced orthodox scholars to change their perspective.

This book is the story of how the most significant, one might say groundbreaking, radical critiques expanded the debate on US imperialism during the Vietnam War and compelled many Americans to reconsider their global role with a greater degree of candor (and a good deal less parochialism). A review of the scholarly literature on American empire, and a rigorous investigation of radical journals, magazines, and protest flyers distributed in Madison (one of the epicenters of the antiwar movement) during the 1960s, reveals two distinct schools of thought on the origins of US imperialism: a Marxist economic determinist strain embodied by the radical New Left and a more nuanced and progressive interpretation promoted by the aforementioned William Appleman Williams and the Wisconsin School revisionists. Consequently, although Williams has frequently been depicted as a "New Left" historian, and distinguished scholars like John Lewis Gaddis and John Patrick Diggins have bracketed the Marxists and progressives together as "allies," the two interpretations were actually quite different; they conflicted radically in a number of ways—divergences that stemmed from a contrasting intellectual approach to domestic reform.[5]

Although Steven Hurst has discussed the methodological differences between Williams and the New Left scholar Gabriel Kolko, much remains to be said about critiques of American empire during the Vietnam War. The following chapters will do this by tracing their origins, exploring their evolution, discussing their strengths and weaknesses, and ultimately tracking the emergence of the critical concept of US imperialism in what was one of the most turbulent, yet fascinating, periods in American history. While student radicals brought the concept of American empire into the public consciousness, New Left critiques were rarely taken seriously by the historical profession (either at the time or thereafter). Their Marxism was objectionable to orthodox scholars: it was foreign, characteristic of the Old Left (so scarcely original), simplistic, and focused exclusively on economic factors. The Wisconsin critique, on the other hand, fused an economic focus with psychological, religious, ideological, and political considerations. It also possessed a distinctly American (or rather, Midwestern) flavor. As a result, the Wisconsin critique was more holistic and ultimately more palatable to orthodox historians and the American public. It was therefore the Wisconsin scholars who took the study of US imperialism into new territory and demonstrated it could be an effective analytical prism through which the origins and manifestations of US foreign policy could be understood.

Whereas the New Left's economic determinism restricted the horizons of their critique, Williams's interpretation was based on the intriguing premise that Americans' historical experience had forged a unique and powerful Weltanschauung (or worldview); this idiosyncratic perspective led US policymakers to interpret and respond to crises in a certain way. The frontier experience, for example, convinced Americans that expansion was both a natural right and the solution to socioeconomic problems (even though this assumption was flawed). The Wisconsin critique therefore fused the ideas of the great progressive historians Frederick Jackson Turner and Charles Beard, who attributed US imperialism to a psychological dependency on expansion and intellectual failure, respectively. Although this was a somewhat abstract thesis, Williams's critique was enhanced substantially by Walter LaFeber and Thomas McCormick, two diplomatic scholars who had been influenced by Williams during their graduate studies at the University of Wisconsin. LaFeber and McCormick made the Wisconsin critique more specific, introduced pragmatic considerations, moderated Williams's polemical language, and added new definitions to describe the complex phenomenon of American expansion.

Williams's personal contribution was so extraordinary because he predated other Cold War revisionists. Although it could be argued that cracks in the Cold War consensus began to appear in the decade before Vietnam when C. Wright Mills and John Kenneth Galbraith critiqued the US socioeconomic structure, orthodox interpretations of US diplomacy remained ubiquitous until Lyndon Johnson escalated the conflict in the mid-1960s. Williams therefore shaped the debate on US imperialism to a significant degree rather than jumping on an existing intellectual bandwagon. He also confronted Americans' traditional antagonism to the very concept of US imperialism unswervingly: because the US constitution was written in the aftermath of a war of independence against what the colonists saw as a corrupt and antiquated British Empire, Williams's work essentially argued that Americans had become what they hated most. Consequently, Williams played an important role in challenging conventional wisdom and, in the words of Walter LaFeber, "opening the possibilities of all kinds of interpretations and analyses" about US foreign policy, which had been "pretty much dammed up" during the first two decades of the Cold War.[6]

In addition, Williams's critique asked orthodox historians to broaden their understanding of what imperialism actually entailed. Until Williams defined economic expansion (in other words, the spread of US exports and capital across the world) as imperial, American historians only equated imperialism with colonialism (the act of conquering territories and governing them directly). Whereas European empires were generally colonial in nature, US policymakers had usually been reluctant to seize colonies, except for a period at the end of the nineteenth century when the United States annexed the Philippines and Hawaii in the aftermath of the Spanish-American War. The orthodox view, therefore, was that the United States could not be considered an imperial nation.

Williams's interpretation was also at odds with important concepts that had shaped American history. For example, his critique questioned the notion of American exceptionalism (the perception that the United States' political and ideological composition made it unique and superior to other nations). When the United States expanded across the Western Hemisphere during the nineteenth century, most Americans regarded this process as a natural right; any suggestion that the annexation of the Philippines and Hawaii had constituted imperialism was therefore rebuffed by orthodox scholars. A sense of Manifest Destiny also pervaded orthodox accounts of America's history. Rather than admitting that the United States had exhibited imperial tendencies like other great powers, US scholars tended to argue that American expansion was a godly duty to civilize other nations and part of a divine plan; the United States was not an empire because "empire was a term of opprobrium" and therefore "a label no self-respecting liberal would wish to claim."[7] Consequently, when intellectuals celebrated "the American Century" after World War II, and the publicist Henry Luce encouraged his countrymen to "accept wholeheartedly" their "duty" to "exert upon the world the full impact of" their "influence," US imperialism was not a concept most Americans recognized.[8] This has remained, to a certain degree, the prevailing attitude in the new millennium. For example, when George W. Bush launched military campaigns in Afghanistan and Iraq, he was at pains to point out that "America has no empire to extend or utopia to establish."[9]

Foreign scholars have found this prevarication hard to accept. For example, the British scholar David Cannadine identified a number of similarities between British imperialism and US expansion during the twentieth century. He cited the way that both nations preached "the unique merits of laissez faire economics and constitutional democracy," which they then "exported overseas so that other places might be similarly improved—not by the imposition of empire but by the gift of freedom." Additionally, Cannadine highlighted the irony that both British and American expansionists believed they were "exceptional" and "providentially blessed"; therefore, he believed that modern US Christians were not so dissimilar to the zealous Protestants of nineteenth-century Great Britain. But the commonalities were not only ideological and religious. Cannadine also claimed that the British and American empires were built on the same foundations of "unrivalled economic superiority" and a "belief in the importance, and sometimes the necessity, of unilateral behavior."[10] However, while the British celebrated "Empire Day" until the late 1950s, no such event has ever appeared on the American calendar. Indeed, considering Americans' aversion to the concept of US imperialism, it would be impossible for one to do so.

The writing of orthodox American diplomatic history during the twentieth century reflected this dilemma. Distinguished diplomatic scholars such as Samuel Flagg Bemis, Julius Pratt, and Ernest May constantly did their best to play down the United States' imperial accomplishments. Instead, they described US economic and territorial expansion in the late nineteenth century as an "aberration," argued American foreign policy was essentially philanthropic, and claimed that the United States became a great power inadvertently and had "greatness thrust upon her."[11] Although these histories did their best to uphold the United States' image as "the prototypical and quintessential anti-colonial nation," Cannadine described this perception as "utter delusion."[12] Instead, he described the United States as "the last authentic western imperial power."[13] During the 1980s an increasing number of (nonradical) American scholars became aware of this evasion too. For example, Amy Kaplan described how the study of US imperialism in the United States had been held back by a "paradigm of denial" that made it difficult for historians to approach the subject objectively.[14]

Of course, Americans' failure to address the concept of American empire in a detached, dispassionate manner was exacerbated by the Cold War. As American intellectuals rallied behind the flag, they characterized the Soviet Union as a malevolent imperial force while American foreign policy was portrayed as an attempt to spread democracy (or an area of freedom) across the world. This was particularly the case during the early 1950s, when McCarthyism made it difficult for dissenting perspectives to emerge. Williams's criticism of US diplomacy, and his portrayal of the United States as an imperial nation in particular, was therefore highly unorthodox and (if one ignores a handful of marginalized Marxist critiques written by American communists) unprecedented within America at the time.

Given this historical context, the emergence of Williams, a scholar who placed America's entire history within the context of economic and territorial expansion, was remarkable. However, when one considers his background and education, Williams's radical disposition was actually quite understandable. Williams was a product of the history department of the University of Wisconsin, which was an oasis of progressivism during the 1950s and managed to resist Cold War intellectual currents to a large extent; it was "just about the only major research university that still valued Charles Beard," a historian whose economic interpretation of American history was fashionable before World War II but became incredibly controversial thereafter.[15] Although it is difficult to demonstrate that Williams's critique was a direct result of his education in Madison, the progressive intellectual heritage of the town and university, plus the unique composition of the UW history department, certainly played a part. For example, Williams's mentor in Madison lectured extensively on US economic expansion. Meanwhile, the history department employed several maverick professors who challenged conventional thinking. Given this context, Madison was definitely one of the places, if not *the* most likely one, for a radical critique of American imperialism to emerge.

Williams outlined his interpretation of US expansion in a series of essays that were published during the 1950s, but it was *The Tragedy of American Diplomacy* (1959) that earned him acclaim from the American left. *Tragedy* was published at a time when intellectual currents showed signs of shifting. The end of McCarthyism, the creation of the National Committee for a Sane Nuclear Policy (SANE) (which campaigned for nuclear disarmament), plus the critical appraisals of US society by Mills and Galbraith led more Americans to question the Cold War liberal consensus. Meanwhile, the emergence of a youth subculture (as expressed in rock music, films, and literature) also attacked the perceived materialism and conservatism of mainstream US society. However, even though outgoing President Dwight Eisenhower warned Americans about the military industrial complex in 1961, few citizens criticized the general thrust of US foreign policy. Indeed, it took what Maurice Isserman and Michael Kazin called "a succession of emotional and political blows," such as the Cuban Missile Crisis and the assassination of President John F. Kennedy, to redirect the "spirit of idealistic commitment away from the official agendas of the liberal establishment."[16] When it came to radical critiques of US imperialism, it was only the escalation of the Vietnam War in 1965 that changed perceptions decisively and enhanced Williams's reputation.

This book will describe the evolution of critiques of imperialism within the context of these momentous contemporary events. As the horrors of the Vietnam War, violence on university campuses, and the social disorder prompted by the civil rights movement caused the radical New Left to seek revolution on the streets, another less conspicuous revolution was taking place: one that ultimately transformed the writing of American diplomatic history. While the New Left imploded and failed to achieve its goals, the Wisconsin scholars actually achieved something tangible: although their interpretation of US imperialism never became as dominant as the orthodox critiques that perpetuated the paradigm of denial, significant aspects of the Wisconsin critique of American empire found their way into post-revisionist interpretations of the Cold War. Furthermore, by demonstrating that empire could be an effective analytical framework for the study of US foreign policy, they ensured that while no consensus on the use of the term "imperialism" has emerged, diplomatic historians have become increasingly prepared to use what Edward Crapol called "the dread word."[17]

When the New Left disintegrated after the Vietnam War, they abandoned the field of US diplomatic history. The Wisconsin scholars, on the other hand, remained firmly committed to the study of American empire. Because they did more than anyone else to transform US imperialism into a valuable field of research—and because their contribution has been recorded somewhat erroneously—their contribution needs to be clarified and illuminated. The Wisconsin scholars were not "New Left" historians.[18] Neither were the progressive and New Left perspectives the same. Their critiques evolved in different directions and they had irreconcilable intellectual approaches. For example, Williams wanted to instigate domestic reform by educating Americans about the need for change; by creating an intellectual enlightenment, he hoped the public would petition the government until meaningful reform could be brought about peacefully and democratically. Although the New Left admired Williams greatly, they repudiated his methods and attacked both the US government and the university. In doing so they charged UW president Fred Harvey Harrington, who tried to deal with radicalism on campus by expelling unruly students, of "repression" and turning the campus from "an armed camp" into a "fully-fledged police state." The hyperbole was extremely revealing. In his previous life as head of UW's history department, Harrington had founded the Wisconsin school of diplomatic history. Indeed, it was Harrington who was Williams's aforementioned mentor in Madison. By accusing such a distinguished progressive scholar of "goose-stepping," the radical New Left had turned upon a pioneer of Cold War revisionism and one of the primary architects of the critical concept of American empire.[19] Is it any wonder, therefore, that the New Left and Wisconsin critiques were different?

1

The Paradigm of Denial

> Empire and imperialism enjoy no easy hospitality in the minds and hearts of Americans.
>
> William Appleman Williams, 1980

The Intellectual Chill

During the 1930s, the social and economic turmoil of the Great Depression created a fertile environment for American dissidents to express radical views. However, the advent of World War II drastically shifted the public mood. Solidarity was the order of the day. The overwhelming majority of academics rallied behind the flag, believing that intellectual cohesion would promote national unity and help the war effort. This in itself was not unusual. After all, academics had also supported government policy during the Great War. But the international environment after World War II was very different from the one that resulted from the conflict three decades earlier—and correspondingly, the intellectual atmosphere was also different. Three decades earlier, the intellectual unity fostered by World War I had quickly dissipated as new insights into the root cause of US intervention emerged. Similarly, many intellectuals became frustrated when leaders failed to meet the high expectations generated by postwar optimism. Continued economic hardship and the findings of the Nye Committee compounded a feeling of disillusionment, thus creating an atmosphere in which dissident expression could thrive. However, in the years following World War II, there was less opportunity to reflect critically on US policies. No sooner had the war ended than another struggle between freedom and oppression developed; Hitler had been defeated, but now the world faced the threat of Soviet communism.

The Cold War seemed to develop quickly—and within five years the United States was fighting another major war overseas, this time in Korea. As a result, the intellectual patriotism that had characterized American scholarship during the war years marched onward into the late 1940s and early 1950s. World War II also produced a change in liberal thought generally. During the New Deal, reform-minded liberals believed that America's greatest socioeconomic problems were "rooted in the structure of modern industrial capitalism." This did not mean that liberalism was anticapitalist, but many liberals believed that US capitalism needed to be reformed to create a fairer and more prosperous nation. However, after World War II, the American economy had changed. Large-scale bureaucracies had consolidated their power, corporations seemed more powerful than ever, consumerism was on the rise, while workers and farmers had organized into interest groups in an attempt to influence public discourse. Alan Brinkley argued that these socioeconomic changes had a profound effect on liberal political and intellectual thought, which became "more coherent, less diverse, and on the whole less challenging to the existing structure of corporate capitalism." As a result, instead of seeking "to restructure the economy," post–World War II liberals wanted to "stabilize it and help it grow." This impulse survived "for at least 20 years" after the defeat of Nazi Germany, thus heralding "the end of reform" and a period of history in which hostility to capitalism and the corporate world was muted.[1] This atmosphere made it difficult for radical sentiment to grow; therefore, few dissident critiques of American imperialism emerged. This was exacerbated by the Treaty of Manila, which granted the Philippines independence in 1946.

This relative paucity of dissent was compounded by the fact that the intellectual left had no obvious champion to turn to. Whereas Charles Beard was known as one of the greatest historians in the United States during the 1930s, his career was in critical condition after 1945. During World War II, Beard's credibility had reached an all-time low as his refusal to acknowledge the genuine security threat posed by Hitler, plus his personal vendetta against Franklin Roosevelt, led even some of his strongest supporters to question his credibility.[2] Beard's calls for the United States to focus on continental matters therefore seemed irrelevant. Instead, leading members of America's critical intelligentsia concentrated on the nation's escalating confrontation with the Soviet Union, which was no longer seen as a brave ally but an intransigent opponent of a new world order based on liberal principles.

The changes in liberal thought, combined with the new international environment, created "a resurgence of popular conservatism" in the United States. Rather than focusing on potential changes to the nation's socioeconomic structure, which might (in the eyes of the left) reverse American expansionism, the new intellectual vogue was "a fervent commitment to internationalism and the struggle against communism, a commitment that at times seemed to overshadow all else."[3] Accompanying this fixation was a fear of "totalitarianism," a term that "served both as the principal theoretical underpinning of scholarly studies of Nazism and communism in the United States, and as foundation of American counter-ideology in the Cold War."[4] By grouping Stalin and Hitler together under the same banner, opinion was quickly mobilized against the Soviet Union. There was even a sense of continuity, as if the fight against communism was simply a continuation of the war against oppressive fascism. Academics even claimed that Nazism and Soviet communism shared one essential characteristic: they both required military expansion to survive. Although this claim was debatable, few had the inclination, or courage, to dissent.

Considering this intellectual climate, it was not surprising that the relativism of Beard and other progressive historians was assaulted. In fact, any historical perspective that was sympathetic to socialism was considered dangerous. Academics were increasingly recruited into government circles to promote a version of events that reaffirmed America's sense of mission. The best examples were Arthur Schlesinger Jr., who worked with the Economic Cooperation Administration and Mutual Security Administration, Gordon Wright, who underwent "a tour of duty" at the National War College, and Ernest May, who served with the Joint Chiefs of Staff. These scholars were briefed to provide "a version of recent history which would justify current policy, linking America's struggles with the Axis and with the Soviet Union as successive stages in one continuous and unavoidable struggle of the Free World against expansionist tendencies." The result was "a step backward for critical distance" from government policy.[5]

The 1950s were therefore a direct contrast to the 1930s. Between the two world wars, Americans became introspective and suspicious of internationalism. But the early Cold War rhetoric created an appetite for US expansion, mainly because most intellectuals believed this was the only way to defeat global communism. Liberal globalists wanted American power to fill the voids left by the waning colonial powers such as Britain and France. The continentalism of Beard was pushed aside as liberals celebrated "the universal desirability of the American way of life."[6] The question of whether other nations actually wanted to adopt US values and embrace American economic expansion was largely ignored; consequently, there was never a debate about whether internationalism could be seen as a form of imperialism. Looking back, Thomas McCormick lamented how those who disagreed with the "narrow definition of imperialism," which equated Soviet interference in Eastern Europe as imperialism (while US internationalism was interpreted as philanthropic), were seen as "treasonous and unpatriotic."[7]

Radicalism within the historical profession as a whole was restrained during the early years of the Cold War. This was illustrated by the preeminence of the consensus historians: a group that included the likes of Richard Hofstadter, Louis Hartz, and Daniel Boorstin. The consensus historians argued that the progressives had been wrong to emphasize class conflict in US history. In contrast, they claimed that America's development "was not all cataclysmic change, abrupt, angry," and "cacophonous." Instead, they argued that "Americans had disagreed with each other, of course, but not irreconcilably or over the basic issues of property and political democracy."[8] Consensus history therefore emphasized America's "continuity and stability"—an approach that ultimately reasserted US exceptionalism.[9] This harmonious and somewhat romanticized view of the past perpetuated the paradigm of denial regarding US imperialism. Furthermore, all interpretations that emphasized economics in general were attacked. This is because, as Walter LaFeber might say, "context shapes the historian's view." Whereas the 1930s were a time of considerable economic hardship, the 1950s witnessed a period of prosperity in the United States; therefore, economics seemed inconsequential during "the good times."[10]

Progressive histories (with their broad interpretation of the nation's past) became associated with Marx during this period. Indeed, many observers "actually confused Beard's work with Marxism."[11] Scholars such as Hartz and Boorstin discredited progressive texts because they hoped to promote an ideological conservatism that might unite the nation and win the Cold War. The result was a genre of history that portrayed "objectivity" as "the official version of events." Reflecting on the intellectual atmosphere of the 1950s in *The Progressive Historians* (1968), Richard Hofstadter admitted that the new "consensus history" that emerged during this period was guilty of homogenizing American history. Although he argued that this "moment of conservative retrospect" was caused by a revulsion to the horrors of World War II (which convinced many Americans that the United States was the last great hope for mankind), he was not afraid to highlight the shortcomings of orthodox scholarship at this time. However, subsequent observers went further in their criticism. For example, while Hofstadter was happy with the term "consensus" history, Peter Novick, whose book *That Noble Dream* has done so much to trace the inherent biases of American scholarship, had another name for it: "counter-progressive" scholarship.[12]

The homogenizing histories of the late 1940s and early 1950s were entrenched by McCarthyism—the obsessive fear of communism that permeated American national life. Ellen Schrecker's *Many are the Crimes*, which explores the various manifestations of anticommunism during the period, described how over one hundred teachers lost their jobs as a direct or indirect result of Senator Joseph McCarthy's witch hunts. This included three scholars at the University of Washington, who were fired after the Canwell Committee accused them of disseminating procommunist ideas in 1953. Although academic freedom was officially supported during this time, Schrecker observed how "previously accepted modes of analysis" such as Marxism "were marginalized," while "whole lines of inquiry simply disappeared."[13] Much of this occurred because of self-censorship. Many scholars suppressed their leftist views for fear of being investigated by the House Un-American Activities Committee (HCUA), which had the power to damage a professor's reputation.

Schrecker contended that when academics were fired, faculty members usually "knew" the accused "were not sabotaging their laboratories or subverting their students," but they "had to go" because their reputations had been "contaminated by communism."[14] Therefore, she argued that the academy fully collaborated with the witch hunts initiated by the right. This perspective is given credence by a close reading of *The Rights and Responsibilities of Universities and Their Faculties*, the document adopted by the Association of American Universities in March 1953. This booklet, which was supposed to demonstrate the integrity of American universities and their commitment to preserving academic freedom, arguably did the opposite. The document demanded that universities "exercise the utmost wisdom in their appointments and promotions" and insisted that university employees "must be diligent and loyal in citizenship" and maintain "integrity and independence" at all times. Any lecturer advocating "communistic practice" or becoming "a propagandist" for the ideology of Russia and its satellites forfeited not only "university support" but also his or her very "membership of the university." Consequently, rather than committing the academy to the exploration of all intellectual vogues, the Association of American Universities dodged the issue of making "progress towards the truth" and simply stressed that "academic freedom" was "not a shield to those who break the law" (a reference to the illegality of membership in communist organizations at the time).[15] In doing so they missed the opportunity to encourage open discussion of communist ideas, which could have been discredited through intellectual argument. Although scholars who wanted to discuss the negative effects of American foreign policy (including the possible existence of US imperialism) were not exclusively communists, American universities allowed those who offered alternative critiques of US diplomacy to become marginalized.

Thankfully, however, dissent was not totally extinguished after World War II. Jonathan Bell has argued that although the Cold War robbed liberals of the "freedom to experiment with left wing ideas without fear" of being "associated with totalitarianism," the general trend toward conservatism actually disguised "a brief flowering of a social democratic impulse." Bell pointed to the initial success of former Vice President Henry Wallace, who received strong backing from former New Deal stalwarts during the early stages of his presidential campaign in 1948. Echoing Beard, Wallace made a link between domestic and foreign policies, claiming that cooperation with the USSR would help to facilitate left-wing social policies at home. To Wallace's supporters, "a Cold War abroad meant the end of the promise of the New Deal at home and the rehabilitation of the right in America."[16]

Furthermore, although the academy itself seemed reluctant to protect the rights of suspected communists, the curtailment of academic freedom did receive some criticism. For example, an article in the *New Yorker* in February 1949 argued that there was "no question" that colleges and universities were "under pressure from alumni and trustees to clean house" and "provide dynamic instruction in the American way of life." The article described how professors were adjusting "their neckties a little more conservatively" and qualifying "their irregular remarks with a bit more care." The author was unequivocal that some of the firings "resembled a political purge"—something that was counterproductive and showed "little real faith in liberty." Instead his article argued that a university could best "demonstrate freedom" by "not closing its doors to antithetical ideas."[17]

The *New York Times* also occasionally gave those who opposed the firing of university professors a voice. In an article titled "Should Communists Be Allowed to Teach?," Professor Alexander Meiklejohn claimed that academic freedom was more important than prohibiting communist ideas from universities. He argued that banning communists from teaching actually "advanced the cause" the authorities were "seeking to hold back" and reminded Americans that when "the advocates of freedom and the advocates of suppression meet in fair and unabridged discussion, freedom will win." Furthermore, Meiklejohn highlighted the hypocrisy of banning discussion of leftist ideology, claiming that those who issued bans "have gone over to the enemy" because "they are not willing to give a fair and equal hearing to those who disagree with us."[18]

Unfortunately for the left, however, the pleas of Meiklejohn were largely ignored. Academics associated with the left continued to live in fear, leading the historian Broadus Mitchell to complain that congressional investigation into academics' backgrounds amounted to "a war against the colleges." Mitchell insisted that no matter how "stigmatized" some "beliefs and associations" had become, they "must be given asylum."[19] Meanwhile, Alan Barth complained in the *Nation*, a flagship periodical of the left, that the activities of HCUA "menaced academic freedom in the most direct and destructive way." Barth contended that the right was essentially seeking to make the church and universities servants of the state, an idea he claimed was actually communist. Instead he insisted that universities must serve as "checks upon the state" and claimed that the academic "purges" threatened "the whole of human freedom."[20]

Arguably the loudest dissident voice during this period was the radical journalist I. F. Stone, who had edited the *Nation* between 1940 and 1946 before working for a series of newspapers including the *New York Star* and the *Daily Compass*. Stone used these publications to express his own dismay about the erosion of academic freedom in the United States. He condemned the sacking of professors on ideological grounds and claimed that HCUA investigations had created an American equivalent of the "Spanish inquisition."[21] Stone also lambasted US policymakers' approach to the Cold War, and criticized the way the mainstream media reported the subject. His usual strategy was to gather official documents and relay information he thought might embarrass the government. In doing so, he often exposed contradictions in US foreign policy and revealed when the government was being economical with the truth.

Stone's quirky political analysis and meticulous dissection of the news enabled him to become America's leading radical journalist during the early Cold War period. After the collapse of the *Daily Compass* in 1952, he established his own publication titled *I. F. Stone's Weekly*, which first appeared in January the following year. Stone used his new platform to censure policymakers and keep alive the tradition of American radicalism that the Cold War had threatened to eliminate. His book *The Hidden History of the Korean War* (1952) demonstrated this approach and confirmed his penchant for discrediting those in authority. For example, the book depicted the decorated General Douglas MacArthur as a warmonger who craved a wider war against China.

However, Stone neither formulated a critique of US imperialism nor used empire as a conceptual framework for the study of American foreign policy. In fact, the intellectual atmosphere of the early Cold War period nearly suffocated debate surrounding American empire altogether. Although the existence of US imperialism had been debated during the 1930s, only a handful of left-leaning publications kept the study of American empire alive during the early 1950s. The best known of these was *Monthly Review*, a Marxist journal edited by Leo Huberman and Paul Sweezy. Many of *Monthly Review*'s writers were openly communist; therefore, they employed Marxist methodology to interpret international events (including the contention that imperialism was an inevitable by-product of capitalism). However, the journal failed to make much of an impression on the academic community or the public at large. Its circulation hovered around the eighty-five hundred mark, a meager readership that reflected the hostility most Americans felt toward Marxism.

The ideological transformation of *Partisan Review* is a good example of how Marxist theories became marginalized during the Cold War. Originally published as a communist publication during the mid-1930s, the journal changed its political persuasion after World War II as news of Stalin's atrocities began to reach American shores. Robert Tomes, whose book *Apocalypse Then* charted intellectual trends between 1954 and 1975, has therefore argued that "the intellectual march to the right was well underway before Senator McCarthy began his zealous prosecutions." Radicals who spoke out against US foreign policy became extremely rare. Even old communists such as James Burnham and Sidney Hook began to preach "militant anticommunism."[22] Meanwhile, the CIA began to supply liberal publications with financial aid to promote official versions of the truth.

However, not all Americans enjoyed living in a society that frowned upon dissent. The ideological rigidity of the early Cold War period fostered a cultural sterility and materialism that irked some citizens. Consequently, although the nation appeared to be mobilized for an anticommunist crusade, tensions bubbled beneath the surface. Dissatisfaction was particularly prevalent among young people. This was reflected by the popularity of rock and roll, which provided a welcome alternative to the manufactured songs that dominated the music industry. Elvis Presley, who defied social norms by using sex appeal to sell records, and film stars like the rebellious James Dean and the brooding Marlon Brando, demonstrated that some young Americans yearned to be free from the social constraints of the day. Indeed, the money generated by films such as *The Wild One* (1953) and *Rebel without a Cause* (1955) illustrated that nonconformity ultimately became a commodity.

The existence of the Beats, who are frequently seen as forerunners to the 1960s counterculture, also demonstrated how the Cold War consensus was not all-pervasive. Emanating from New York and then San Francisco, the Beats rejected cultural norms entirely: they rejected corporate materialism, experimented with drugs, explored their sexuality, and discovered alternative religions. The Beats' goal was to redefine US values and embrace a new culture that shunned soulless careers in corporate America. As a result, they offered young people "an exotic alternative to the buttoned-downed world around them." By the late 1950s, social outcasts and the intellectually curious began to gather in pockets in American cities. Significantly, college towns and campus cafeterias also developed "their own mini-versions of North Beach or Greenwich Village."[23] Although few Americans took these people seriously (and they played no real political role), many of these disaffected youths became the political agitators, civil rights activists, and antiwar protestors of the 1960s.

Beat generation writers also played a significant role in the broader cultural insurgency that gradually eroded the Cold War consensus. Jack Kerouac's *On the Road* (1957) and William S. Burroughs's *Naked Lunch* (1959) became cult literary hits alongside other nonconformist classics such as Normal Mailer's *The White Negro* (1959). Meanwhile, some comics and magazines also began to adopt a more subversive attitude. The former portrayed distasteful images of exaggerated violence, while *Mad Magazine* moved into the political world by poking fun at what Mark Lytle called "the pomposity and self-serving rhetoric of authority." Although comics, films, magazines, and rock music had little direct effect on intellectual currents in the United States, they demonstrated that the Cold War consensus was not impregnable. For example, *On the Road* and *Naked Lunch* became the focus of obscenity trials that ultimately liberalized publishing laws in America. Furthermore, this cultural radicalism suggested that dissent in the early Cold War period was actually "widespread but muted."[24]

More significant to the debate on US imperialism, however, was the increasing propensity for intellectuals in the mid to late 1950s to question both America's socioeconomic structure and the hard line taken against the Soviet Union. The 1954 Army-McCarthy hearings demonstrated to liberal Americans that the anticommunist witch hunts were vacuous and hysterical. The notion that the government was infested with communist spies therefore lost credibility. Meanwhile, the prominent journalist Walter Lippmann remained an outspoken critic of containment and reiterated his argument that the United States should respect the Soviet Union's desire for a security zone in Eastern Europe. Radical publications also began to emerge. For example, a group of New York intellectuals including Irving Howe founded the radical journal *Dissent*. Although *Dissent* was critical of the CPUSA (the American Communist Party) and its support for Stalin, the publication opposed McCarthyism, criticized cultural conformity, critiqued contemporary politics, and promoted democratic socialist values.

New ideas, which seemed radical at the time, also began to flourish in academic circles. Kenneth Stampp's *The Peculiar Institution* (1956) revolutionized the study of slavery in the United States. Whereas orthodox histories had depicted slavery as a benign system, Stampp highlighted how African Americans resented slavery and regarded it as oppressive. Intellectuals also began to undermine the Cold War consensus by critiquing the hierarchies of American power. The emergence of the radical sociologist C. Wright Mills, whose influential book *The Power Elite* (1956) argued that power lay in the hands of an interconnected minority from the political, military, and corporate worlds, was one such example. *The Power Elite* bemoaned the existence of privileged individuals who moved seamlessly from corporate America and the military into government and back again. Mills believed members of this elite engineered forays into the political world in order to manipulate policy and satisfy the aspirations of their respective groups. Because the elite transcended party politics, Mills argued that ordinary citizens were essentially excluded from American democracy.

The economist John Kenneth Galbraith also provided a powerful critique of America's socioeconomic landscape. In his seminal book *The Affluent Society* (1958), Galbraith argued that while the United States was enjoying a period of economic growth, the prospect of perpetual prosperity was uncertain. He claimed that the personal fortunes accrued by wealthy Americans were not being reinvested in society; consequently, projects to improve domestic infrastructure and public services remained underfunded. Galbraith attacked corporate America for concentrating almost exclusively on increasing production rather than technological innovation. He also criticized the proliferation of nuclear weapons; this tapped into public fears over the Soviet Union's successful test of the first intercontinental ballistic missile in 1957. Concerns about the nuclear arms race were reflected by the formation of SANE, a political group that attracted pacifists and old leftists from the New Deal era. Although membership of SANE remained small during the 1950s, its very existence showed that some Americans were dissatisfied with government policy and anxious about the future.

Aberrations and Absentmindedness

Although intellectuals had started to critique America's socioeconomic structure in the late 1950s, the concept of American empire itself remained taboo. Other than Paul Sweezy, whose Marxist critique of US imperialism blamed state monopoly capitalism for America's postwar expansion, American intellectuals prudently steered clear of the subject. This was a contrast to international trends, where the various manifestations of economic imperialism were discussed freely. For example, the British scholars John Gallagher and Ronald Robinson argued in "The Imperialism of Free Trade" (which was published in *The Economic History Review* in 1953) that colonial empires were no longer fashionable because free trade secured economic benefits without the need for formal political arrangements; this was a perspective William Appleman Williams shared.

Significantly, however, the work of foreign scholars in the 1950s had little impact on the writing of American diplomatic history within the United States. Instead, orthodox critiques of US expansion remained narrow, insular, and defensive in nature; in fact, they adhered to the twin concepts of US exceptionalism and Manifest Destiny, which justified expansionism and interference in other nations' affairs. Seymour Martin Lipset, the foremost expert on US exceptionalism, has argued that Americans see themselves as "the New Israel" and a shining example to mankind. Lipset also claimed that Americans are "utopian moralists, who pressed hard to institutionalize virtue," and "view social and political dramas" as "battles between God and the devil."[25] Orthodox critiques of US imperialism before the Vietnam War substantiated this view. Indeed, discussions of American expansionism were usually placed within broader histories that stressed the benevolence of US foreign policy and emphasized the civilizing effects of American power. When topics like the Spanish-American War were discussed (or America's annexation of Pacific islands in the late nineteenth century) they were treated as footnotes in the nation's history; either that or they were portrayed as short lived and out of rhythm with the philanthropic course of American history (as represented in recent times by the Atlantic Charter and the Good Neighbor Policy).

The intellectual atmosphere created by the Cold War entrenched this outlook. Orthodox historians rallied against the Soviet Union and claimed that empire was "them, not us."[26] The announcement of the Truman Doctrine in 1947, which declared the United States' desire to "assist free peoples to work out their own destinies in their own way," ingrained Americans' altruistic self-image.[27] Imperialism, which violated self-determination and exploited weaker nations, was obviously incompatible with the United States' philanthropic aspirations; consequently, the overwhelming majority of intellectuals as well as the American public remained hostile to the very concept of US imperialism—a hostility that, in the words of David Cannadine (the expert on British imperialism), had been a constant theme in US political and popular discourse. Cannadine believed that "American presidents behave like imperialists" but "never admit to being imperialists"; as a result Americans were unable to escape the following logic: "Empire, which others do, is 'bad,' but because America doesn't 'do' empire, it is therefore 'good'; and because it is 'good,' it cannot admit to being imperial"; therefore a self-perpetuating cycle of denial was established that characterized orthodox accounts of US expansion.[28]

Before the Vietnam War, histories that ingrained this paradigm of denial were ubiquitous. These orthodox interpretations emulated Samuel Flagg Bemis's influential book *A Diplomatic History of the United States* (1936), which did its utmost to describe America's imperial turn at the end of the nineteenth century in benign terms (there was certainly no suggestion, for example, that the Spanish-American War was part of a broader expansionist pattern). During the 1890s, the United States annexed Hawaii, launched the aforementioned war against Spain over the future of Cuba, and wrestled the Philippines from Spanish control; the Philippines were annexed as a result, while a loose protectorate was established over the Cubans. By the end of the century, the United States had expanded to its western continental borders and established an insular empire that embraced not only Hawaii and the Philippines but also Wake, Guam, and the islands that became known as American Samoa. Realizing he could not ignore these events, Bemis attempted to explain them away as somewhat inconsequential. His solution was to call this pivotal period in American diplomatic history—a time when the United States announced itself as a global power—a "great national aberration."[29]

A Diplomatic History of the United States claimed that US policymakers conquered the Philippines because of a unique set of circumstances that came together by accident. Bemis argued that US policymakers instigated the Spanish-American War without considering the fate of indigenous populations; therefore, the Philippines were annexed as an afterthought, because Americans simply did not know what else to do with the Filipinos after defeating Spain. Furthermore, Bemis contended that the Democrats only voted to annex the islands because it was the fastest way to settle the matter; this enabled the Democratic leader, William Jennings Bryan, to shift the political agenda to his favorite issue (the future of free silver) as soon as possible. Consequently, US imperialism after the Spanish-American War could be attributed to a combination of "adolescent irresponsibility" and chance.[30] According to Bemis, Americans were not even aware of the economic benefits of territorial expansion until after the conflict, so no imperial master plan could have existed.

The Cold War and McCarthyism exacerbated the need for historians to handle this imperial turn with delicacy. With the Korean War still fresh in the public's mind, Julius Pratt's *A History of United States Foreign Policy* (1955) addressed the issue of US expansion, but in a manner that praised its benevolence and philanthropic instincts. Similarly, Pratt's *America's Colonial Experiment: How the United States Gained, Governed, and in Part Gave Away a Colonial Empire* (1950) claimed that imperialist sentiment in America was only temporarily ascendant for a short period of time (an argument that supported Bemis's aberration theory). He denied that the United States had been consistently expansionist throughout its history and instead argued that American imperialism had been characterized by "haphazard and occasionally inconsistent implementation." Furthermore, in a passage that reaffirmed US exceptionalism, Pratt asserted that US foreign policy had always been "aimed steadily at the material and educational advancement of the colonial peoples and the development of their capacity for self-government." Therefore, the nation's colonial aberration was not only short lived but also "benevolent" and "accepted by those living under it."[31] This line of argument seemed easier to believe after the Philippines were granted independence in 1946.

Meanwhile, Robert Osgood, another prominent historian of the 1950s, argued that while the United States had acted in "an imperial way" during the nineteenth century, the nation's empire building was caused by a temporary surge of nationalism, self-assertiveness, humanitarianism, and Manifest Destiny. He concluded in *Ideas and Self-Interest in America's Foreign Relations* (1953) that "the American people arrived at the centre of the stage of world politics by entering a war to free Cuba and vindicate national honor, fighting a victorious crusade for Manifest Destiny and the American Mission, acquiring a far-flung empire and then forgetting about it."[32] Once again, this interpretation of the 1890s stressed the benevolence of American intentions abroad while ignoring the negative aspects of US imperialism, such as the suppression of the Filipino insurrection that claimed thousands of lives.

Osgood's work was a typical example of orthodox US diplomatic history during the early Cold War period. The book argued that once the 1890s had finished, Americans once again retreated into isolationism, believing that "the imperial responsibilities of ruling over an alien people seemed incompatible with traditional isolationist self-interest and contrary to the democratic and humanitarian values for which they had entered the war." Once this became apparent, Americans developed a sense of shame for their country's actions, bemoaning that her "better instincts had fallen prey to sheer power lust" and good intentions gone awry. Osgood therefore described the late 1890s as "a travesty upon the national mission" and claimed that utopians once again became ascendant over imperialists at the dawn of the American century.[33]

Although Osgood's interpretation may seem old-fashioned today, it was typical of the 1950s. The nation's most visible historians reassured their readers that American foreign policy was guided by a sense of moral mission, and that any episode when the United States appeared to act in self-interest was an aberration. For example, in his intriguing essay "Cuba, the Philippines, and Manifest Destiny" (1952), Richard Hofstadter attributed US expansion to a transitory "psychic crisis" created by the frustrations of economic depression and the end of the domestic frontier.[34] The author claimed that an elite group of imperialist politicians led by Theodore Roosevelt and Henry Cabot Lodge were able to manipulate the public into supporting an imperial war against Spain thanks to a short-lived but irresistible elixir of public emotions. Hofstadter believed that genuine humanitarian concern for the people of Cuba fused with a jingoistic aggression caused by anxiety about the future. The result was a public craving for war that President McKinley found impossible to ignore. Hofstadter denied that it was the lobbying of business or commercial interests that prompted US intervention in Cuba but, rather, this unique set of psychological conditions. Once Americans had vented these frustrations on the Spanish, the desire for war and overseas expansion apparently abated, thus creating an anti-imperialist backlash.

The Challenge to Orthodoxy

The critiques of Bemis, Osgood, Pratt, and Hofstadter, parochial as they were, nourished the prevailing paradigm of US imperialism. These scholars were prepared to entertain all manner of overly simplistic theories (it was all down to chance) or somewhat convoluted explanations (it was a fleeting psychic crisis) rather than contemplate the potential role played by economic and material interests. However, not all American scholars were prepared to accept orthodox hypotheses. Immersed in the complex intellectual environment of the time was William Appleman Williams, a young scholar who thought differently. Williams was a former naval officer who received his PhD from the University of Wisconsin at the beginning of the 1950s. Because Williams was neither a prominent journalist like Lippmann nor an award-winning writer such as Mailer, few Americans outside the academic community knew his name. Yet the Wisconsin scholar eventually became one of the most influential American diplomatic historians of his era. Those who knew Williams described him as "an individualist, who was not afraid to state his opinions." Although this intransigence sometimes irked his colleagues, "he was loved by many people because of his frankness and openness." However, of his many qualities, Williams will be best remembered as an inspiration—not only to those he taught and those who worked alongside him but to Cold War revisionism in general. His friend and colleague at Madison, Harvey Goldberg, once admitted, "I used to rummage around Bill's wastebasket to find ideas."[35]

Williams became a radical figure in the late 1950s because he was the first serious American diplomatic scholar to challenge orthodox histories of the late nineteenth century. While he accepted that "the classical ideas about American foreign policy are not all wrong," since the United States had been "anti-imperialist in some respects at different times" and came to "active involvement in international affairs by degrees," he emphasized how Americans considered expansion "essential to mitigate economic clashes by providing an empire for exploitation." He therefore argued that Americans adopted an expansionist foreign policy during the 1890s to "solve existing troubles" and prevent future economic "difficulties."[36] In Williams's eyes, the Spanish-American War was anything but absentminded or an aberration: a consensus existed on the need to expand, with the only real debate being whether colonialism was the best way to achieve this. Williams argued that US policymakers eventually decided to reject colonialism; instead, they attempted to obtain economic benefits while avoiding the burdensome responsibilities of formal government. They executed this plan by promoting the Open Door Policy (which sought to eliminate international trade barriers) across the world; the hope was that the removal of protectionist tariffs would enable powerful American corporations to dominate international markets.

Williams argued that the Open Door became the priority of US statesmen throughout the twentieth century; consequently US economic expansion was at the heart of American plans for the post-1945 world. This was obviously a highly controversial contention because it equated American anticommunism in the Cold War with a broader attempt to actively expand US global trade. Williams argued that at the end of World War II, American policymakers transformed the Open Door from "a utopian idea into an ideology" that they persuaded other nations to accept. He argued that this was an "imperial" approach that only succeeded in spurning on "a dynamic opposition" (of which the Soviet Union was the most obvious example). Furthermore, Williams claimed that this "American attitude left the Russians with but one option: if they did not accept American proposals, they were confronted by American hostility." Therefore, the Wisconsin scholar contended that the United States was largely responsible for causing the Cold War; because US policymakers were preoccupied with facilitating US economic expansion and extending the Open Door to Eastern Europe, they ignored "the Soviet Union's traditional and philosophical fears of foreign and capitalist antagonisms."[37]

Williams argued that American fears of Soviet hostility were misplaced—not least because Russia's sacrifices during World War II had rendered the nation weak and unwilling to fight the west. According to Williams, Stalin merely wanted to "establish a basic security perimeter in Europe, the Middle East, and Asia" and to "induce other peoples to accept communism by the force of persuasiveness and example" rather than by military might. However, because American policymakers assumed their vision was benevolent, and believed that "those who did not recognize and accept that fact were not only wrong" but "incapable of thinking correctly," the United States pressed ahead with a containment strategy that ultimately divided the world into two competing spheres.[38] Of course, all of this was a direct contradiction to orthodox interpretations of the Cold War, which contrasted American humanitarianism with Stalin's intransigence and blamed Soviet expansion in East Europe for causing international tensions.[39]

Williams believed that by promoting the Open Door, opposing spheres of interest, and combating alternative economic models, American policymakers created "an empire of economics, ideology, and bases." Although he claimed that many countries had initially "welcomed" this empire as "a policy of assistance and friendship with no strings of absentee ownership attached," they eventually sensed that "its optimum goal was to institutionalize American expansion." Williams predicted that these nations would ultimately rebel against what he described as "the subordination of their own cultural, political, and economic life"; this was a process he believed had already begun. Instead of facilitating economic expansion, Williams beseeched US policymakers to promote "an open door for revolutions," in which America would allow nations "to achieve their own aspirations in their own way." Williams argued that because US policymakers saw indigenous revolutions as part of a Soviet inspired conspiracy, they felt compelled to intervene militarily overseas to prevent communism from consuming nations that would otherwise, in American eyes, be free. Williams explicitly warned against such "crusades to save others" lest the United States become bogged down in "the many as yet unknown revolutions" that would doubtless appear as the developing world freed itself from European colonialism.[40] Of course, when the United States became embroiled in what appeared to be a civil war in Vietnam, Williams's critique seemed vindicated in the eyes of the left.

Not surprisingly, however, orthodox critics strongly criticized Williams's work. For example his first book, *American-Russian Relations, 1781–1947* (1952), was criticized by O. T. Barck Jr. in the *American Historical Review* for being "decidedly uneven" and "influenced by sources which present primarily one side of the picture."[41] The reaction to Williams's third book, *The Contours of American History* (1961), was so mixed that Keith Berwick claimed "seldom has a work of serious history aroused so much antagonism."[42] Consequently, although American intellectuals had begun to challenge the Cold War consensus during the 1950s, Williams's interpretation was still far too radical for most tastes. Indeed, those close to him feared that his ideas might be too controversial. For example, Fred Harvey Harrington, his mentor at the University of Wisconsin, initially advised Williams not to publish his seminal work *The Tragedy of American*

Diplomacy (1959) in case it ruined the young scholar's reputation. Harrington was especially concerned about his protégé because the only American historians who challenged orthodox accounts of US foreign relations at the time were Marxists such as Paul Sweezy, who had been subpoenaed because of his alleged connections to communists and cited for contempt of court.[43]

Although Williams was not strictly a Marxist, his admiration for Charles Beard was highly unorthodox. After World War II, when the Cold War penetrated the academic community, progressive methodology was frowned upon because its broad approach had parallels to Marxism (which also emphasized broad social changes). Consequently, any book that promoted a general economic or social view of history, and placed all events within the context, was considered to be ideologically dangerous. Williams's predicament was not helped by critics misreading his work. In his review of *Tragedy* in *Political Science Quarterly*, James P. Warburg accused the book of promoting "economic determinism."[44] It was not long before HCUA became suspicious of his activities and requested the unpublished manuscript of *Contours*. While Williams escaped with his job intact (and a subpoena was eventually dropped), the Internal Revenue Service harassed the Wisconsin scholar over his taxes, and he remained an intellectual pariah in the eyes of orthodox contemporaries. Yet none of this deterred him. While the majority of liberal and conservative scholars rallied behind the flag, Williams's opposition to American foreign policy was unwavering; he chose instead "to walk alone."[45]

It was only in the 1960s, when the power of HCUA had diminished and cultural, political, and academic dissent became more widespread, that Williams found more allies in the history profession. This was the decade when radical critiques of US imperialism finally became more prevalent—thus facilitating an energetic assault on the paradigm of denial. Although Williams had developed his critical concept of American empire during the 1950s, his audience was initially limited. Furthermore, while other dissidents like C. Wright Mills had written about foreign policy as well as socioeconomic structures, they had failed to articulate a holistic critique of US imperialism. It was only a series of traumatic events during the early 1960s that changed matters—and of course, this process was accelerated in the middle of the decade by the Vietnam War, which sparked critical appraisals of US foreign policy in general.

It was during these early years of the 1960s that several graduate students who had befriended Williams at the University of Wisconsin launched their careers. Many of these were instrumental in forming the left-leaning journal *Studies on the Left*, which published its first issue in Madison in 1959 (the same year *Tragedy* was published). Like Williams, the original editors of *Studies* wanted to educate Americans about the need for reform, so that change could occur organically and democratically. Several UW students also embraced Williams's critique of US imperialism. The best examples were Walter LaFeber, Thomas McCormick, and Lloyd Gardner, the scholars who, alongside Williams, became known collectively as the Wisconsin School revisionists. Benefiting from time spent with Williams socially (which often included dinner, followed by alcohol-fueled debates into the early hours), the Wisconsin Scholars adhered to the central premise of Williams's critique but conducted additional research and added their own insights—modifying and enhancing the thesis set out in *Tragedy*.

Unlike Williams, LaFeber, McCormick, and Gardner began their careers at a time when social, political, and intellectual radicalism was finally gathering some momentum. Consequently, although Williams's friends were pioneers in their field—and they helped to inspire subsequent radicals to use imperialism as a conceptual framework for the study of American foreign policy—their work was representative of the gradual increase in dissent within the United States in general. Even though political activism climaxed during the second half of the 1960s, social discontent became widespread before Lyndon Johnson sent combat units to Vietnam. The focus of this dissent was undoubtedly the civil rights movement. It was in 1960, after the sit-ins in Greensboro, North Carolina, that the Student Nonviolent Coordinating Committee (SNCC) was formed. Later that year, Students for a Democratic Society (SDS) came into existence (although its iconic Port Huron Statement was not published until 1962). Indeed, it was this discontent over civil rights that led to the iconic August 1963 march on Washington, in which Martin Luther King Jr. delivered his famous "I Have a Dream" speech to over two hundred thousand Americans.[46]

This growing penchant for political activism was particularly rife on university campuses. In May 1960 five thousand students at Berkeley jeered "Sieg heil" as police prevented a sit-in designed to disrupt HCUA investigations in San Francisco's Bay Area. Berkeley was a hotbed of dissent at the time because it was more racially diverse than other campuses; therefore, the students were more sensitive to the civil rights struggle. Alongside radicals at the University of Wisconsin (Madison) and the SDS activists at Harvard and Brandeis, Berkeley became a beacon of dissent in the early to mid-1960s. This was highlighted by the Free Speech Movement that emerged in the middle of the decade. Mark Lytle has argued that the protest against HCUA, plus a subsequent protest when Malcolm X was banned from visiting the Berkeley campus, demonstrated that "the Cold War consensus was losing some of its power to silence."[47]

The cultural insurgency that had begun in the late 1950s also continued at a pace. Books such as Joseph Heller's *Catch-22* (1961), in which the protagonist escapes military service, "stripped the official voices of the nation of their authority" and revealed "the absurdities and arbitrariness" of power in the United States.[48] Meanwhile, Stanley Kubrick's film *Dr. Strangelove* (1964) used black humor to poke fun at the military while conveying the considerable unease many Americans felt about the nuclear arms race. These fears had been crystallized by the Cuban Missile Crisis of October 1962, which seemingly took the world to the very edge of catastrophe. In the aftermath of the crisis, many citizens questioned whether the rivalry with the Soviet Union was in the nation's (and indeed the world's) best interests.

This political and cultural radicalism was complemented by an increasing intellectual dissidence. For example, the *New York Review of Books* (first published in 1963) "energized intellectuals" and helped to create "a mood of insurgency" in New York and the Northeast.[49] Meanwhile, the *Village Voice* expanded its circulation and brought its critique of politics and current affairs to a broader audience. Consequently, the transformation of the United States from a nation obsessed with the Cold War crusade, where consensus reigned and academic freedom was reined in, to a country where the intelligentsia was prepared to probe, criticize, and question authority accelerated rapidly. Indeed, one could argue that the very concept of change itself became appealing during the early 1960s. This was demonstrated by the presidential election of 1961, in which the young, energetic, and Catholic John F. Kennedy defeated Richard Nixon (a politician who embodied traditional white, Protestant America). Many citizens interpreted Kennedy's victory as a significant break with the past; it also gave hope to the civil rights movement. Meanwhile, Kennedy's creation of the Peace Corps, which became "a great incubator of political radicals," suggested that US foreign policy might change for the better too. When Kennedy was assassinated, his death "eroded faith in traditional politics" and "marked a rite of passage into a world full of tumult and tragedy."[50]

However, although the emerging intellectual radicalism provided an alternative to the Cold War consensus, it was the Vietnam War that led to a fundamental reappraisal of US foreign policy and made critiques of US imperialism more prevalent. The war shook many Americans' faith in US philanthropy and led intellectuals to question the nation's anti-imperial image. There was no single event in the conflict that revolutionized mainstream thinking or stimulated a sudden surge of radical dissent (rather the level of opposition seemed to grow gradually in proportion to the escalation of the war). However, two particular events certainly intensified general antiwar sentiment. The first of these was Operation Rolling Thunder in February 1965 (the extensive bombing campaign against North Vietnam). The intensity of the raids shocked many Americans and helped the New Left achieve a degree of "national recognition." The second event was the Tet Offensive in 1968, which demonstrated the enemy's ability to mount a coordinated attack on several urban targets simultaneously. Although American troops successfully repelled these attacks, the surprise nature of the offensive undermined the credibility of US officials (whose optimistic appraisals of the war seemed unrealistic) and undermined hopes that the war could be won quickly. To critics of the war, the Tet Offensive represented liberal intellectual failure and "the final collapse of a long, mistaken policy."[51]

As well as politicizing thousands of young people, Vietnam made them question the underlying forces that drove US foreign policy. Many believed the government's assessment of the conflict was nonsensical; indeed, some even argued that official announcements were "a fraud of Hitlerian proportions."[52] It was no surprise, therefore, that dissatisfied Americans turned to alternative interpretations such as Williams's *Tragedy*. However, the Wisconsin scholar provided his students, and the antiwar movement as a whole, with more than a mere critique of the war in Southeast Asia; he presented a different interpretation of America's entire development—one that contextualized the Vietnam War as part of a broader history of US imperialism. This was a radical departure from the orthodox critiques of Bemis, Pratt, and Osgood, who had denied the existence of any long-term imperial pattern. It was also a radical contrast to contemporary critiques of US foreign policy such as Senator William Fulbright's *The Arrogance of Power* (1966) and Arthur Schlesinger Jr.'s *The Bitter Heritage* (1966).

Liberal opponents of the conflict in Southeast Asia claimed that the war was the wrong war in the wrong place. Others blamed tactical misjudgments for America's failure to stabilize South Vietnam. Williams, on the other hand, claimed there were larger issues in play. He argued that war was in fact logical, even if he believed it was palpably immoral. This was because Williams regarded the conflict as an imperialist war waged to protect a loosely defined American empire. From this perspective, US foreign policy in Vietnam was actually a rational war in a logical place. After all, he believed that US policymakers regarded the preservation of a capitalist (and anticommunist) regime in South Vietnam as key to their strategic vision for Southeast Asia—a region they allegedly wanted to incorporate into a pro-American global capitalist system.

Because Williams's critique was written before the Vietnam War, his prediction that America would become bogged down in foreign wars unless policymakers reassessed their Weltanschauung (or worldview) seemed somewhat prophetic. When President Lyndon Johnson began to increase the number of American troops in Southeast Asia during the 1960s without tangible success, antiwar scholars regarded Williams as their "patron saint"; after all, Williams was (at the time) the most prominent intellectual to have emphasized the alleged failures of American foreign policy.[53] Indeed, Williams's work soon became "virtually required reading" for students who protested against perceived US atrocities abroad.[54] As a result, *Tragedy* became one of the seminal texts of the Vietnam War era. It was the first comprehensive revision of American diplomatic history during the Cold War and "an iconoclastic attack upon conventional wisdom."[55] The book was therefore an intellectual catalyst that ultimately inspired a generation of dissident literature.

Although critics assaulted Williams's work for being at best "too personal and idiosyncratic" or at worst "solemn nonsense . . . divorced from reality," orthodox liberals and conservatives ultimately proved unable to suppress Williams's influence.[56] Having read *Tragedy*, the radical elements of the antiwar movement became convinced that US policymakers had failed to understand the tides of history. Instead, they hailed Williams as an intellectual doyen whose "uncompromising defiance of all of the fashionable currents of opinion" had provided an alternative manifesto for American conduct abroad.[57] In their biography of Williams titled *William Appleman Williams: The Tragedy of Empire*, Edward Rice-Maximin and 1960s radical and former University of Wisconsin student Paul Buhle described how *Tragedy* was used as ammunition at antiwar rallies. They recalled how demonstrators clutched copies of Williams's books and underlined key passages, while orators crammed *Tragedy* before mounting the stage.[58] These scenes were repeated across the United States during the mid to late 1960s—and as the antiwar movement grew, the New Left political movement produced a number of radical scholars who used history as a political weapon.

New Left radicals such as Gabriel Kolko, Harry Magdoff, a young David Horowitz, and a generation of radical students who passionately opposed the war drew inspiration from *Tragedy* and composed their own critiques of US imperialism. The result was a new strain of radical history that contextualized the Vietnam War as the latest of many attempts to preserve and expand global capitalism. If the war was lost, policymakers feared Japan and the rest of Asia would likely fall to communism; the Japanese may have been nefarious villains to US policymakers approximately twenty years earlier, but now they were considered to be a vital bastion of democratic capitalism and the key to the balance of power in the Pacific. The radicals argued that if Southeast Asia and Japan abandoned capitalism, the network of trade and investments the United States had done so much to build since 1945 would be in jeopardy. For the New Left, this capitalist network was best described as an economic empire: an empire that provided international markets for American industry and investment opportunities for US-owned corporations (thus sustaining America's domestic prosperity). Furthermore, they argued that the establishment of this empire—and the wars waged to protect it—were an inevitable by-product of American capitalism.

As we shall see in subsequent chapters, Williams's critique differed from the New Left interpretation because he attributed US imperialism to intellectual failures rather than the expansionist nature of capitalism. Similarly, while the New Left activists admired *Tragedy*, their strategy to end the war and secure domestic reform was also fundamentally different. Whereas the energetic and passionate young dissidents who opposed the Vietnam War often protested in a vociferous and mutinous manner, Williams reacted in a more measured and philosophical way. Rather than embracing the era's mood of rebellion, Williams hoped that the power of his writing and, indeed, his teaching could help to save the United States from itself—and ultimately save the lives of American soldiers fighting in Vietnam. Consequently, although Williams "anticipated, encouraged and explained the attack of conscience suffered by the nation during the 1960s," he passionately opposed the confrontational tactics ultimately adopted by SDS.[59] Those who have characterized him as "a senior member of the New Left" were therefore wrong.[60] His approach, one might say, was radically different from the more anarchic elements of the radical left.

Williams was undoubtedly an "intellectual hero" of the antiwar movement, but claims that he was the "godfather" of the New Left are erroneous.[61] The Wisconsin scholar was a patriotic American who remained nostalgic about the society in which he grew up. The counterculture was an anathema to him. In fact, he craved a return to his childhood days in the midwestern rural town of Atlantic, Iowa. Williams was also something of a philanthropist, who craved international harmony and a moral American foreign policy. Ironically, he also seemed to adhere to the notion of American exceptionalism: he wanted the United States to be a shining beacon of benevolence and an example to mankind and strongly believed that the nation should aspire to such a role. The problem, he believed, was that US diplomacy had been subverted by what he regarded as a tragically flawed national Weltanschauung.

Williams believed that US expansion not only prevented developing countries from improving their standard of living but also paralyzed socioeconomic reforms at home. According to Williams, the only way Americans could escape this destructive cycle, and fulfill the ideals of their better selves, was to abandon their flawed Weltanschauung and redistribute wealth within the United States—in other words, nothing short of comprehensive socioeconomic reform would do. Williams became frustrated at the United States' inability to lift poor people out of poverty. In short, he believed that the country he loved could, and should, do better. However, whereas the unlawful protestors of the New Left occasionally leaned toward anarchy, Williams's dissidence was intellectual. The Wisconsin scholar did not want to destroy American society; he wanted to reform it democratically via peaceful means. Williams had a high regard for US institutions and believed that raising the income of working-class Americans would increase domestic demand and mollify the craving for economic expansion overseas.

But where did Williams's critique come from? To those who were familiar with the progressive histories of the 1930s, the primary features of Williams's critique (and indeed his whole intellectual approach) would have seemed familiar. Indeed, the Wisconsin scholar's perspective might have been unique in the context of the 1950s, but it was more than a little reminiscent of left wing histories written during the Great Depression. Therefore, to trace the roots of the Wisconsin critique, and to unearth the origins of the debate on American expansion in general, it is necessary to delve into critical interpretations of US expansion before the Cold War. The 1930s provided a fertile environment for radicals to express their views. In fact, many of the cornerstones of Williams's critique—the yearning for domestic reform, the belief that capitalism could be reformed to avert imperialism—derived unmistakably from the work of Charles Beard and other progressive histories composed during the first half of the twentieth century.

2

Pushing the Boundaries

> It would seem in the national interest to lay more emphasis on eliminating backwardness from the American nation than . . . securing more moral obligations to other races.
>
> Charles Beard, 1935

The Progressives

During the 1950s, dissidents like Williams were isolated voices struggling to be heard. In the words of historian Robert Tomes, anticommunism became "a fundamental and unquestionable assumption of political life." Stringent anti-Marxism permeated the academic community at a rapid pace, a process that was entrenched by the defection of prominent intellectuals to government ranks. As a result, observers have concluded that "the mutually exclusive lines between government policymaking and intellectual discourse became blurred." Furthermore, an unofficial system of self-censorship emerged, since academics were frequently rewarded for praising Washington's approach. Orthodox historians either did not worry or it did not occur to them that "mutual self-advancement" can sometimes take place "at the expense of the truth."[1]

Dissidents in the early years of the Cold War therefore served a valuable purpose. They challenged prevailing assumptions and asked Americans whether the confrontation with the Soviet Union was actually in the national interest. However, it would be wrong to suggest that Williams and his radical contemporaries emerged from nowhere. Historians on the left had already written alternative interpretations of American expansion during the first half of the twentieth century. These scholars were the first historians to use imperialism as a conceptual framework to interpret American history—therefore they set an important precedent that Williams was keen to follow. The most famous of these intellectuals was the seminal progressive historian Charles Beard. Although the progressive historians were not exclusively focused on empire as an issue (their main priority was actually to broaden the horizons of the US history profession by considering social and economic factors), they identified a relationship between economic interests and politics long before Williams began teaching at the University of Wisconsin. Furthermore, it was pre-Cold War scholars who first argued that foreign policy might be influenced by material interests—whether this involved the interests of a particular industry or the upper class in general.

Because they challenged the orthodox view that domestic and foreign policies were formulated to serve the majority of citizens, progressive ideas were frequently received with outright hostility by America's privileged minority. This was not surprising since the accusation that governments were primarily concerned with extending the power and wealth of the ruling classes unsettled those in high places. This has been noted by many historians, including Clyde Barrow, who claimed that the US plutocracy and judicial establishment disliked progressive intellectuals because they "exposed" their "best kept secrets" to "the restless masses."[2] Although Barrow's claim implied an unlikely conspiracy, there is little doubt that the progressive scholars moved history into what Richard Hofstadter called "the controversial political world." Pointing out that the three most famous progressive scholars—Turner at Wisconsin, V. L. Parrington at Oklahoma, and Beard at Columbia—were all drawn into university controversies and left an institution "under stress" (because their radicalism upset the conservative sensibilities of their respective academic boards), the likes of Beard took the discipline of history from a "gilded age . . . marked by its aloofness from, if not hostility to popular aspirations" into an intellectually vibrant and socially relevant environment.[3] The 1920s were also the time when "a modern critical intelligentsia was emerging" in the United States. Socialists like Beard thrived in this intellectual environment, since "there was an increasing acknowledgment by historians that the writing and teaching of history, when not narrowly antiquarian, inevitably had political implications."[4]

Before the progressive movement, history in the United States was traditionally written as a storytelling narrative that reaffirmed American exceptionalism. History was therefore romanticized and patriotic, propagating the idea that the United States was guided by providence and a sense of moral mission. When reflecting on this period in American historiography, observers have often lamented the lack of critical insight and the paucity of professionalism. For example, Peter Novick's *That Noble Dream* complained that "most of the distinguished historical work" at the end of the nineteenth century "was written by men without formal training," while even those books "universally acclaimed by the professional historical establishment, continued to be produced by independently wealthy amateurs."[5] Meanwhile, Richard Hofstadter argued that nineteenth-century history books were purely "works of art," composed by authors who prioritized the eloquence of their writing style over interpretative and analytical substance.[6]

The emergence of professional and politically minded historians like Beard changed this. At the beginning of the twentieth century, the socioeconomic changes brought on by the industrial revolution and the end of the domestic frontier (plus the period of prolonged economic turmoil that followed) inspired the progressive historians to look critically at America's past. Instead of using history to celebrate the national mission, Beard and the progressives wanted to identify the factors that had shaped America's social and economic history. Although the majority of historians remained rooted in the orthodox narrative tradition, the progressives attacked these "consensus" scholars, whose dominance at the beginning of the twentieth century was "in some ways surprising, for there was never another time in American history in which, overall, there was so little consensus." Unlike their orthodox contemporaries who remained "serene and untroubled in their celebration of traditional pieties," the progressives refused to ignore recent socioeconomic controversies such as the populist revolt, the free-silver campaign, and trade union violence.[7] They also started to question whether American expansion was the result of something other than Manifest Destiny.

After the trauma of World War I, progressives began to assess US foreign policy from a more critical standpoint. Although Beard was initially a supporter of Wilson's decision to fight Germany, he later became cynical about America's role in world affairs, arguing that business interests were ascendant over humanitarian concerns. This placed Beard alongside the so-called Peace Progressives, a bloc of dissenting senators who promoted "an alternative to corporatism that combined anti-imperialism, economic diplomacy and anti-militarism." The Peace Progressives opposed Wilson's internationalism because they believed it "represented a foreign policy controlled by businessmen and international bankers."[8] Although Beard was slow to come round to this point of view, he ultimately became a champion of those progressives who lamented the influence of business interests in US diplomacy. This continued in the vein of radical progressive politicians such as Robert La Follette and William Borah, who constantly opposed what they saw as imperial interventions in Latin America and the Caribbean—militaristic excursions that served corporate interests and violated US traditional values.

Although Beard had not articulated a critique of American imperialism at this stage, he agreed with dissident politicians that American interests would be best served by influencing other nations through the power of example (rather than direct military intervention). However, Beard's time would come. In the first two decades of the twentieth century the work of another progressive historian, Frederick Jackson Turner, provided the most influential critique of US expansion. Although Turner was not as radical as Beard (his perspective influenced politicians such as Woodrow Wilson), his thesis predicted that imperialism would be central to America's future. Consequently, any discussion of the historiography of American empire in the twentieth century must begin with an analysis of Turner's pioneering work.

Frederick Jackson Turner and the Frontier Thesis

Of all the progressive historians, Turner and Beard had the greatest influence on the work of William Appleman Williams. Although other progressive scholars such as V. L. Parrington and Carl Becker also managed to reach a broad audience, when it came to the subject of US imperialism, Turner and Beard provided the pivotal ideas that shaped the Wisconsin critique of American empire. As Turner had established his national reputation in Madison, Williams was more than familiar with the progressive scholar's frontier thesis; therefore by focusing on US expansion Williams was following in his footsteps somewhat. The key tenets of Turner's thesis were outlined in *The Frontier in American History* (1920), which argued that American democracy had been founded within the context of continuous territorial expansion. The book included Turner's renowned essay "The Significance of the Frontier in American History," which claimed that "the existence of an area of free land, its continuous recession, and the advance of American settlement westward, explains American development." Turner believed that US history was unique because of "the peculiarity of American institutions" that had "been compelled to adapt themselves to the changes of an expanding people." He also asserted that territorial expansion was inherent in Americans' national psychology: "that coarseness of strength" that was "combined with acuteness and inquisitiveness" and a "practical, inventive turn of mind." Similarly he claimed that the nation was moved by a "restless nervous energy"—claiming that American "frontier individualism" had created an exceptional democracy because of the people's "antipathy to control."[9]

Significantly, Turner's frontier thesis also stated that Americans saw expansion and freedom as inextricably linked. This begged an important question: if expansion was a vital ingredient of freedom and democracy, would America continue to expand now that the western frontier had closed? Turner answered in the affirmative: "He would be a rash prophet who should assert that the expansive character of American life has now entirely ceased. Movement has been its dominant fact, and, unless this training has no effect upon a people, the American energy will continually demand a wider field for its existence." Turner also put forward a fascinating theory that the frontier offered "a gate of escape from the bondage of the past."[10] This was a key proposition that influenced radicals during the late 1950s and early 1960s, particularly Williams. As we will discuss in chapter 4, Williams was very much a product of his Madison education. The University of Wisconsin was an institution that traditionally encouraged close relationships between the schools of history, economics, and political science. This eclectic intellectual environment proved to be a breeding ground for new ideas—and although many of Turner's were somewhat vague and hard to substantiate, they certainly resonated with Williams. The implication that Americans turned to expansion to escape from domestic problems was a prime example. Here was a vague hypothesis for which there was little tangible evidence, yet it proved to be a powerful concept that formed a central pivot in Williams's critique of American imperialism.

The events of the late nineteenth century were not lost on Turner, who discussed the conflict in another essay that appeared in *The Frontier of American History* called "Contributions of the West to American Democracy." Turner interpreted the Spanish-American War as evidence of the expansionist tendencies of the American people. "Having completed the conquest of the wilderness, and having consolidated our interests, we are beginning to consider the relations of democracy and empire. . . . The battle of Manila . . . broke down the old isolationism of the nation and started it on a path the goal of which no man can foretell."[11] Turner's words were relevant to subsequent critiques of American imperialism, because they implied that US expansion would be infinite. Williams and the New Left scholars in the 1960s also predicted that American imperialism would be limitless, although the New Left based their reasoning on the Marxist assumption that capitalism would always require a growing sphere of existence, whereas Turner's and Williams's critiques were primarily concerned with psychological triggers.

By placing US foreign policy at the end of the nineteenth century into the same context as the nation's frontier expansion, Turner had constructed the first Progressive model of American imperialism. He was convinced that the United States' emergence as "an imperial republic with dependencies and protectorates" was "the logical outcome of the nation's march to the Pacific."[12]

Although observers have criticized Turner, claiming his arguments were "a series of very broad assertions, very vaguely put," they have also acknowledged "a core of merit" in his analysis. For example, Richard Hofstadter complained that *The Frontier in American History* ignored other factors that may have contributed to the nation's development ("the frontier had a big maw, but it cannot be made to ingest everything") but simultaneously praised "the core of Turner's insight" if not the formulation of his ideas.[13] It is easy to agree with Hofstadter in this instance, since it is almost impossible to prove that the impact of the frontier on the American psyche drove the nation's extracontinental imperialism. However, this does not prevent one from being intrigued by Turner's hypothesis. Furthermore, it cannot be denied that "The Significance of the Frontier in American History" became influential over time. Turner's ideas reached a wide audience across America, captivating scholars, politicians, and the general public alike. Consequently, the emergence of Turner's frontier thesis must be appreciated as a hugely significant moment in the historiography of US imperialism.

It should also be noted at this point that some of Turner's ideas were formulated amid the backdrop of the anti-imperial protests that occurred at the end of the 1890s. Although these anti-imperialists did not develop systematic critiques that reexamined US development through the prism of expansion, their arguments cannot be ignored when assessing the historiography of US imperialism. The anti-imperialists were wary of annexing the Philippines, or any other extracontinental territories, because they feared that American colonial expansion would propel the United States "into the vortex of international power politics, contradict its democratic principles, and reverse the whole thrust of its history." As many Americans were thankful for their geographical isolation from the perceived corruption of European politics, they feared that an active role in world affairs would lead to needless wars and unnecessary expense. Dissidents also raised objections on "constitutional, diplomatic . . . and historical grounds," claiming that the Philippines were incompatible with the US political system.[14] Meanwhile, there was the moral issue of whether it was right to conquer less developed nations and impose American values upon them.

The anti-imperialists were a diverse group who opposed US expansion for a host of conflicting reasons. In fact, Robert Beisner argued in *Twelve Against Empire* that there was no such thing as a typical "anti-imperial position." Those who dissented even came from different political backgrounds, as demonstrated by the schism between the Democrat Mugwumps (a group that included Carl Schurz, William James, and E. L. Godkin) and the dissident Republicans (who were led by Senator George Hoar and the businessman Andrew Carnegie).

However, their diversity did not prevent them from reaching a wide audience at the end of the century, particularly during the key years of 1898 and 1899. "Hundreds of prominent politicians and private citizens denounced American imperialism in newspapers, magazines and pamphlets, made countless speeches on the subject, fought the acquisition of Puerto Rico, Hawaii, and the Philippines in Congress, organized anti-imperialist leagues and associations . . . all in the name of restoring the United States to the haven of safety and rectitude from which it had been rudely dislodged." However, these anti-imperialists differed from many of those who protested against the Vietnam War in the 1960s because they were opposed to "belligerent diplomacy in general as well as actual expansionist projects."[15] Furthermore, although some anti-imperialists opposed US expansion on moral grounds, others (such as Senator Hoar) did so because they were racists who believed the annexation of foreign peoples would dilute the racial purity of America. The New Left would have found this position abhorrent.

Nevertheless, it is possible to argue that the late-nineteenth-century anti-imperialists did influence later critiques of US foreign policy in some ways. For example, they argued that America would be better served by influencing foreign nations through the power of example rather than through conquest—this was a key characteristic of the Wisconsin critique of American diplomacy during the Cold War. But more importantly, the anti-imperialists at the turn of the century established a trend whereby foreign policy was seen as a product of domestic sociopolitical issues. Although they did not develop this theory to the same extent as the intellectuals who followed them, those who opposed the annexation of the Philippines frequently saw a connection between US expansion and the problems facing America itself. For instance, Beisner described anti-imperial criticisms as "a commentary on the forces transforming America in the last third of the nineteenth century," claiming that dissidents saw "imperialism as both an example and a product of a large number of unfortunate and dangerous developments that had taken place since the Civil War."[16]

The Emergence of Charles Beard

Few historians considered foreign policy in the context of domestic factors more than Charles Beard; consequently, it is no surprise that Beard influenced Cold War critiques of US imperialism. Whereas Turner had concentrated on psychological and geographical dimensions, Beard introduced economic factors into the study of United States history. This made Beard a considerably more radical and controversial figure. Orthodox historians during the first half of the twentieth century generally celebrated the national mission and presented a romanticized view of America's past. Therefore, Beard's seminal work, *An Economic Interpretation of the Constitution of the United States* (1913), which claimed that the constitution was framed to protect the material interests of the propertied class, created something of a storm. Indeed, the book has since been described as "unquestionably the most controversial historical work of its generation."[17]

World War I accelerated changes in the historical profession and created a sympathetic audience for radicals like Beard. Because the war was both a traumatic experience and another reversal of the United States traditional policy of isolationism, the public began to ask fundamental questions for the first time since the anti-imperial debates at the turn of the century. For instance, people began to ask who specifically benefited from US intervention. Was the war in the best interests of the United States or just in the interests of munitions makers? Similarly, Wilson's internationalism was much debated (as was Americans' rejection of the League of Nations). Beard confronted these issues directly. The progressive scholars did not want historians to be mere chroniclers of events; rather, they wanted to analyze America's dilemmas and suggest solutions. In doing so, they engaged with the public and helped to shape and reflect popular opinion.

Consequently, Beard had a profound effect on the US historical profession. This has been noted by several critics, including Richard Hofstadter, who acknowledged that "Turner's conception of the frontier thesis and Beard's of the economic interpretation of politics gave a connected meaning to the multiple events of American history." Although Turner and Beard's hypotheses were somewhat vague and generalized, their arguments somehow generated a "mythical appeal" that "reached outside academic walls."[18] As a result, progressive historians reached a new audience and tried to influence politics. For example, by the 1930s Beard's books were clearly aimed at the government, which he hoped to influence through cutting critiques of both American society and the nation's foreign policy. President Franklin Roosevelt even invited Beard to the White House so they could discuss his ideas.

The use of history to promote a political agenda was a new phenomenon during the 1920s and 1930s. Before this time, historians usually tried to adopt a stance of objective detachment. However, historians like Charles Beard believed true objectivity was impossible. Instead, he strongly favored "relativism"—the belief that a scholar can only compose history that is "relative to the setting in which it was written." The period between World War I and II was characterized by a struggle between orthodox historians and their relativist challengers. Relativists assaulted the American historical consensus, which observers have since described as a "convergent, celebratory historiography" that promoted "an overwhelmingly affirmative stance towards the American experience."[19]

Although the relativists were disliked by orthodox scholars, Beard and the progressives won the battle for prominence within the historical profession between the world wars. This was because economic critiques resonated with the public at large. The onset of the Great Depression made many people look for scapegoats, which they often found in the form of supposedly greedy business interests and corrupt or incompetent government officials. This public cynicism was particularly evident between 1934 and 1936, when the Nye Committee investigated the causes of America's involvement in World War I; the committee eventually concluded that bankers had pressured Wilson to intervene in order to protect their loans abroad. This appeared to confirm suspicions that private interests worked against the true interests of the American people.[20]

However, although the 1930s was a time when the socioeconomic structure of the United States drew much criticism, few scholars actually addressed the seemingly related issue of American imperialism. Progressive historians had demonstrated that domestic politics and economics were linked (and how foreign policy could also be manipulated to serve private interests), but the majority of intellectuals did not attempt to construct a sophisticated critique of American empire. For example, Harry Elmer Barnes became famous for his tirades against Franklin Roosevelt's foreign policies, but he never placed his criticisms within the broader context of US imperialism. The only scholars who did so were Charles Beard and the lesser-known Marxist historian Scott Nearing.[21]

Before we examine the Beardian concept of American empire, and how Beard inspired subsequent radicals like Williams, it should be noted that the progressive historian was himself influenced by John Hobson, the renowned expert on global imperialism. As an Englishman, Hobson had been able to write candidly about America's ascent to global power without fearing for his reputation. His book *Imperialism: A Study* (1902) stated unequivocally that Americans' sense of mission was "clearly subordinate to the driving force of the economic factor." Hobson had warned that "the adventurous enthusiasm of President Theodore Roosevelt and his Manifest Destiny and mission of civilization" must not "deceive" the world, for it was America's "sudden demand for foreign markets for manufactures and for investments" that was "avowedly responsible for the adoption of imperialism as a political policy and practice." Hobson even insinuated that private industrial interests played a primary role in dictating policy, claiming that "it was Messrs. Rockefeller, Pierpont Morgan, and their associates who needed imperialism" and "fastened it upon the shoulders of the great Republic of the West."[22]

Hobson's critique of US imperialism could not have contrasted more with Americans' self-image. He argued that policymakers from industrialized nations may have used "noble phrases, expressive of their desire to extend the area of civilization, to establish good governance, promote Christianity, extirpate slavery, and elevate lower races," but overall they were "primarily engaged in business," and they were "not unaware of the utility of the more unselfish forces in furthering their ends." Hobson therefore believed that US exceptionalism was a myth. He even argued that Americans' very belief in their distinctiveness was unexceptional. "The French Chauvinist, the German colonialist, the Russian Pan-Slavist, the American expansionist, enter the same general conviction with the same intensity, regarding the capacity, the destiny and the rights of their own nation." The English scholar claimed that every powerful nation provided allegedly "scientific" reasons why their nationality was superior to all others; therefore, Americans were exactly the same as other powers by claiming they were unique.[23]

As an American, it was difficult for Beard to be as blunt as Hobson. However, the progressive historian was certainly influenced by Hobson's work. Not only did Hobson and Beard agree that economic considerations drove US imperialism; Beard was also fascinated by Hobson's contention that governments (including the United States) used territorial and economic expansion to serve "the double purpose of securing private material benefits for favored classes of investors and traders at the public cost, while sustaining the general cause of conservatism by diverting public energy and interest from domestic agitation."[24] Although Beard never explicitly claimed that those with wealth and power used imperialism as a deliberate tactic to evade domestic upheaval, his critique certainly claimed that economic expansion was an outlet that circumvented the need for domestic socioeconomic reform.

Like Hobson, Beard argued that imperialism was pursued by the ruling classes to solve the problem of overproduction. This was a predicament caused by the industrial revolution, which created a manufacturing boom that saturated American domestic markets. Beard contended that the US government, in collusion with business leaders, decided to chase overseas markets for their products rather than redistributing wealth within America itself. Consequently, when faced with the choice of either slowing production, sharing a greater percentage of their profits with workers, or exploiting new markets overseas, the ruling elites chose the latter course—not only because it was the most lucrative option but also because it entrenched their personal wealth and privileged social status.

As a result, Hobson concluded that imperialism was not strictly necessary. This was a departure from the Marxist theory that imperialism was an inevitable stage of capitalism. Like Beard and Williams after him, Hobson argued that "the inevitability of imperial expansion as a necessary outlet for progressive industry" was "a fallacy," since it was "the mal-distribution of consumer power" at home that prevented "the absorption of commodities and capital within the country." Rather than falling back on the "depraved choice of capitalism," Hobson claimed it would be more responsible and moral to restrict foreign trade and redistribute domestic wealth.[25] Although Beard and Williams had a slightly different twist on this matter, arguing that Americans chose imperialism because they wrongly assumed that economic expansion was the only solution to America's economic ills, Hobson influenced dissidents to reject the Marxist dogma that imperialism and capitalism inevitably went hand in hand.

Beard and US Expansion

Many historians have discussed the relationship between Williams and Beard—and considered their contribution to the debate on US imperialism. The prevailing opinion, as reiterated by Andrew Bacevich in *American Empire* (2002), is that "Beard first identified the underlying logic of American expansion" and Williams "went a step further, urging Americans to contemplate the implications of their imperium."[26] While this is generally true, their relationship was actually more complex than that. Williams accepted much of what Beard wrote, but he also differed on many fundamental issues. Similarly, it is wrong to credit Beard alone for revealing the triggers behind American expansion, for as we have seen, his critique of US imperialism bore many of the hallmarks of Hobson's earlier interpretation. However, this is not to argue that Beard did not have a substantial influence. Beard was the first highly visible American scholar to highlight the expansionism of the US economy—and as such his critique demands a great deal of attention. Similarly, like the dissidents who succeeded him during the Cold War, his interpretation was idiosyncratic as well as passionate and patriotic.

During the 1920s and 1930s, Beard's books were tailor-made for a time of "muckraking," when, in the words of Walter Lippmann, "the national mood had grown so suspicious that . . . the public had a distinct prejudice in favor of those who made accusations." Beard was therefore one of many scholars who contributed to the general debate in the country at large, when "almost every aspect of American life, from sex, religion, and race relations to foreign policy, the regulation of business, and the role of the Courts, was being reconsidered." In these turbulent times, Beard adopted the role of "the public moralist" who was not afraid to abandon perceived objectivity if he believed he was writing for a good cause. Consequently, his books displayed a "polemical edge" and an "activist zeal" that was unprecedented among historians at the time.[27]

Beard always identified "a close relationship between the structure of the state and the economic composition of society." Although he admitted in *The Economic Basis of Politics* (1922) that "definite political consequences" do not "inexorably flow from the total economic situation," there was little doubt in his mind that economics and politics had always been "inextricably linked" and had "reciprocal" influences upon each other. Because economics and politics were interrelated, and economic interests were essentially selfish in nature, Beard doubted that American society could operate harmoniously. Conflict between various interest groups was therefore inevitable, as each sought political control to further its interests. Given this interpretation of society, it was no wonder that Beard believed economic factors frequently influenced foreign policies as well. Because he claimed that "economic interests will come to expression in political power," it surely followed that the political bodies that formulated foreign policies would have taken economic factors (both foreign and domestic) into account.[28]

From the beginning of his career, Beard argued that foreign policy was formulated according to material interests. However, it was not until the 1930s that Beard made the effort to "systematically formulate a theory of foreign policy that was anchored in his economic interpretation of American history."[29] This model, which largely framed US diplomacy in terms of imperialism, was expressed in a number of books starting with *The American Leviathan: The Republic in the Machine Age* (1930), *The Idea of National Interest* (1934), and *The Open Door at Home* (1934). Beard's primary assertion was that America had always been an expanding nation, in terms of both overseas trade and territory. Initially, the Founding Fathers made territorial growth a priority, but it was not long before this movement was accompanied by calls for "a consolidation of commercial, manufacturing, financial, and agricultural interests at home," plus "the promotion of trade in all parts of the world."[30] Beard believed that industrialization during the nineteenth century accelerated this process, for production increased at such a pace that the domestic market alone did not suffice as an outlet for US manufacturing. Beard claimed this economic development had a huge impact on politics, since "new economic facts produce new political facts."[31] Therefore, the government's priority became the acquisition of international markets to satisfy the economic interests of its citizens. This would be achieved through "the engines of diplomacy" and "the defense of that trade by a powerful navy."[32]

In 1930 Beard's *The American Leviathan* (which he wrote in conjunction with his son William) described how "from its formation" the United States government "has promoted, in a more or less methodical fashion, the foreign trade of its citizens." This was achieved through the granting of "bounties, subsidies, tariffs and discriminating legislation" (against competitors). Although this process gathered pace after World War I, the approach also existed during the eighteenth and nineteenth centuries. In fact, Beard claimed that "one of the prime purposes of the Fathers in framing the Constitution was to afford protection and assistance to American commerce and industry."[33]

The link between the domestic economy and foreign policy was apparent throughout Beard's major works. For example, *The American Leviathan* stated that "American manufacturers had fairly saturated the domestic market" by the end of the nineteenth century, a development that had multiplied "the pressure" on the government to assist in "commercial promotion" as businesses "feverishly" sought "additional outlets in all quarters of the globe." In response to this pressure, the US government made the expansion of overseas commerce its number-one foreign policy objective. Beard claimed that "diplomatic and political intervention in support of American undertakings abroad" was "organized into a fine art." The United States annexation of the Philippines was apparently one striking illustration of how the government used foreign policy for "the development of American trade."[34]

The argument that the United States usually seized economic opportunities when they arose, while ignoring possible repercussions, was a premise that dominated Beard's interpretation of American foreign policy. This was the central thesis of both *The Idea of National Interest* and *The Open Door at Home*, a two-part study that outlined the classic conception of America's international interest, assessed its validity, and then offered a hypothetical alternative. Beard argued that American governments since the 1890s had pursued economic expansion abroad because the policy was deemed "necessary," "possible," and "desirable" to the national interest. Beard attributed this to a deeply held belief among US policymakers that economic growth abroad was the only way to prevent "an impasse or deadlock" in the domestic economy.[35]

Beard argued that America's devotion to the Open Door, the strategy of removing prejudicial tariffs and encouraging international free trade, demonstrated Washington's intention to extend US economic influence throughout the world. He defined this policy as "pushing and holding doors open" to American trade "in all parts of the world with all the engines of government, ranging from polite coercion to the use of arms."[36] This entailed forcing other nations to accept an influx of US products (whether industrial, agricultural, or both) without imposing prejudicial tariffs. The United States also encouraged the export of capital overseas, which included loans to lesser developed nations or investment by American companies in business ventures abroad.

By using this strategy, Beard claimed the Open Door was employed to exploit opportunities in regions where American influence was strong, such as Latin America, but also to attempt to expand commerce in areas where the US strategic position was relatively weak, as in China. Because American policymakers feared that the competition among major powers would ultimately divide China into spheres of interest (which would close vast areas to American trade), the Open Door presented itself as a compromise solution, which would supposedly preserve Chinese sovereignty while "thrusting America into the European balance of power in the Far East."[37] However, Beard argued that the Open Door was more than just an economic policy. This was because "the continuous economic expansion of foreign markets for American manufactures, capital, and agricultural produce" was not only considered necessary, possible, and desirable but was also regarded as "part of the process of destiny and Almighty God." This introduced a new element into critiques of US imperialism: the fundamental conviction shared by Americans that their economic expansion and growing international influence was preordained by a higher power. This enabled the United States to justify its imperialism, for "whatever may be won by ingenuity, by the influence of wealth, negotiation, and permissible intrigue, by diplomacy and naval pressure, belongs of right to American citizens and corporations."[38] This assertion that US expansion was generated not only by perceived economic necessity but also by religious ideological beliefs was a topic explored subsequently by Williams, whose own critique of US imperialism concurred with Beard's hypothesis.

The contention that economic and ideological motives drove American expansion was central to Beard's interpretation of US history. However, his overall synthesis possessed a further dimension that we must discuss: this was the author's suggestion that social factors also played a significant role in the formulation of expansionist US foreign policies. Like many of the prominent dissidents who followed him, Beard argued that the property-owning classes promoted US expansion to further their own wealth. The progressive scholar believed this was morally bankrupt—therefore, rather than pursuing a course of imperialism to solve overproduction, Beard argued it would be more socially responsible to redistribute wealth within American society itself:

> There are numerous opportunities to do good at home which could supply outlets for swelling passions of sacrificial virtue. There are millions of illiterate and degraded people, young and old, now living in the United States. There are millions of American people, even in prosperous times, who are lacking the security, sanitary conveniences, medical services, educational opportunities, and habits of industry which American statesmen of the industrial school are eager to supply to the "benighted" in distant and foreign places. It would seem

> in the *national* interest, therefore, to lay more emphasis on eliminating backwardness from the American *nation* than to make plans for wrestling new "benighted" areas from Great Britain, France, or Japan for the purposes of securing more moral obligations to other races.[39]

This was Beard's plea for an Open Door at home. It was an appeal that resonated with subsequent dissidents during the Cold War, most notably Williams, who also beseeched the government to concentrate on domestic reform rather than indulging in reckless imperialism to solve domestic economic ills.

Beard also influenced future dissidents by claiming that US economic expansion not only exacerbated inequality at home but also increased the disparity between rich and poor abroad. This was a radical and controversial perspective, for his orthodox contemporaries insisted that foreign peoples touched by US imperialism had "fared well in the main."[40] Whereas policies such as the Open Door were traditionally presented as benevolent strategies to preserve the "full sovereignty" of less-developed nations in the face of "foreign encroachments," Beard argued that US economic expansion was motivated by self-interest. Scholars like Bemis might have argued that foreign countries were "ingratiated" by American expansion and saw the United States as "generous," but Beard doubted whether unrestricted (or free) trade could produce anything other than misery and subjugation for the world's poor.[41] Instead, he argued that "vegetable civilizations have been subordinated to the commodities of mineral civilizations. . . . With their control over heavy industries and huge capital accumulations, they practically dominate the vegetable economies of the world and hold them at their mercy under a regime of free and equal commerce." Meanwhile, Beard claimed "there is good ground for believing that the well-organized and ruthless machine civilizations would use their power of exploiting the weaker and unorganized agricultural and raw material regions to the limit."[42] Therefore, far from aiding the development of poorer nations, the progressive scholar firmly believed that America's "free-trade empire" would never result in equality and stability.

When Beard's views became unfashionable during the Cold War, debate focused on the apparent isolationism of his progressive views. However, this allegation does him a disservice. Beard was actually a continentalist, who believed that the United States' economic and security interests would be best served by focusing on the northern reaches of the Western Hemisphere. Furthermore, Beard was not a pacifist like many true isolationists. In fact, he explicitly argued the nation should not hesitate to fight wars when its vital interests were threatened. What made Beard controversial was his assertion that the chances of having to fight such a war would be dramatically reduced if America concentrated its vital interests at home rather than in distant lands.

Calling Beard an isolationist and the author of an "isolationist treatise" was expedient, but it was an unfair portrayal. Yet orthodox contemporaries seemed to persist with this characterization because his radical views seemed provocative.[43] For example, Beard assaulted Bemis's interpretation of the Spanish-American War by arguing that America's seizure of an extracontinental empire in 1898 cannot "be accurately described as a historical accident" because "the policy was the upshot of a long term chain of actions and leadership extending back over more than half a century."[44] He underlined this point six years later in *A Foreign Policy for America*, when he forcefully reiterated that "to ascribe" the nation's "imperialist adventurism . . . to 'fate,' or 'destiny' or 'cosmic tendency' is to resort to a mysticism on the level with witchcraft or superstition . . . and to surrender the possibility of rational analysis."[45] Beard was equally unmoved when it came to Bemis's aberration theory. Although he agreed that US imperialism during the 1890s was a "break from the historical US policy" (which he saw as continental Americanism), he did not believe that the United States returned to isolationism at the beginning of the twentieth century. Instead he argued that the Spanish-American War was "the first war of commercial empire" (not the only war), while the period from 1897 to 1913 witnessed "a sharpening" and "intensification" of economic expansion.[46]

Beard's Influence on Williams

Beard's refusal to believe that US imperialism at the end of the nineteenth century was an aberration was embraced wholeheartedly by Williams during the 1950s. Like Beard, the Wisconsin scholar also saw the Spanish-American War as the culmination of decades of economic expansion. It is not surprising, therefore, that critics such as John Patrick Diggins have argued that Williams's interpretation of US imperialism "goes back to Charles Beard" and was "scarcely original."[47] Williams actually admitted his debt to Beard. For example, in the acknowledgments section of *The Contours of American History* (1961), Williams expressed his desire to "acknowledge formally" his "respect for and indebtedness to Charles Austin Beard." The Wisconsin scholar described Beard as "a man of rare intellectual capacity" and a "great historian," before declaring that "it was one of the most illuminating aspects of our time" that the Pulitzer Prize Committee had "yet to find the intelligence or the courage to honor him."[48]

However, it would be unfair to say that Williams and the Wisconsin scholars were mere imitators of Beard. They all had their own individual perspectives and idiosyncrasies. Nor would it be accurate to say that they were only influenced by Beard. Thomas McCormick, for instance, wrote about a "power elite" in a similar vein to C. Wright Mills.[49] Indeed, while Williams himself admitted his admiration and affection for Beard's work, he was also at pains to point out that "my own analyses and interpretations differ from his."[50] What has confused some historiographers, and made them believe that the Wisconsin scholars were mere clones of Beard, is the fact that Beard's emphasis on the psychology of US policymakers was borrowed, to a large extent, by Williams. This does not simply refer to the varying personalities of American presidents, but rather, it takes into account a particular mindset that governed the behavior of successive administrations, regardless of the personalities involved.

In *The Open Door at Home*, Beard referred to what he described as "a crisis of thought" in America, a problem that had apparently hindered the nation's attempt to recover from the "economic crisis" of the 1930s. Beard contended that during the late nineteenth century, policymakers believed that "the country had reached a plateau of permanent prosperity and could find ever-expanding markets for the goods that flowed from factory and farm." But once the Great Depression began to tighten its grip, Americans believed that their only "escape" from stagnation was a renewed attempt to expand abroad.[51] Consequently, both the US public and the government came to the conclusion that economic expansion, as represented by imperialism and the Open Door policy, was the most important aspect of the national interest.

According to Beard, this conviction became ingrained in the American psyche, even though the question of its validity was "neglected in public discussion." This led US policymakers to pursue an unproven strategy, which not only jeopardized the prospect of prosperity at home but also forced US expansionism onto foreign peoples. Bearing in mind the economic chaos that afflicted the United States in the early 1930s, Beard concluded that Americans' faith that expansion would solve America's economic ills had proved to be "a false prophecy." Consequently, he berated politicians and businesses for failing to recognize the "internal contradictions in thought" inherent in the strategy of spreading the Open Door across the world.[52]

This analysis was strikingly similar to the causes of US imperialism identified by Williams in *The Tragedy of American Diplomacy*. Like Beard, Williams was convinced that the United States prioritized economic expansion because leaders assumed it was the only way to solve the crisis of overproduction; if there was not enough domestic demand for American manufacturing and agricultural produce, markets would have to be found overseas. Williams believed that this fundamental assumption guided American leaders whenever important foreign policy matters arose. For example, in going to war with Spain in 1898 (and annexing Hawaii and the Philippines) American politicians spoke publicly of their desire to help less-developed nations, but their actions were actually motivated by their conviction that expanding trade would ameliorate economic stagnation.

Yet a closer look at the work of Beard and Williams actually reveals an important disparity. Beard's *A Foreign Policy for America* and *The Idea of National Interest* blamed the government and business interests for driving US economic expansion. Beard even argued that the government deliberately manipulated the public into supporting war in 1898 (he believed most Americans were unaware of the economic benefits of imperialism). This key tenet of Beard's interpretation was diametrically opposed to the Wisconsin school critiques that emerged in the 1960s. In books such as *The Roots of the Modern American Empire* (1969), Williams claimed that the agricultural community joined industrialists in creating a public consensus that demanded economic expansion overseas. Williams argued that "the majority of the population played a vital part in the evolution and adoption of the imperial policy at the end of the nineteenth century." Consequently, he concluded that "American imperialism was not forced on the majority by a domestic elite, any more than it was imposed on the country by outside forces or foreign nations."[53]

Many historiographers have either ignored such fundamental differences or have failed to recognize them; instead, they chose to emphasize the similarities between Williams and Beard. For example, Diggins's *The Rise and Fall of the American Left* claimed that Williams "and other New Left historians extended the Progressive-Marxist line of reasoning to the Cold War." This statement perpetuated two myths simultaneously. First, it implied that the progressive historians were Marxists—an argument that does not bear close scrutiny. Marxist historians believed that US imperialism was an inevitable consequence of the nation's capitalist economy. Beard on the other hand believed (like Williams after him) that economic expansion would be unnecessary if US policymakers redistributed wealth within the United States and raised the purchasing power of ordinary Americans. Second, Diggins's analysis implied that 1960s radicals simply reiterated a single "line of reasoning" that was merely borrowed from scholars like Beard.[54] This wrongly suggested that the Cold War critiques of US imperialism and earlier progressive interpretations were homogenous. There is no doubt that 1960s radicals were influenced by Beard, but the extent to which they emulated earlier critiques varied.

It is easy to see why Diggins fell into this trap. After all, the methodologies of Beard and Williams were extremely similar. Both men had a penchant for broad interpretations of the past and both argued passionately that an enlightened socialism could solve America's ills. Indeed, many of the criticisms leveled at Beard also applied to Williams. For example, Peter Novick's main concern with Beard's work was its "loose and inconsistent" formulation, which resulted in "convoluted" theories tainted by "ideological preconception." Similar accusations were made by Williams's detractors, who complained about the "ambiguity" of his major works. Critics even used remarkably similar language to chastise both authors. For example, Richard Hofstadter argued that Beard's presentation of history was "somewhat conspiratorial" and displayed a "selective use of historical facts."[55] Meanwhile, Robert Tucker discussed whether Williams and other 1960s radicals conveyed "a conspiratorial version of American foreign policy" and employed "double standards."[56]

However, these similarities have simply masked important divergences. The fact that Beard and Williams both advocated broad interpretations of American history and emphasized economic factors does not mean that their interpretations were one and the same. The Wisconsin critique of US imperialism was arguably more radical than Beard's. This is because Williams, McCormick, and LaFeber believed that the United States had been expansionist throughout its history, whereas Beard occasionally identified periods of hiatus. LaFeber's *The New Empire* (1963), for example, argued that several "years of preparation" preceded the Spanish-American War; therefore, the annexation of the Philippines was simply the climax of a long period of economic expansion.[57] The Wisconsin scholars argued that this expansion continued during the twentieth century, when Wilson's internationalism helped to propel American imperialism. Beard, on the other hand, had a different point of view. The progressive scholar argued in *The American Leviathan* that the Philippines and other territories were taken "without much thought as to the larger political consequences."[58] Furthermore, he believed that Wilson's internationalism marked the end of America's imperialist phase—a phase that had been characterized by the "promotion of foreign commerce with government aid, under the aegis of an expanding sea power."[59]

The Marxist Alternative

It is important to recognize that there was no singular consistent critique of American imperialism before World War II. For example, the Marxist scholar Scott Nearing was a contemporary of Charles Beard but had a very different take on the forces that drove American expansion. Nearing was arguably the most well-known American Marxist intellectual of the 1920s and 1930s. Writing at a time when many Americans suspected that business leaders had induced

US entry into World War I, Nearing's views resonated with those who craved a Marxist solution to the nation's problems. However, whereas Beard's fame gave him personal access to politicians, Nearing was a more reclusive figure. This was because Nearing's Marxist ideology and his association with the American Communist Party made him unpalatable to many Americans, including the major publishing companies, who shunned his work. Although this hindered Nearing's ability to reach a wider audience, his antiestablishment reputation made him a cult figure on the radical left.

Considering his Marxist leanings, it is not surprising that Nearing focused on the subject of income distribution during his early years as an intellectual. However, World War I deeply affected the young scholar. He soon came to believe that capitalism was the main evil in American society—and the primary reason why the United States had entered the war. Feeling that income distribution was too narrow a field, he turned his attention to the "new study of war, revolution, imperialism and civilization" that "spread across the entire field of social history."[60] Nearing felt deeply ashamed of America's participation in what he regarded as a wasteful conflict. Although imperialism was not his specialty, he was able to "shift his analysis of unearned income to a conception of economic surplus" and "reorient his conception of the American plutocracy to a universalized view of the ruling class in all industrialized societies"; this reinforced his belief that war was a feature of capitalist economies.[61]

Although Nearing had little standing within the academic community (he was quickly dismissed from his first teaching job at the University of Pennsylvania), his Marxist views attracted a following on the left. His appeal lay in his suspicion of bankers, which was inspired by the apparent link between the pattern of US overseas investment and American foreign policy. Like Hobson, Nearing believed that bankers and financiers were the driving force behind US imperialism. He quoted Hobson directly, agreeing with the English scholar that "private interests" used "the machinery of government" to protect "economic gains outside their country" (a policy that exacerbated inequalities of wealth and embroiled the United States in needless wars).[62] Nearing also agreed with Hobson that imperialism was the product of competition between the world's major industrial powers. However, whereas Hobson (and Beard for that matter) argued that imperialism could have been avoided, Nearing revealed his Marxism by insisting that "the system of competitive capital makes war inevitable." Therefore, he believed that Beard's plea in *The Open Door at Home* (1934) was a forlorn hope.[63]

Nearing's most famous work, *Dollar Diplomacy: A Study in American Imperialism* (1925), which he cowrote with Joseph Freeman, attempted to demonstrate the relationship between American economic interests abroad and the protection afforded to them by the US government. Although *Dollar Diplomacy* was "a wholly descriptive . . . documentation of the imperial stage of American capitalism," and was therefore not primarily concerned with class struggle, Nearing's contempt for the economic elites that allegedly promoted imperialism was nevertheless clearly evident. Taking a typically broad Marxist perspective, *Dollar Diplomacy* contextualized US expansion during the 1890s as part of the global evolution of capitalism, an inevitable pattern that Nearing believed America could not escape: "Economic necessity dictates that every modern industrial society must develop foreign markets for its surplus products; must control sources of food, fuel, minerals, timber, and other raw materials; must secure business opportunities for the investment of surplus capital. . . . This process of discovering foreign markets, of establishing permanent foreign economic interests and of exercising political pressure upon the regions in which the economic interests exist, has found its chief expression in Europe, yet it is not peculiar to any nation, but corresponds to a certain stage in the development of economic surplus."[64]

This passage demonstrates Nearing's application of Marxist-Leninist theory to the United States. He argued that Americans had always taken lands to satisfy the nation's economic requirements. Nearing claimed that the government had expanded its territorial boundaries to meet the needs of southern slavery before the Civil War—then, as the end of the nineteenth century approached, US foreign policy was used to seize extracontinental lands. Although the bulk of US industries were still focused on exploiting domestic markets at this time, others (such as the sugar industry) were branching out into Cuba and Hawaii. According to Nearing, this "produced a change in American diplomacy," for the "United States was reaching the point which had driven European countries into the Far East and Asia"; in other words, because America's economy was developing along similar lines to the Europeans, the US government followed the European example by seizing foreign markets for its businesses and stimulating overseas capital investment.[65] The result was the establishment of an American empire that by 1900 had embraced Samoa, the Philippines, Guam, Puerto Rico, and Hawaii.

Dollar Diplomacy also argued that the spread of US capital throughout Latin America (and subsequently Europe after World War I) made imperialism unavoidable. This was because United States investors would "apply to the United States Government for support" whenever they did not receive "satisfactory treatment." In a number of cases, this practice resulted in armed intervention, with the "armed forces of the United States" intervening "in the internal affairs" of the lesser-developed nation to resolve difficulties; Nearing gave Haiti, Santo

Domingo, and Nicaragua as examples. Occasionally, this policy also involved outright military conquest (as in the Philippines) or the purchase of the disputed territory (as happened with the Virgin Islands). Nearing stressed that these developments occurred "without consulting the wishes of the populations" that were "transferred to American sovereignty," while "military occupation" frequently ceased "after a territory" had "accepted United States control."[66]

The above analysis demonstrates the contempt Nearing had for US capitalism and imperialism in general. But what did he suggest as an alternative? To answer this question, it is necessary to delve a little deeper into his mind. In *Scott Nearing: The Making of a Homesteader*, John A. Saltmarsh quoted Nearing as saying that "the ruling class of the United States" had become "the ruling class of the world"; consequently, Nearing believed that reform of the American socioeconomic system would go a long way to eradicating the international phenomenon of imperialism in general.[67] However, Nearing believed that a redistribution of wealth (as suggested by Beard in *The Open Door at Home*) was not enough because the problem of capitalism would still remain. After all, Nearing believed capitalism made war and imperialism inevitable. Therefore, he suggested a radical alternative whereby American political institutions would remain but the economic system of communist Russia would be implemented within the United States.

Since Nearing was devoted to the social ideas of communism, but rejected the Bolshevik form of political organization, he believed that if America's superior democratic institutions were fused with the Russian economic model, an equitable and productive socioeconomic system would result. This new breed of socialism could then be exported around the world, supported by a world federation that promoted both democracy and worker-controlled production. Nearing's philosophy, therefore, should not be described as Leninist. Although Nearing saw capitalism as the world's primary evil (and called for its abolition), he was also a devoted pacifist; Nearing rejected Lenin's assumption that violent struggle was the only way to wrestle power away from the capitalist ruling classes. Instead, Nearing advocated peaceful reform of American society and a "long struggle of educating the worker towards a revolutionary social consciousness."[68] Interestingly, this approach had more in common with Williams's vision for reform than with the Marxists who comprised the activist New Left during the 1960s. These activists, who attempted to create a revolution on the streets, emulated Nearing by claiming that imperialism was an inevitable consequence of capitalism, but they rejected his model for reform.

Nearing's idiosyncratic vision for change demonstrates that radical scholars before the Cold War had diverse views. It also shows that subsequent radicals did not always follow their example—although, as we shall see, the contrasting critiques of Beard and Nearing created two contrasting camps regarding the origins of US imperialism (camps that future dissidents generally belonged to). Beard was essentially a socialist who wanted to redistribute wealth within the United States—a shift he expected would mollify imperial urges. Meanwhile, Nearing was a Marxist with a capital *M*; therefore, he attributed the causes of US imperialism to different factors and dedicated himself to an alternative vision of domestic reform. Although both scholars emphasized the role played by economics in US expansion, their critiques actually differed in significant ways because their interpretations originated from separate ideologies.

Existing scholarship that emphasizes continuities in the historiography of American empire (without recognizing these subtle nuances) consequently gives a false sense of homogeneity. As subsequent chapters will demonstrate, Beard had a greater influence on the Wisconsin scholars than Nearing because he attributed US expansion to the intellectual failures and false assumptions of US policymakers. Nearing, on the other hand, was more inspirational to Marxist New Left historians like Gabriel Kolko and David Horowitz because he was an economic determinist. Overall, Beard and the Wisconsin scholars portrayed American imperialism as an unfortunate tragedy; they believed that economic expansion was unnecessary and could have been avoided. The Marxists, meanwhile, saw US imperialism as a necessary and inevitable quest to protect an expanding global economic network.

Even then, however, these two contrasting camps were not entirely distinct. After all, Williams's critique of US expansion possessed a somewhat Marxian (if not pure Marxist) flavor. Furthermore, it must be acknowledged that Beard's and Nearing's critiques had some commonalities too: both dissidents described how economic groups led the United States into conflicts that served their individual interests rather than the general welfare. Although this was a stock subject of Marxist historians, Beard's *The Economic Basis of Politics* also explained how "manufacturing, commercial, financial and agricultural interests" became "closely linked in their fortunes to the fortunes of politics."[69] Because political decisions ultimately had a large bearing on their profit margins, Beard asserted that business interests would always seek influence with politicians through party donations and other methods.

Beard explored this subject in *The American Leviathan*, which not only described how Congressmen represented local business interests but also stated that a president's "origins, his training, his affiliations, and his (initial) profession" determined which "types of ethical aspirations and economic interests" he represented.[70] Four years later, in *The Idea of National Interest*, Beard went further by claiming that the government came "to lean very heavily upon a distinct body of men" who moved "in the same environment and associated by ties of friendship, favor, family, class, and business relationship."[71] By suggesting that US foreign policy was formulated to serve the interests of wealthy elites, Beard's critique occasionally slipped over into the world of Marxists. However, it must be stressed that Marxists like Nearing and Horowitz went much further than Beard: Horowitz's *Empire and Revolution* was essentially a polemic denouncing US foreign policy as part of a global conspiracy to enslave the poor.

Toward the Cold War

There is little doubt that critiques of American expansion written before the Cold War had a significant influence on radical interpretations of US imperialism during the 1950s and 1960s (even though this influence was not entirely pervasive). The assertion that US expansion was a long-term phenomenon, plus the emphasis on economic triggers, are prime examples. The progressive scholars and Nearing dedicated themselves to a broad interpretative approach to diplomatic history that clearly inspired the radical scholars we will examine in subsequent chapters. Early dissidents like Beard and Nearing also influenced subsequent radicals through the power of example: they dismissed rhetoric that characterized US diplomacy as benevolent, they were not afraid to criticize their country, and they began to attack the paradigm of denial surrounding American imperialism.

Although Beard conceded that the perceived morality of US diplomacy appealed to the public—the majority of whom did not realize the economic value of extracontinental territories—he concluded that "material interests" usually dominated policymakers' thoughts. "The assumption that the pursuit of material interests is the prime mover [has not been] rejected or modified in any way. To be sure, ethical phrases, such as the white man's burden and moral obligation, were freely and loosely used in the new literature of policy, but in practice they were treated as useful affiliates of material interests, not as independent and often opposing primordials."[72] Pre–Cold War critiques of American empire therefore set a precedent by arguing that the selfless dimensions of US foreign policy were mostly used for propaganda purposes. The quest to civilize and develop poorer nations was a supplementary concern. The process worked thus: "When a policy or an act had been deemed desirable, . . . the appropriate mandates of moral obligation were drawn upon to substantiate, support or provide justification for the deed."[73]

The scholars who criticized US foreign policy in the first half of the twentieth century also inspired Cold War radicals because they were not afraid to use the term "imperialism." This struck a blow against the orthodox scholarship that claimed that America was a unique anti-imperial nation. In fact, Beard's *A Foreign Policy for America* remains one of the best examples of how historians criticized the United States for its self-interested expansionist ambitions. Beard was particularly scathing of the men who orchestrated US foreign policy during the end of the nineteenth century, particularly Alfred Thayer Mahan, that great promoter of US naval power. *A Foreign Policy for America* described Mahan and his entourage as "imperialists who drink with wine of the lust for power," who might have justified US imperialism with "history, politics and religion" but in reality were motivated by "the pure materialism of biological greed."[74]

Finally, the interwar radicals also inspired their Cold War counterparts by resisting the overwhelming criticism they received. For example, Chester W. Wright in the *Journal of Political Economy* once accused Beard of using only "the facts that bear out the author's point of view," while O. G. Libby claimed in the *Mississippi Valley Historical Review* that Beard's work appeared "somewhat like a partisan appeal to class prejudice" and displayed a "lack of perspective."[75] Some critics even disputed Beard's whole understanding of international relations, pointing out that the United States did not have the freedom of action Beard assumed. For instance, Jesse S. Reeves reminded him that "national interest as secured by diplomacy involves an adjustment with the national interests of other states."[76] This criticism continued during the Cold War when Richard Hofstadter praised Beard for warning Americans about "the dangers of overreaching themselves," but dismissed his whole conception of international relations as "wrong."[77]

It is understandable why Beard was criticized so heavily in the 1940s. Curiously, he abandoned his economic framework and chose to make personal attacks on Franklin Roosevelt for supposedly abusing his power and misleading the public into war. As an alternative to intervention, Beard had proposed a policy of continentalism (the restriction of US activities to the North American continent). The problem with continentalism was that it assumed America's geographical isolation from Europe guaranteed the nation's security—this ignored "the emergence during the war of carrier-based transoceanic aircraft" and "the rise of Nazi Germany," which was an "unmistakable global threat."[78] Furthermore, Beard's intransigence on the issue, plus his personal attacks on a popular wartime president, made the progressive scholar appear "petty, silly and stubborn."[79]

Nevertheless, the demise of Beard's reputation did not dissuade the Wisconsin scholars from using important aspects of his interpretation. After all, Beard helped persuade them that although all history "cannot be 'explained' in economic terms, . . . in great transformations in society . . . economic 'forces' are primordial or fundamental, and come nearer 'explaining' events" than any other factors.[80] However, perhaps Beard's greatest influence was his refusal to accept that economic expansion served the national interest. "If a nation depends upon for its standard of life, vital interests outside its jurisdiction, which it cannot dominate and defend, then it does not and cannot possess economic security."[81] Williams agreed with this assessment wholeheartedly and concurred that US imperialism diverted attention away from much-needed domestic socioeconomic reforms. This was a tragic situation that, perhaps more than any other factor, inspired Williams's most famous book, *The Tragedy of American Diplomacy.*

3

Madison as a Melting Pot

A special place at a special time.
William Appleman Williams, 1990

Why Madison?

Before we reach for our analytical hats and scrutinize Williams's critique of US imperialism, it is important to explore the full intellectual context in which the Wisconsin scholars emerged. Studying national circumstances is not enough. To get the full picture, one must delve into the local intellectual context too; this means understanding the University of Wisconsin's intellectual heritage, recognizing the distinguished but somewhat unconventional scholars who taught history at UW during the 1950s and 1960s, and appreciating Madison's progressive history. After all, in the words of Walter LaFeber, "it was difficult for a PhD candidate not to think of himself as somehow a part of the Wisconsin progressive tradition."[1] Once this true context has been established, it will emerge why, of all the academic institutions in the United States, Madison was the most likely place for a radical critique of US imperialism to emerge during the Cold War. This process will also illuminate the origins of the Wisconsin interpretation and help to explain what made it unique.

The first thing to emphasize is that UW, which lies scenically alongside the tranquil banks of Lake Mendota in Madison, was held in high regard by the academic community during the 1950s and 1960s; this was particularly true among those who valued a challenging intellectual environment that encouraged original and unconventional thought. Students applying to study history were particularly aware of the university's progressive heritage and its standing within the history profession. For example, when Williams arrived at Madison in 1947, he believed that UW was "probably the best on-campus liberal arts faculty" in the United States.[2] When Thomas McCormick joined the University of Wisconsin a decade later (a period he described as the university's "heyday"), he considered the history department to be "clearly the best in the country by far. . . . It was something else."[3] Meanwhile, Walter LaFeber turned down an offer from Harvard to study for his PhD in Madison. When weighing up which university to choose, he sought the advice of his old college professor, Robert Bowers. Having studied at UW under Merle Curti, Bowers told his young protégé it was "no contest—go to Wisconsin," a decision LaFeber has described as "the best professional advice I have ever received."[4]

As intelligent and freethinking young scholars, LaFeber and McCormick were among hundreds of bright prospects who made what could be described as an intellectual pilgrimage to Madison during the Cold War. In his recent book *Beyond the Frontier*, David S. Brown described how "the Madison experience" made the University of Wisconsin "for a long time" something of "a mythical destination for intellectually curious young people"—a place that many considered to be "the eternal city of Midwestern historical writing." It was, after all, where Frederick Jackson Turner composed his frontier thesis and became "the founding father of modern professional writing."[5] Madison also became, alongside Berkeley (where the Free Speech Movement blossomed), an epicenter of the antiwar movement in the mid-1960s. University of Wisconsin students protested against not only the US intervention in Vietnam but also the university's alleged collusion with Washington policymakers; the students particularly resented UW administrators' compliance with the Selective Service System (the method by which the government selected young men to fight in Vietnam). Believing that the academic integrity and heritage of the university had been violated, the young demonstrators took a stand to show their commitment to "the ideals of the university," which they described as "the search for truth through independent study."[6] The intellectual heritage of the University of Wisconsin, it seems, was something worth fighting for.

However, the University of Wisconsin had become "an intellectual haven for the radical intellectual" before the Vietnam War.[7] Its reputation was cemented in the 1950s when the history department resisted the intellectual conformity that characterized the early Cold War period, becoming a bastion of independent and often radical thought. It therefore attracted students with a penchant for political activism. When the protest movement gathered momentum during the 1960s, the UW was already primed. Madison witnessed what was the largest peace demonstration in the nation's history in 1965, but the most notorious protest occurred in October 1967 when UW students demonstrated against Dow Chemical—a tragic event that ended in violence. This demonstration, which sought to prevent Dow from recruiting on campus, was significant in the national antiwar movement because "it caused by far the most reverberations" of any student demonstration at the time and "marked the point where the tactics of protest changed."[8] However, although this episode of student activism was the most vociferous witnessed in Madison, radicalism at UW was hardly new. In fact, the student strikes that took place after the Dow demonstrations between 1967 and 1970 followed in the footsteps of similar strikes during the 1930s. The Vietnam crisis might have been different to the economic emergency during the Great Depression, but students in Madison reacted in similar ways.

Although UW was not the only campus where student activism thrived during the 1960s, the radicalism in Madison was unique. This is because it obscured a deeper and more significant intellectual radicalism. While former student Paul Buhle recalled that "the 1960s" in Madison, "as a sentiment or political mood, lasted longer than nearly anywhere else," he was also keen to point out that UW's dissidents were not as "anti-intellectual" as they were in other American towns and cities.[9] For example, Madison was home to two intellectually creative radical journals: *Studies on the Left*, which was established by UW students (and initially guided by Williams), and subsequently Buhle's own journal *Radical America*, which "translated the inarticulate concepts of the day into categories for analysis"—something the more militant members of the New Left often failed to do.[10] Furthermore, the original editors of *Studies*, which included James Weinstein, often turned away from activism in the hope of creating social and economic revolution through the power of intellect and ideas. The student experience at UW, particularly for those who studied history, was therefore distinctive, and for some, life changing. The personal journey of Thomas McCormick is testament to this: "When I arrived at UW as a graduate student I was a Republican who admired Eisenhower, but UW changed me."[11]

In *History and the New Left*, Buhle speculated that Madison's location and "scenic beauty" reflected "as its lakes do the sky on a perfect day, the possibilities of a better life." Although the idea of young idealists being inspired by their surroundings might seem romanticized, it was somehow more feasible than fanciful. After all, geography has certainly played a part in the evolution of the university and its intellectual heritage. Because Madison was a tranquil haven isolated from large metropolitan centers, the University of Wisconsin escaped the bitter arguments that divided the Old Left in the first half of the twentieth century. As a result, its professors and students were able to develop a fresh approach. Similarly, it was Madison's midwestern isolation that nourished the university's progressive roots and enabled UW to escape "the general stultifying atmosphere of Cold War America." While intellectuals elsewhere rallied behind the flag, Madison remained "a verdant intellectual oasis of the Midwest." The town also possessed a "fusion" of American and European culture that encouraged its citizens to resist monopoly, embrace social-intellectual currents, and dedicate themselves to grassroots political action.[12]

Brown's *Beyond the Frontier* contextualized the University of Wisconsin as being part of a broader midwestern voice that profoundly influenced historical writing in the United States. The book traced an intellectual tradition that stretched from Turner to Beard, and Williams to Christopher Lasch—men he collectively described as "children of the Midwest" who displayed "a faint but unmistakable provincialism."[13] Brown argued that as midwesterners, these distinguished scholars thought differently from cosmopolitans. For example, they were suspicious of eastern power and frustrated by its liberal internationalism, which they believed had led to an imperialist foreign policy. Instead they cherished progressive, democratic, and populist ideas and were occasionally inclined toward isolationism.

The University of Wisconsin itself was the heartbeat of Madison's progressive and democratic tradition. Indeed, the town's progressive politicians wanted to use UW as "a laboratory for democracy" and a resource for science, agriculture, social policy, and creativity that would aid the government and enhance the lives of Wisconsin's citizens.[14] Close links between the university and the city gradually evolved into a concept known as "the Wisconsin Idea," which sought to involve university academics in the running of the state. As the twentieth century progressed, the Wisconsin Idea expanded in scope and came to embody the restriction of corporate influence and the sustenance of democratic polity. It also questioned post–World War II liberalism, which many midwesterners blamed for consolidating the power of elites in US national life; at UW and in the broader community of Madison, the majority of citizens craved a more idealistic and egalitarian socioeconomic structure than the one corporate capitalism had created.

Although the university played an important role in the community during the nineteenth and twentieth centuries, and was home to many exceptional scholars of English, economics, sociology, and political science, it was the history department that built up the greatest national and international reputation. The department initially became famous because of Turner, whose work on the American frontier put UW on the map. After 1945 distinguished historians like Merle Curti and Williams further enhanced the reputation of both the department and the university as a bastion of progressivism. In doing so, they entrenched UW's "distinctive school of thought," which David Maraniss has described as "democratic" and "scornful of the eastern establishment" as well as being "somewhat isolationist."[15] When the Cold War stifled intellectual freedoms during the 1940s and 1950s, the University of Wisconsin was consequently able to resist. Instead of bowing to consensus history, UW's scholars expressed themselves freely, knowing that the university's dedication to independent scholarship and, crucially, the support of the UW administrators, ensured an environment in which they could think differently.

Because progressive scholarship was still revered in Madison during the Cold War, UW was the ideal place for Williams to develop his controversial interpretation of US imperialism—a critique that assaulted the paradigm of denial and criticized American foreign policy in a manner that shocked orthodox contemporaries. Even Williams's mentor, Fred Harvey Harrington, who later became the president of the university, described Williams's interpretation of US diplomacy as "pro-Russian" in appearance because it "found no fault with the Russians" while "finding lots of fault with US foreign policy."[16] A perspective this radical would have been discouraged at most universities, but because the progressive tradition was alive and well at UW, and the Cold War consensus held little sway, a critique of US expansion that fused the ideas of Turner and Beard was not considered odious.

This chapter will delve into the unique intellectual atmosphere in Madison that profoundly affected Williams, McCormick, and LaFeber. It will identify the personalities who inspired the Wisconsin scholars and explore the factors that shaped their critique of US imperialism; this will include a brief look at Madison's progressive history and the unconventional makeup of the UW history department during the 1950s (the period when Williams began his career). Between 1950 and 1956 members of the Old Left found in "the safe haven" of Madison "a means and a reason to rewrite history from the inside out" and a "political calling" to stand up to McCarthyism and promote civil liberties. Williams was very much immersed in this intellectual atmosphere when he wrote *The Tragedy of American Diplomacy*; he was inspired by Turner's legacy and influenced by the professors who instructed him. Williams was also determined to create a new intellectual radicalism in Madison that remained faithful to UW's intellectual traditions. He nurtured this new radicalism, which moved away from the Old Left between 1956 and 1965 and laid down "barricades against the threats to existence posed by the Cold War," by helping Madison students to establish *Studies on the Left*.[17]

The Radical Tradition

The relevance of Turner's frontier thesis to the historiography of American empire has already been discussed. However, we have yet to consider Turner's conception of history and his approach to studying the past—both of which influenced the Wisconsin scholars. Turner regarded history as a movement, and he believed the historical profession had much to learn from sociology as well as geography and demography. This was a conviction that Williams shared. During his time at UW, Williams read as widely as possible and increased his knowledge of other academic subjects. In many ways, this is why *Tragedy* read like a work of intellectual rather than diplomatic history. Williams did not want his approach to be constrained by the norms of his profession; he saw himself as more than just a diplomatic scholar.

Williams was also influenced by the subjects Turner chose to teach and research. Turner's advanced course on "The History of the West" at UW portrayed the advance of settlements across the continent as a movement. This dovetailed with two other courses Turner taught, which appeared under the banner "The Economic and Social History of the United States" (one course that went to 1789, and another focused on the period between 1789 and 1850). As the course literature described, Turner wanted his students "to treat economic and social topics in relation to the general movement of national history."[18] This novel approach helped UW, through Turner and his work, to make "a permanent mark on the writing of American history."[19] It also encouraged Williams to think broadly and place individual events within a broader historical context or pattern.

However, although Turner's approach became a hallmark of the history department at UW, it was John Bascom, the president of UW from 1874 to 1887, who established the University of Wisconsin's general intellectual approach. In the opinion of Merle Curti and Vernon Carstensen, who chronicled the history of the University of Wisconsin in *The Wisconsin Idea*, Bascom represented "in many ways the most humanistic traditions of his time" and promoted "the unity of all knowledge." Bascom wrote about seemingly diverse topics such as psychology, Christian ethics, economics, and political economy—he argued that "knowledge was inseparable and shouldn't be fragmented."[20] As a result Bascom instigated a broad university curriculum and thought seriously about how the university could contribute toward the life of the state. He therefore became the first proponent of the Wisconsin Idea, which envisaged UW as "a democratic, public institution serving the public interest."[21] For example, Bascom hoped the university's agricultural school would help the state to prosper.

But Bascom was not only dedicated to creating an enlightened society with the university at its heart—he also championed the cause of academic freedom. This sentiment remained important after Bascom's death and became increasingly relevant to the university during the 1940s and 1950s, when the onset of the Cold War and McCarthyism threatened to stifle intellectual dissent. A plaque at the top of Bascom Hill, one of UW's most recognizable landmarks, still reminds students and visitors of the historical importance of academic freedom to the university. The plaque reads: "We Believe That the Great State University of Wisconsin Should Ever Encourage That Continual and Fearless Sifting and Winnowing by Which Alone the Truth Can Be Found." These words were written by the Board of Regents in 1894 to defend a UW professor accused of teaching pernicious ideas. The plaque informs readers that "sifting and winnowing represents the ideological backbone of American higher education: that teachers and students should be free to search for the truth." These values were not just important to Bascom; they were also cherished by students and professors at UW.

Consequently, when Williams began to articulate his critique of US imperialism in the 1950s, an interpretation that challenged prevailing intellectual currents, incurred the wrath of orthodox contemporaries, and risked investigation by HCUA, Williams was very much upholding the traditions of his university. Indeed, it could be argued that Williams was upholding the traditions of the state of Wisconsin itself—after all, the history of the university and the state were inextricably linked. For example, Bascom also had a profound influence on one of Wisconsin's favorite political sons, Robert La Follette, who was governor of Wisconsin from 1901 to 1906 and thereafter a nationally renowned US senator. Indeed, La Follette's autobiography paid homage to Wisconsin's democratic tradition and the influence of Bascom on local government.

The state of Wisconsin has a long tradition of radicalism. At the end of the nineteenth century, industrialization and migration from rural areas to urban centers caused an upsurge in social dissent. This period of transition enhanced Wisconsin's reputation for radicalism and enabled La Follette to make a name for himself as a champion of ordinary citizens. Indeed, he soon earned the affectionate nickname "Fighting Bob," which reflected his determination to resist the power of corporations and stand up for ordinary citizens. During the first quarter of the twentieth century La Follette, who was described by David Thelen as "one of the most respected radicals ever," became a "hero to millions" as he launched a campaign against privilege and concentrated wealth. He became a Republican senator in 1906 and ran for the White House in 1924 as the nominee of the Progressive Party he had formed. Although he ultimately failed to become president, "Fighting Bob" won the state of Wisconsin and came second in a further eleven states. During his long political career, La Follette was credited with shaking "the conservative bastion of the Senate"; meanwhile, his leadership of the radical progressive "insurgency" before World War I left a lasting impression on the US political landscape.[22] His son, "Young Bob" La Follette, followed in his father's footsteps, narrowly losing to Joseph McCarthy in the Wisconsin Republican primary in 1946.

In many ways, Wisconsin scholars like Williams shared the wish of "Fighting Bob" to "dethrone corporate control of government." Williams also agreed with La Follette's stance that American foreign policy had become an instrument of big business; therefore, it was not surprising that both men believed US intervention in World War I had been a mistake. In the aftermath of the Great War, La Follette claimed that the League of Nations was an attempt to build "an iron ring of conservative governments" around the world.[23] Williams concurred with this sentiment throughout his career—like "Fighting Bob" he believed that US foreign policy was often designed to secure foreign markets for American exports. Consequently, when Williams began to challenge orthodox liberal scholarship during the Cold War, expressing views that were often similar to the discredited Henry Wallace, he became another in a long line of "exemplars of Madison's progressive tradition."[24]

While the rest of the academic community turned its back on progressive thought during the Cold War, the University of Wisconsin remained hostile to the consolidation of corporate influence in post-1945 America and the intellectual consensus that bolstered it. McCarthyism barely touched the history department in Madison at all; this was somewhat ironic as Wisconsin was, after all, Joseph McCarthy's home state. Madison's intellectual heritage, which made UW "a laboratory for the uses of history," enabled the university to resist the academic purges of the 1950s to a large extent. Meanwhile, it was politically difficult, if not impossible, for McCarthy himself to lead a crusade against the left in Wisconsin.[25] The University of Wisconsin, therefore, retained "a general sense of estrangement from prevailing currents."[26] Paul Buhle has even argued that "the Leviathan state" found its historical and "scholarly nemesis" in Madison.[27]

It must have pained McCarthy to know that one of the primary hubs of intellectual dissent was based in Wisconsin, but there was little he could do about it. It was far too risky politically for the senator to create enemies in his own backyard. Looking back at the period forty years later, Williams reflected that "McCarthy was shrewd enough to know that he would be destroyed quickly at home if he ever launched a full frontal attack on the University of Wisconsin."[28] Madison's academic leaders quickly grasped this fact and were able to take liberties that were impossible for other academic institutions across America. For example, Owen Lattimore, the editor of *Pacific Affairs*, a journal published by the Institute of Pacific Relations, was invited to speak at UW even though McCarthy's supporters had portrayed him as a communist and a traitor. This infuriated the right, who had blamed the Institute of Pacific Relations for the fall of China to communism.

Although it must be reiterated that Madison was not the only center of radicalism during the Cold War—for example, dissidents from the Beat generation and the labor tradition gathered in San Francisco, while New York radicals recruited from the New School and the East Village—UW was the heart of intellectual radicalism in the early years of the Cold War. While Arthur Schlesinger Jr. and Reinhold Niebuhr led the liberal/conservative consensus that discredited Beard and other radicals, UW's historians retained a deep respect for the progressive doyen, believing Beard's work helped scholars to develop a greater understanding of America's past. Diplomatic historians like Fred Harvey Harrington, who was Williams's mentor, saw great merit in Beard's theory that foreign policy was "a way of helping the well-to-do people to get what they wanted." Harrington was also attracted to Beard's concept of imperialism as "a push from the business people" of the United States. However, it was not just the diplomatic historians who owed a debt to Beard. Most historians at UW adopted a "liberal approach to history" and subscribed (to varying extents) to Beard's assertion that "economic factors determined the way in which decisions were made in American history." For example, Curti was very much an admirer of Beard, while Merrill Jensen's work on the articles of confederation was certainly "Beardian." The Madison historians cared little that the eastern establishment "didn't like it."[29]

Harrington's arrival at UW was particularly significant in the emergence of the Wisconsin critique of US imperialism. Although he had left UW in 1940 to take up a position at Arkansas, he returned in 1944 at a time when interest in US foreign relations was surging (primarily because of World War II). In an interview he gave for the University of Wisconsin Oral History Project in 1985, Harrington admitted that he was initially nervous about the prospect of teaching in Madison. However, he soon developed a flair for lecturing and inspired several budding diplomatic scholars during his second stint—including, of course, the likes of Williams, McCormick, and LaFeber. Alongside Curti (who arrived in 1942) and Jensen (1944), Harrington became an important member of a burgeoning group of UW historians. The department also recruited a European intellectual historian, a Russian historian, and even an expert on China; therefore "a world history department" was established.[30] This enhanced UW's national standing and its reputation for broad thinking.

In his interview for the UW Oral History Project, Harrington attributed the Madison historians' admiration of Beard to their backgrounds. "We were products of the depression. . . . We were deeply impressed by the fact that the American capitalist system had come into some disrepute and that it was important to analyze some of the economic factors that had brought on the depression. . . . Thus we tended to be against the traditional interpretations, which tended to be descriptive and highly patriotic." Harrington also admitted that although he had considered himself to be a New Dealer in the 1930s, he was at one time tempted to "go the whole hog" and become a communist. However, despite "flirting" with the Socialist Party he ultimately remained "a left-wing New Dealer" like many of his colleagues at UW. He believed this position knitted with the department's existing "Beardian pattern."[31]

It is interesting to note that some UW scholars opposed American intervention in World War II. Although the conflict "was a war in which the American people were certainly very patriotic," and "there was a good deal of pressure on one to be silent if one did not agree with the main position," neither William Hesseltine nor Curti were naturally inclined to support US involvement. Although Curti eventually came round, Hesseltine remained "very outspoken" against the war and received similar criticism to Beard.[32] Meanwhile, Curti and Howard Beale were also "strongly against discrimination against blacks" and firm "believers in racial equality . . . and also, to an extent, pacifism." This demonstrated that the Madison scholars were often "very strongly agreed on things which were really minority positions in the country at large."[33] The history department at UW therefore consisted of several historians who followed their convictions and were unfazed by criticism; Williams therefore fitted in perfectly.

The controversy these historians created soon attracted like-minded scholars to Madison. By the late 1940s and early 1950s the department became "distinguished" by bringing in scholars who were "not acceptable in other places." Harrington described some of these people as "peculiar."[34] For example, UW appointed E. A. Ross after he had been sacked by Stanford and also employed Beale, who had a reputation for being difficult. As a result, the history department could call upon a diverse and talented group of historians who embraced a number of different views. Reflecting on his time as a student in Madison, Williams claimed he was attracted to UW precisely because the history department offered "teachers as different as Jensen, Harrington and Hesseltine" who "all demanded more than one's best" and "hired young radicals without batting an eye."[35]

It must be remembered that the "towering figure" in American diplomatic history at the time was Samuel Flagg Bemis, a man Harrington described as "a straight old-type historian" who was more of a "State Department type" than a Beardian. Although a vigorous conservative called William Campbell had joined the Board of Regents in the 1940s, and wanted UW to become more patriotic and shed its reputation as a bastion of liberalism and radicalism, in the words of Harrington "he certainly wasn't going to get" such a perspective from Madison's former New Dealers. Consequently, as the UW history department grew, it had "as large an impact on diplomatic history as anybody"—but not in the way that Campbell intended.[36] Instead, the conservatives on the Board of Regents winced as the progressive heritage of the history department survived and the Wisconsin critique of American imperialism gradually evolved.

The Education of the Wisconsin Scholars

During the 1950s, history at UW became as strong as it had been in the early twentieth century when Turner was the most famous historian in the country. The history department established a reputation as "the Big Red Machine" that produced graduate students who regularly "beat out the competition" for prominent positions in history faculties across the United States.[37] After Fred Harvey Harrington became chairman in 1952, the department assembled an "illustrious cast" of scholars.[38] In addition to Curti, Hesseltine, and Jensen, who were already at Madison, William Taylor arrived to teach foreign policy, Harvey Goldberg was recruited to provide expertise in French social history, John R. W. Smail was hired to teach Southeast Asian studies, and George Mosse, who became a prominent radical speaker on campus, arrived to lecture on European history and nationalism. The department was also complemented by other "formidable intellectual powers," such as the disillusioned former Marxist Paul Farmer and a historically aware sociologist called Hans Gerth, who had fled Nazi Germany during the rise of Hitler. Gerth introduced "a cosmopolitan learning and a depth of feeling for twentieth-century tragedy congruent to the historians' message," an approach that inspired both Williams and the radical sociologist C. Wright Mills.[39]

At first glance, senior UW figures such as Curti, Jensen, and Beale appeared to be "throwbacks to an earlier era." This was because of their progressive leanings and their belief that the historical role of dissent had been neglected in American history. For example, Jensen's work "bemoaned the demise of the agrarian democratic impulse" and emphasized how the state had violated the autonomy explicit in the Articles of Confederation.[40] Meanwhile, Beale subscribed to Beard's theory that history could be used to solve public problems, while Curti praised the progressive tradition in an address to the American Historical Association in 1953. Of the senior historians at Madison, Curti was the most influential. His progressivism was understandable from his past: Curti had been a student of Turner's at Harvard, and he once heard the socialist hero Eugene Debs make a speech in Boston (an experience he found inspiring). As a result, Curti became an enthusiastic proponent of social change who was wary of both Cold War liberalism and US militarism.

Williams's critique of US imperialism, and indeed his whole intellectual approach, imitated these UW scholars to a significant extent. He embraced the department's progressivism, focused on the agrarian community like Jensen, agreed with Beale that socioeconomic problems could be solved through intellectualism, and shared Curti's suspicion of militarism and his enthusiasm for social reform. However, it was Harrington who had the greatest influence on Williams and the Wisconsin revisionists—not only because he was the chairman of the history department at UW between 1952 and 1955 (and therefore the man "who built the modern history department") but also because it was Harrington's approach to US diplomatic history that inspired the Wisconsin critique of American empire.[41] After all, it was Williams's mentor who convinced his students that economic expansion was the reason why the United States became involved in world affairs.

Although the UW history department contained a number of capable instructors during the 1950s, Harrington's role was crucial—not that Harrington himself liked to admit it. In his interview for the UW Oral History Project, Harrington singled out Hesseltine and Curti as the scholars who "contributed most to the training of excellent students" and was very modest about his own achievements. When asked about Williams, LaFeber, and McCormick, he simply said, "I helped them some, but they were very good when they came to Madison."[42] However, Harrington's former students were in no doubt about Harrington's influence on their academic development. For example, McCormick has described Harrington as a "Socrates" and "a brilliant seminar tutor."[43] Meanwhile, LaFeber has said that "the opportunity to work with Fred" was one of the main reasons he chose to study in Madison. Indeed, when Lloyd Gardner decided to move from Harrington to Williams for his PhD work, LaFeber stayed with Fred because he greatly "admired his published work" and "his unbelievable political skills in both the university and the profession."[44]

When reading the Wisconsin scholars' work, one is struck by the extent to which Harrington's influence is clear. Harrington not only "fuelled the revisionist theory of history" that "put emphasis on economics" but also (in a similar manner to Turner) encouraged budding historians to consider the value of other subjects in their research—particularly psychology and sociology (two disciplines that Williams in particular applied to his interpretation of US expansion).[45] Harrington expressed an interest in economics and US imperialism from the beginning of his career. Although he decided against researching empire in his PhD dissertation because Curti was already working on something similar, this was something of an anomaly. "Imperialism formed the basis, of the things I did much later," and "I worked on this imperialism business ever since."[46] He also taught a course at UW on America's diplomatic and economic relationship with Russia. This is significant because Williams's first book, *American-Russian Relations, 1781–1947*, discussed this very subject.

However, it was Harrington's course on American foreign relations at UW that earned him national recognition. In 1937 the course had just thirty-five students, but the onset of World War II created a surge of interest in the subject. By the early 1950s the numbers had soared to over four hundred. This was not all due to current affairs: Harrington himself had become a highly polished and engaging teacher; his lectures drew a considerable audience and were sometimes broadcast on local radio. As a result, Harrington managed to attract what he called "an exceptional group of graduate students." He didn't demand or expect these students to agree with his assertions; instead, he encouraged them to think for themselves—offering criticism to coax students into challenging their preconceptions. Harrington summarized his approach as letting "people follow their own line," which is why, he believed, "some of my historians turned out to be left-wing historians and others did not."[47]

Having said that, the subject matter Harrington discussed in his seminars displayed a clear progressive leaning. In fact, when LaFeber, McCormick, and Lloyd Gardner arrived in Madison, they regarded Harrington as "a bit of an anachronism" because, like the American history group at UW in general, he emphasized economic factors when the overwhelming majority of diplomatic scholars no longer did so.[48] A look at the description of his third-year undergraduate course, which appeared in *The Bulletin of the University of Wisconsin Catalog* in 1957, hinted at his progressivism: "American Foreign Relations 1775 to Present. Description: 'The United States in its relations with the outside world, emphasizing public opinion and the economic, social, political forces that have determined American foreign policy.'" One can tell from this extract that Harrington saw US foreign policy as far more than a moral calling. He also ran a postgraduate course titled "Studies in American Expansion Overseas."[49] His approach, therefore, was quintessentially Beardian.

Although the relationship between Harrington and Williams was not always smooth—they clashed on several occasions, including a time when Harrington allegedly recommended McCormick for a job at Michigan without consulting his colleagues—Williams's approach to history was remarkably close to that of his mentor.[50] For example, Williams agreed with Harrington's conviction that history had often "neglected to use the talents of persons in other disciplines," and that historians should be more interested in politics, economics, psychology, anthropology, and the sciences. Williams also shared Harrington's determination "to make history a literary field as well as a scientific one" and to "address a larger audience"—in other words, "to be popular as well as correct" and "interesting" as well as "clear."[51] When Williams wrote *Tragedy* and later *Empire as a Way of Life*, he was criticized for failing to use footnotes meticulously (which some believed neglected his duty as a historian). Instead, he often employed emotive rhetoric and used generalized arguments to convey his point. This was evidence, perhaps, that Williams was writing for a lay audience as well as the academic community.

In 1957 Harrington decided to take a job as assistant to UW president Edwin Broun Fred; this was a move to the administrative side of university life that ultimately saw him become president himself. This created an opening in the history department that Williams, as a former pupil of Harrington, eagerly filled. Reflecting on his decision to take the job, Williams explained that he was attracted to UW because "the progressive tradition was alive and well" despite the dominance of consensus history on the national stage. He also appreciated the department's "commitment to critical intellectual excellence" and relished the prospect of becoming "an intellectual and political activist in the academic and general community."[52] Williams also admired the fact that UW's intellectual heritage was "anchored in a social conception of society" that rejected the "individualistic ethic" and went beyond the New Deal and the progressivism of other states.[53] Madison had a history of resisting the eastern government's "imperialistic demands," and Williams wanted to be part of the struggle against an American society that worshiped "abundance" as the "end goal."[54]

By joining UW, Williams believed he was "on the edge of a new radical consciousness that could make a significant contribution to changing society for the better." He was also excited at the prospect of working in a city where the progressive Weltanschauung was "shared" by academics and nonacademics of all classes (rural as well as urban)." Furthermore, the quality of students at UW, many of whom had parents "of an old left persuasion" was another incentive. Williams found that these students were "intelligent, willing to work hard," and were "proud bearers of an activist tradition." Like Harrington, Williams regarded the university's students as "a powerful yeast in the Madison brew"—a vital ingredient that made UW "a special place at a special time."[55]

From the history department's perspective, Williams was the ideal candidate to replace Harrington. Although he was more committed to political activism than his predecessor, Williams generally shared Harrington's conception of US foreign relations—particularly its emphasis on economic triggers and expansion overseas. When Harrington was a graduate student he omitted economic factors from his work as his instructor, Henry Steele Commager, predominantly stressed intellectual history. However, Harrington found that the economic interpretation resonated with him; therefore, when he turned his hand to teaching he always ensured he had "this economic interpretation rather vigorously at hand."[56] The young Williams was equally fascinated by economic factors, and although he certainly did not neglect intellectual history, he shared Harrington's penchant for challenging orthodoxy.

As an admirer of Beard and a student of Harrington, it was not surprising that Williams emphasized economics in his teaching. Although his work could arguably be described as Marxian (in other words, aspects of his interpretation were somewhat reminiscent of Marx), he was more interested in the psychology of American expansionism (as explored by Turner) than economic determinism. In "The Significance of the Frontier in American History," Turner had framed the evolution of the United States in terms of westward continental expansion; he believed Americans had a psychological dependency on expansion because they linked the frontier with freedom itself.[57] Williams agreed with this general sentiment and fused it with Beard's economic interpretation of history, which asserted that US imperialism resulted from policymakers' mistaken belief that economic expansion would prevent overproduction. This was a broader interpretation than Marx's narrow determinism.

Williams believed that Turner's work was significant because he provided the first psychological interpretation of America's imperial turn at the end of the nineteenth century (the moment when the United States became "an imperial republic"). Turner claimed that the frontier had offered Americans "an escape . . . from the bondage of the past"—an opportunity to evade the imbalances of their society through constant expansion.[58] Williams was fascinated by this theory. As the 1950s progressed, he adopted this hypothesis and applied it to his fresh concept of US imperialism. Williams even wrote an essay titled "The Frontier Thesis and American Foreign Policy," which was published in *The Pacific Historical Review* in 1955. Williams claimed that "Turner's concept that America's unique and true democracy was the product of an expanding frontier" had provided "American empire builders with an overview and explanation of the world." Williams quoted Turner directly, particularly his contention that "the perennial rebirth" provided by expansion provided a "fluidity to American life" without which "fissures begin to open between the classes, fissures that may widen into chasms."[59] Consequently, although Williams's evolving critique of US imperialism was certainly pioneering, it was clearly influenced by the intellectual heritage of the UW history department and the great scholars who had worked there.

The Intellectual Approach

It is too simplistic to argue that the Wisconsin critique of American empire started and ended with Williams. As we shall see in chapter 5, the students Harrington and Williams influenced did not simply regurgitate *Tragedy*: they actually composed their own individual interpretations of US expansion that emphasized political, economic, and psychological factors to varying extents. However, all these scholars shared one important thing in common: an approach to historical inquiry that was clearly shaped by their Madison education. When McCormick and LaFeber arrived at the University of Wisconsin, the history department boasted a fine national reputation. They realized that UW provided excellent teaching and research assistantships, and they knew that everywhere their PhDs went, they "talked about Wisconsin" affectionately. Other universities like Harvard and Berkeley obviously attracted good students too, but in the words of Harrington, "their draws were a little different." Harrington believed this was because UW possessed "a Charles Beard kind of department" that questioned conventional wisdom.[60] When McCormick was asked why he chose the University of Wisconsin he was unequivocal. "I came to UW to be part of the Wisconsin intellectual tradition, . . . to take ideas seriously and question conventional thinking."[61]

It is important to remember, however, that the Wisconsin tradition was more than just progressivism. It was also shaped by midwesterners' traditional suspicion of the federal government and the radical heritage of Wisconsin as a state. McCormick summarized this intellectual approach as adopting "a critical state of mind"; to follow the University of Wisconsin intellectual tradition, "one didn't have to follow a set pattern of axioms, but it did mean a kind of state of mind—that is, you questioned everything and dug for assumptions underneath too. It was all about nurturing an inquiring state of mind, which, implicitly, means ending up having a critical state of mind."[62] As a result, the Wisconsin scholars all went beyond Turner and Beard, even though they were "Beardian in the old sense" (in other words, their critiques were influenced by Beard's *The Open Door at Home*). In terms of diplomatic history and the study of US imperialism, this meant looking "a little behind 'foreign policy' to see what pressures were operating."[63]

When he instructed the talented group of graduate students that became the Wisconsin revisionists, Harrington hammered home the necessity of taking a "broad view" of American diplomacy. This involved looking at "pressure groups" and the motivations of those "who make decisions on what our foreign policy is going to be." This differed from the orthodox approach that was often restricted to "the official change of notes" between the United States and other countries. The study of US foreign relations at UW in the 1950s under Harrington (and then Williams) therefore meant examining the influences that determined foreign policy, "whether they're economic pressures like businessmen or labor groups, whether they're like pressures from religious people" or even "ethnic groups."[64]

Because the Wisconsin scholars were attuned to the Wisconsin intellectual tradition, they addressed the issue of US imperialism without bowing to Cold War orthodoxy. While orthodox contemporaries equated imperialism, with its pejorative associations, solely with colonialism, the likes of LaFeber and McCormick thought differently. "Equating imperialism only with colonialism, in a narrow way, was just an intellectual game they (orthodox scholars) played to avoid confronting the centrality of American expansion to US history. It was their way of saying 'yes, we were imperial for a period of time, but this was a very short period and an aberration'; after all, as soon as America got an empire, we started devising ways to give it back." The Wisconsin scholars agreed that the United States rarely sought formal governance over foreign lands, but they believed this disguised policymakers' desire to secure economic hegemony. Madison, as an academic refuge, gave them the freedom to make such radical claims—and because they were different from the Marxists, they regarded themselves as belonging to a unique "school."[65]

The emergence of this distinct Wisconsin School was evident in the pages of *Studies on the Left*, the journal established by UW students in 1959. In many ways, the contents of the journal and its history reflected the difference between the Wisconsin scholars and the Marxist New Left in general (although the journal's intellectual outlook eventually changed when it left Madison for New York in 1963). Perhaps this was not surprising as many of the original editors, which included Gardner, were familiar with Williams on a personal level as well as an academic one. Williams actively helped the editors establish the journal by providing intellectual support and encouragement. He convinced them to think of history as creating a usable past; he also wrote an article on Samuel Adams for the third edition.

Although it was a coincidence that *Studies* was launched in 1959, the same year that Williams's *Tragedy* was published, the timing was fitting. Like *Tragedy*, the first edition of *Studies* discussed the crisis of the 1890s with reference to America's "developing imperialism." It also examined how the diplomacy of

"Open Door Expansion" (which Williams believed was the basis of US expansion in the nineteenth and twentieth centuries) was designed to prevent territories (in this case, Morocco) from falling into the hands of rival empires.[66] Not surprisingly, the first edition of *Studies* gave *Tragedy* a glowing review, praising Williams's analysis as "incisive" and claiming that "all open-minded readers who follow his argument carefully will be convinced of its validity."[67]

However, *Studies* focused on a great deal more than foreign policy. Among other subjects, it discussed US consumer culture, the decline of the older Marxist left, the rise of new protest movements, plus the corporate economy. The editors of *Studies* were highly concerned by this latter issue as they disliked the consolidation of corporate power that had occurred since 1945. They argued that "twentieth-century liberalism, insofar as it is not merely rhetorical, is a system of political ideas consciously developed to strengthen the system of large-scale corporate capitalism." As a result, they portrayed Cold War liberalism as "corporate liberalism"—an ideology they believed was also responsible for driving US expansion and militarism across the globe. Like Beard and Williams, the editors craved an alternative ideology and a more progressive society that put "man and his social needs at the centre."[68] If this could be established, they believed economic expansion overseas would become unnecessary.

The editors of *Studies* also disliked the pressure to conform to "academic objectivity" as defined by orthodox Cold War scholarship. Instead, they rejected the "prevailing trends" and sought to create a new radical intellectual consciousness that could unite the disparate elements of the American left. Although they admired the socialism of the Old Left, and some of them had once flirted with communism, they "were able to leave behind such antiquated debates as Trotskyism vs. Stalinism and pursue fresh ideas in Madison." The progressive heritage of the university and their contact with scholars like Curti and Williams inspired them to develop their "own conceptions of the necessity for radical scholarship."[69] They also hoped that *Studies* could act as a forum for leftist causes like inequalities of wealth, privilege, power, and the growing power of elites.

Ultimately, however, the journal lost its way during the mid-1960s. This occurred after its move to New York when, under the influence of more activist scholars such as Staughton Lynd and Tom Hayden, the journal became more of a voice of the New Left; as a result it placed a greater emphasis on reporting the activities of the protest movement. Although *Studies* sold ten thousand copies at its peak, the growing antiwar movement regarded its content as too intellectual and dry. The new editors therefore changed its approach to reflect the escalating activism (and Marxism) of SDS. Consequently, those who had been with the journal from the beginning, such as James Weinstein, believed that the journal abandoned its original vision to bring about social change through intellectual enlightenment.

The changes at *Studies* were significant because they highlighted the difference between the Wisconsin intellectual tradition and that of the New Left. As we shall see, Williams became critical of the New Left by the mid-1960s—believing that their tactics were counterproductive and anti-intellectual. Although activists like Lynd and Hayden were optimistic that direct action could change America and inspire revolution on the streets, Williams and *Studies'* Madison editors believed reform was impossible without an intellectual enlightenment within the United States. Instead of risking violent confrontation with authority, which might turn moderate Americans away from the left, the scholars from Wisconsin wanted to educate the US public about the need for reform; they hoped this would create a mass movement for change that the government would find impossible to ignore.

The demise of *Studies* reflected the broader contradictions and divisions within the New Left generally. According to McCormick, who wrote for *Studies*, the journal always struggled to define itself: was it a "servant of the movement" (whether this was civil rights or the Vietnam War) or was it simply "a place where radical socialist scholars could come to publish scholarly work they'd never be able to publish elsewhere?" The journal therefore fell between "being intellectual," on the one hand, and being "supportive of specific movements" on the other. The Madison editors understood that there "was a need for an academic radical movement," but they recognized that *Studies* could not fulfill its original purpose as a critical and objective intellectual forum if it became too closely tied to (and identified with) the protestors and SDS.[70] After the move to New York, the editorial board was divided as to what purpose the journal should serve. Like the broader New Left, these divisions undermined *Studies* and ultimately defeated it. The journal folded in 1967 owing to infighting and financial strife.

The death of *Studies* coincided with the demise of an enlightened approach to socioeconomic reform at UW itself. If the radicalism of the history department during the 1950s was characterized by independent scholarship and a fledgling attempt to unite the left intellectually, radicalism on campus in the 1960s (particularly in the later half of the decade) manifested itself in an altogether more belligerent manner. The Vietnam War and the rise of the New Left created civil unrest throughout the United States, but the effects were amplified in Madison. The peaceful model for social change envisaged by the Wisconsin revisionists was consequently abandoned. Instead, a more confrontational and activist radicalism became more prevalent among students—a mood exemplified by the protests against Dow Chemical in 1967, the subsequent wave of student strikes protesting against UW administrators' perceived collusion with police, and the fatal Sterling Hall bombing of August 1970, when a bomb ripped through the Army Math Center (a building protestors had targeted as an alleged instrument of US imperialism).

The violence that polarized UW during the 1960s was particularly tragic because the student dissidents had initially set out to uphold the Wisconsin intellectual tradition but lost their way. For example, in 1967 the radical publication *Connections* reminded its readers that Madison had always prided itself on "its liberality and tolerance" and had a tradition of "battling the forces" of the "evil right."[71] *Connections* also depicted UW as a utopia for "cosmopolitan, moral and open-minded" people and a "safe haven" or "asylum" for radicals.[72] However, although the relationship between the faculty and the radicals had been harmonious during the 1950s, the Dow protests complicated matters and put UW's administrators in a difficult position. The history department also became exasperated with unruly students disrupting departmental meetings; student participation in these meetings was eventually banned. Consequently, the relationship between radical students and the university broke down. Indeed, some radical groups actually declared war on the university. This obviously sullied the intellectual atmosphere that had blossomed during the previous decade.

As we shall see in chapter 6, the New Left believed activism was necessary to instigate revolution on the streets. If this resulted in violence, they believed it was a price worth paying. The Wisconsin scholars disagreed with this strategy because it contradicted their entire intellectual approach—one that hoped to create a peaceful revolutionary movement by uniting the left through intellectual discourse. Williams in particular believed the student radicals' penchant for protest had become "anti-intellectual" by the late 1960s, while McCormick reflected that the New Left "no longer took ideas seriously."[73] Fortunately, however, the Wisconsin scholars' critique of US imperialism enjoyed greater longevity than their intellectual approach. As the New Left increasingly turned to violence and more simplistic determinist interpretations of US foreign policy during the late 1960s, the Wisconsin interpretation became more sophisticated and ultimately more accepted and influential. It is the specifics of this critique, which enshrined the best intellectual traditions of the University of Wisconsin, that we shall turn to next.

4

Williams and the Wisconsin Critique

Empire is as American as apple pie.
William Appleman Williams, 1970

The Making of Williams

It seems strange that a young scholar embarking on an academic career should promote a Beardian interpretation of history at a time when the influence of the left was on the wane. But neither the contemporary intellectual vogue nor the potential ramifications of expressing leftist hypotheses seemed to deter William Appleman Williams from attacking US foreign policy during the 1950s. Although Charles Beard had died in 1948 with his reputation damaged by what his critics saw as a personal vendetta against Franklin Roosevelt, Williams was keen to apply Beard's general thesis on US expansionism to the Cold War era. As a result, he contextualized America's struggle against communism in relation to the broader problems faced by US society and the economy after World War II.

Williams's approach might have been highly unorthodox in the political climate of the 1950s, but it was actually typical of the academic institution with which he will be forever associated. As we explored in chapter 3, Williams was a graduate student at the University of Wisconsin between 1947 and 1950, where he was influenced by Fred Harvey Harrington and a department renowned for its progressivism. He then returned to teach at Madison in 1957, where he promoted a Beardian interpretation of American history in his lectures and seminars—particularly the contention that foreign policy was a product of domestic socioeconomic and political conditions. To the liberal scholars who dominated American intellectual life in the 1950s, Williams was therefore an anathema. His devotion to unfashionable progressive formulations seemed ideologically contentious. Orthodox contemporaries were upset by his criticism of American Cold War policies—particularly his insistence that a malevolent US imperialism had caused international tensions.

Williams's disenchantment with American diplomacy, which he believed was primarily designed to further US economic expansion, led him to dismiss orthodox perceptions of the nation's global role. During the 1950s, liberal and conservative scholars depicted the United States as the champion of liberty protecting the world from a malevolent Soviet imperialism. They focused on ideological factors (contrasting US democracy with Russian totalitarianism) and discussed the impact of different personalities within the White House. Williams on the other hand claimed that fleeting political pressures and private agendas were largely irrelevant. Because he used imperialism as a conceptual framework through which he interpreted American history, he saw the Cold War as a by-product of US policymakers' determination to extend the Open Door into Eastern Europe—a strategy he believed a defensively minded Soviet Union was determined to resist. According to Williams, economic expansion was the priority of all US presidents from the late nineteenth century to the present day, irrespective of party or personality.

It is hard to pinpoint when Williams became radicalized and adopted his unconventional intellectual outlook. However, Williams's experiences as a child, his exposure to combat in World War II, and his education in Madison (in particular) all contributed to his progressive mindset. Williams grew up in Atlantic, Iowa, a small town with strong links to both the National Grange and the Northern Farmers Alliance during the nineteenth century. The town was also steeped in what David Brown described as midwestern "Plain-states populism"—a tradition that Williams followed, to a large extent, by imitating the populists' hostility to, and suspicion of, the metropolis.[1] Atlantic was predominantly an agricultural community that sent its produce to far-flung lands to sustain its economic well-being. Williams became conscious of his home town's reliance on these foreign outlets as an adolescent, and he came to see trade routes as giant tentacles expanding across the world. As he matured and completed his graduate studies in Madison, Williams began to perceive US foreign policy as the means by which policymakers extended and protected these outlets to global trade.

But how does one describe a living, breathing global trade network? Orthodox liberals wrote about "essential American interests" (a term that embraced both foreign economic outlets and strategic bases that safeguarded

US national security), but Williams, like the Wisconsin School revisionists who followed him, was not satisfied by this term.[2] Meanwhile, he did not believe that Americans were "only incidentally concerned about real or imagined interests abroad."[3] Williams saw US economic aggrandizement as continuous, deliberate, and, in many ways, self-interested. Furthermore, he believed this economic expansion had often had an adverse effect on the developing nations it touched. Consequently, when it came to defining the network of international trade and investments established by the United States, Williams believed only one word would do: "imperialism." Although he believed this imperialism differed from the colonialism of European powers, the Wisconsin scholar argued that the United States had frequently fought brutal yet ostensibly necessary wars to protect this empire. He also began to regard Atlantic as a vulnerable outpost that "lay at the mercy of powerful commercial forces beyond its control." Williams therefore dedicated his scholarship to challenging "the imperial tectonics of Cold War liberalism," in the hope that he might protect towns like Atlantic, reverse the social changes brought on by modern capitalism, and transform US society into a community that replicated his home town.[4]

As a typical "blue-eyed Iowa socialist," Williams believed that modern capitalism and imperialism threatened midwestern values by promoting a selfish individualism.[5] He regarded such egocentric behavior as an abhorrence that undermined society and exacerbated inequalities. Instead, Williams wanted Americans to enjoy an idyllic life similar to the one he had experienced in Atlantic—a town he remembered as having a strong community spirit and few underlying tensions. Reminiscing about his childhood, Williams recalled that Atlantic was "a network of interlocking communities," which had "two extended families—a strong civil community based on a political economy of agriculture, manufacturing, and commerce . . . and a primary peer group of children" who were reared by a larger group of relatives. Children in Atlantic were therefore not raised in a nuclear family environment. Instead they "became familiar with birth, illness, and death in our own and friends' families." Furthermore, there were few boundaries of class or race. Williams recalled fondly how "all the children" in his "neighborhood peer group" regularly played "with children who were richer and poorer than ourselves." Therefore, as Williams grew up, he "dealt regularly with blacks, Jews, Italians, and farm children." Society was therefore cohesive, caring, and harmonious.[6]

Williams also reflected that Atlantic's children were brought up to respect traditions and value the community in which they lived. He enthused that "parents shared a value system that expected children to exercise their minds and bodies in many kinds of activity, and participate in the community at large on a reciprocal basis." Religion also played a role in town life, which helped the townsfolk to view the community spirit "as a moral imperative." The supposed selfish individualism of capitalism therefore played no part in Williams's upbringing. In fact, Williams boasted that he "learned to say 'no' to himself in the name of the community, . . . or in the contemporary idiom, . . . learned that doing one's own thing was capitalism's most sophisticated form of cooptation."[7] The perception that something was wrong with US capitalism also affected Williams emotionally. Like many towns across the Midwest during the 1930s, Atlantic suffered from the economic and psychological effects of the Great Depression. Consequently, one can see why the concept of community was so important to Williams, and why he feared that capitalism could sometimes result in social alienation.

Although a military career can jeopardize a young man's socialist sensibilities, Williams's experiences had the opposite effect. In fact, Williams subsequently criticized radicals for "mocking the camaraderie of the American Legion" and other military groups; he argued that critics missed "the far more significant point that such men found their primary, if not only, sense of experience of community in the military." Williams believed that his two years at Kemper Military School, his three-year spell in the US Naval Academy, his two years at sea, and an unfortunate year recovering from serious injury in various hospitals, had given him not only "a visceral awareness of serious illness, injury, and death" but also a sense of "the interdependence of human beings." By the time he left the hospital he had come to the conclusion that life must be used "as creatively as possible."[8] Williams intended to do this by devoting his talents to the study of history and the creation of a better society.

Williams's quest began in the American south between 1945 and 1946 (the two years before he enrolled at the University of Wisconsin) when he worked as a political activist supporting the black community's struggle for economic and social justice. Williams later described this period as "unquestionably a major experience in my life," for it taught him about social isolation and routine violence and gave him an insight into the plight of poor and oppressed people.[9] He also learned valuable lessons about the tactics of political activism—particularly the value of gaining support among the white working and middle classes. Consequently, when the protests against the Vietnam War began in the 1960s, Williams emphasized how important it was for the New Left to win over moderate Americans.

When Williams arrived to teach at the University of Wisconsin he continued to be a political activist. A perusal of the *Daily Cardinal* (UW's left-leaning newspaper) throughout the 1960s demonstrates his involvement in a variety of humanitarian pursuits. When rallies against US foreign policy or the manufacture of nuclear weapons took place, Williams was invariably involved. For example, he supported the Committee to End the War in Vietnam and often spoke at open meetings that discussed events in Southeast Asia. Like many UW students, Williams also called for self-determination for the Vietnamese. In August 1965 the Wisconsin scholar spoke at a ceremony marking the anniversary of the Hiroshima bombing, which he described as "a lesson in what America should not do."[10] Not surprisingly, Williams also spoke out against the CIA's recruitment campaign on campus. Joining fellow radical professors like George Mosse at a protest rally in November 1967, Williams claimed the CIA should use their own facilities for interviews. Because these discussions amounted to "a contractual marketplace relationship," Williams argued they had "no moral or logical right" to conduct them at a "public forum" like UW.[11]

However, it is important to note that Williams disagreed with the minority of students who took their protests further and demonstrated violently. Williams's broad intellectual approach might have seemed Marxian, but he disagreed with the Marxist-Leninist approach of instigating social change. Consequently, when Williams addressed another audience on behalf of the Committee to End the War in Vietnam in 1965, he proposed that students protest by submitting policy recommendations to the government and organizing teach-ins across the country to spark an intellectual debate about the war. Therefore, even though Williams argued strongly that it was "the duty of citizens" to "make a stand" against US foreign policy and "question the underlying assumptions" of policymakers, he always stressed that protests should remain peaceful.[12]

Williams believed that the best way to challenge US diplomacy and create social change in America was through reasoned argument. If the government's policies could be exposed as intellectually bankrupt, and the overwhelming majority of citizens could see their flaws, then change would occur organically without violent upheaval. This was a contrast to the New Left radicals who wanted to incite revolution on the streets. Williams's psychological disposition was therefore quite distinct, and his writing displayed, in the words of Brown, "a curious mixture of dialectical materialism and Midwestern militancy."[13] Williams had a penchant for activism (up to a point) and was a fierce debater—Thomas McCormick recalled how the Wisconsin scholar "could be unpleasant to argue with if his position was entrenched"—but words were the only weapons that Williams was prepared to use.[14]

During his graduate studies Williams won a scholarship to travel to England for a special seminar on Labor Party economics. He used this time to enjoy the company of European socialists and came to appreciate "the problems faced by left liberals coming to power" in "a capitalist political economy." Williams also began to address "the question of how one organizes a social movement to change the structure of society."[15] He eventually concluded that greater welfare and a more equitable society was possible without violent revolution and the overthrow of capitalism. The best way was to educate citizens and then present the government with an undisputable case for socioeconomic reform. Williams was therefore "an analyst" as well as a scholar and a political agitator. Although he was always "immersed in the documents" during his time in Madison, Williams preferred to think broadly rather than being caught up in the miniscule; of his major works, only his fourth book, *The Roots of the Modern American Empire*, included a vast array of footnotes. When he taught at Wisconsin he preferred to teach American foreign relations between 1781 and 1900 and left John DeNovo to teach the twentieth-century course. This was because "his approach worked better" in the eighteenth and nineteenth centuries, where he was able to make broader generalizations about American history.[16]

Williams believed it was his job to teach people "how to think, not what to think."[17] Instead of instructing students to absorb themselves in individual events, Williams encouraged them to look at the bigger picture and contextualize events within the broadest possible framework. It was apt, therefore, that the Wisconsin scholar's courses focused on global revolutions, the nature of capitalism, and how events such as the Spanish-American War of 1898 were part of greater historical forces (rather than simply focusing on the war itself). Williams's lectures for his course on American history from 1865 reflected this approach. For example, instead of studying the New Deal as a subject on its own, Williams's lecture on the subject was titled "The New Deal Sustains American Capitalism"; other lectures in the course included "Making Peace in a Revolutionary World" (which examined the Versailles Treaty) and "Imperialism and Global Reform."[18] Remember, this was a course on American history—even when teaching United States history, Williams was keen to broaden the discussion.

The Wisconsin scholar also seemed determined to encourage students to think about history itself in broad terms. Studying the past for the sake of it seemed futile—and he let his students know this from the beginning. In the literature for his American history course, he explained to his undergraduates how history could be seen as "a way of learning how we humans operate." He also announced his intention to help students "learn about" their "own society" and help them make "sense out of our history."[19] While Williams reassured people that he was "not primarily interested in persuading you I am right," his former teaching assistant Thomas McCormick described how students were often spellbound by his lectures—and as a result he "changed a lot of folks around."[20] McCormick himself admitted that he was impressed. After hearing him lecture for the first time, he recalled how he and LaFeber turned to one another and commented on Williams's "amazing performance," before joking, "Yeah, but if we ever buy into his assumptions, we're dead!"[21]

Although McCormick believed that Harrington was just as responsible as Williams for changing his own perspective (McCormick was the president of the Young Republicans before he became a revisionist), Williams enjoyed a closer relationship with his graduate students. This was partially because of the younger man's fondness for late night socializing. Harrington himself admitted as much, claiming that Williams had "much more time" for his students on a personal level and "was much stronger on rapping with graduates—that is, he was quite willing to spend the whole night."[22] According to McCormick, Williams was "an extraordinarily charismatic guy" who was great company. Although he was "a difficult person in many ways" and "could put you in your place," he was also a "wonderful character" who was popular with students and fellow professors alike.[23] When Williams left Madison in 1967, John Salapatos, the assistant to the chairman of the history department, told *The Daily Cardinal* that not only was Williams "a pioneer" in the study of American foreign relations, but he was also "loved by many people for his frankness and openness."[24] This openness was perhaps his most enduring quality, and it explains why he never shied away from controversy. When it came to his critique of US imperialism, Williams wrote candidly without worrying about possible repercussions.

Williams Establishes His Critique

Although *Tragedy* was the book that brought Williams acclaim from the left, the hallmarks of his critique had begun to take shape beforehand. For example, the primacy of economic factors in Williams's work was clearly evident in his first book, *American-Russian Relations, 1781–1947*, which was published in 1952 (two years after he received his doctorate). The book drew attention to the broader context of the Cold War by examining the rivalry between the United States and the Soviet Union before World War II. Williams concluded that American actions before 1945 were partly responsible for causing the Cold War; therefore, the United States must shoulder a large proportion of blame for creating the current crisis. In particular, the book emphasized how American financial and industrial interests had come to influence foreign policy. Williams believed these forces drove US economic expansion overseas, where America met conflicting Russian economic interests. Consequently, Williams argued that

Americans had long perceived the Russians as economic rivals and had adopted a hostile attitude accordingly.

The same year, Williams wrote a controversial essay titled "A Second Look at Mr. X," which was published in *Monthly Review* after the liberal journal Foreign Affairs had rejected the article because it was too inflammatory. Originally written as a postscript to *American-Russian Relations,* Williams used this critique of George Kennan's containment theory to dissect American policy in the Cold War thus far. He argued that containment would only harden Cold War tensions and that the Soviet Union had "persistently wooed the United States in the search of an understanding that would serve to decrease the probability of conflict." Most significantly, however, Williams criticized Kennan's entire view of history. "The 'X' Article contains two signal weaknesses: Kennan's failure to probe the relationship between economic forces and foreign policy; and his attempt to analyze the history of the world since 1917 (and make recommendations for the present) without acknowledging, or addressing himself to, the fundamental challenge that the Bolshevik Revolution presented to the Western world in general. . . . For the challenge of contemporary Russia is far more than that of a giant military machine: the Soviet Union is equally potent as the symbol of a fundamental critique of capitalist society that is currently the basis of action in many non-Russian areas of the world." This extract demonstrated Williams's approach to the Cold War. Rather than seeing tensions as an ideological struggle, the Wisconsin scholar identified the rivalry as a tussle between two competing economic systems. In addition, Williams dismissed popular notions of American isolationism, adding that "political and economic (and in some cases military) intervention in Latin America, Europe, and China is not isolationism."[25]

The alleged myth of isolationism was a subject close to Williams's heart. He devoted an entire essay to the theme in 1954, when *Science and Society* published "The Legend of Isolationism in the 1920s." Williams argued that Republican leaders of the interwar period were actually internationally minded expansionists seeking markets in both Latin America and Asia. He portrayed these men as faithful followers of the Open Door policy, which increasingly attempted to expand US economic activity overseas. They were not "imperialists in the traditional sense of that much abused term," because they wanted to avoid the old trappings of politico-economic exploitation. Instead they sought the "internationalization of business," with capitalist countries coming together through a combination of common bonds, assumptions, and purposes.[26]

A year later, Williams introduced his concept of the American Weltanschauung (or worldview) in an essay called "The Frontier Thesis and American Foreign Policy" (1955). The essay described how Americans came to see the world as an area to expand into—a mindset that ultimately brought the nation into confrontation with the Soviet Union. Williams declared that the United States had "been a consciously and steadily expanding nation since 1890" owing to the mindset created by Turner's hugely influential frontier thesis and the unashamedly imperial aspirations of Brooks Adams. Williams argued that Adams used his political connections (he was friends with Henry Cabot Lodge and Theodore Roosevelt) to further the imperialist agenda among the nation's large banks and corporations. Williams claimed that Turner and Adams believed the end of America's continental frontier (and its abundance of free land) constituted a national crisis—and because this moment coincided with a terrible cycle of crippling depressions and social upheaval, they believed salvation lay in the search for new frontiers, the most obvious of which were overseas economic markets. Williams contended that Turner's frontier thesis and Adams's *The Law of Civilization and Decay* provided Americans with a reassuring "nationalistic worldview that eased their doubts, settled their confusions, and justified their aggressiveness" in times of crisis. Williams claimed that these beliefs permeated American psychology and inevitably found their expression in foreign policy. Consequently, Turner and Adams did much to "Americanize and popularize the heretofore alien ideas of economic imperialism and the White Man's burden."[27]

In many ways, *The Tragedy of American Diplomacy*, which was published in 1959, brought Williams's previous work together. The book was a comprehensive revision of American history from the perspective of economic expansion. All the ingredients that characterized his early essays were there: the crisis of overproduction, policymakers' faith in the Open Door as a solution to this problem, plus the expansionist tendencies that Turner believed were ingrained into the American psyche. Williams even explored the theory that Americans linked foreign business opportunities with freedom itself. The result was an "iconoclastic attack upon conventional wisdom" that, according to the well-known diplomatic historian Paul Hogan, "revolutionized the writing of American diplomatic history."[28] However, critics on the right were not so kind. One observer lambasted the Wisconsin scholar's "cavalier treatment of his sources" and dismissed his work as "solemn nonsense."[29] Williams's book therefore became a controversial text that divided scholarly opinion.

Tragedy began by tracing the origins of American imperialism back to James Madison and Thomas Jefferson. The book contended that "having matured in an age of empires as part of an empire, the colonists naturally saw themselves in the same light."[30] This statement alone was contentious, for historians have disagreed over whether the Founding Fathers acted in an imperial manner. Julius Pratt, for example, argued that early American continental expansion was not imperial because it did not consume peoples of alien cultures (other than Native Americans, whose numbers were small), while "new areas were placed under a unique species of temporary colonial government known as the territorial system."[31] However, Williams disagreed with Pratt and argued that early American leaders were most certainly imperialists, for they developed a deliberate strategy to make democratic republicanism work within a large state through an imperial foreign policy. This plan was based on the premise that "expansion was essential to mitigate economic clashes by providing an empire for exploitation and development."[32]

Williams argued that American history reached a crucial juncture when westward continental expansion was no longer possible. The Wisconsin scholar asserted that the majority of the American people (especially farmers and tobacco and cotton traders) actively demanded economic expansion during the economic crises of the 1890s because they believed the US economy would stagnate unless new frontiers were found. Therefore, a "broad consensus in favor of an expansionist foreign policy" emerged "as a solution to existing troubles and as a way to prevent future difficulties."[33] This contradicted Beard because Williams "assigned economic causality to (working class) groups generally worshipped by the intellectual left."[34] Whereas Beard blamed economic elites and the government for driving US imperialism, Williams believed that public opinion drove economic expansion; the Wisconsin scholar agreed that economic elites were in favor of the strategy, but he believed it was the will of the American people that ultimately proved irresistible. As a result, Williams argued there was no debate in the United States as to whether foreign markets were actually required. The only argument concerned "what kind of expansion to undertake."[35] Expansion was, after all, not merely desirable but also considered necessary.

Although Williams argued that US policymakers were prepared to use military force to secure economic expansion, he stressed that their preferred method to achieve this was the Open Door policy. This was the economic strategy of free trade, which was originally conceived by Secretary of State John Hay to exploit economic opportunities in China. The Open Door sought to prevent the implementation of tariffs that hindered American exports; it therefore enabled US manufacturing and agricultural products to reach foreign markets unopposed. Although this strategy ideally suited the United States because of the nation's great economic strength, the Open Door also enabled Americans to claim the moral high ground: US policymakers portrayed the absence of tariffs as a means to ensure "fair field and no favor" in international markets.[36]

Williams declared that the Open Door became so important to US economic expansion that it became *the* "strategy of American foreign policy in the twentieth century." This contradicted orthodox scholarship at the time, for history had not been kind to the Open Door: the policy was usually considered an abject failure because it had not secured the fabled China Market for American exporters, nor had it worked as a means of acquiring markets without military force. However, Williams disagreed with this assessment. He argued that the strategy was in fact "a brilliant strategic stroke which led to the gradual extension of American economic and political power throughout the world" without the pitfalls of colonialism.[37] For example, the approach had allowed William Jennings Bryan and President Grover Cleveland to control trading ports in Hawaii without having to annex the islands.

According to *Tragedy*, promoting the Open Door across the globe became a key aspiration of US policymakers during the twentieth century. Williams believed this was especially the case during the administration of Woodrow Wilson. Although Beard believed that Wilson's internationalism represented a hiatus in US expansion, *Tragedy* depicted the architect of the League of Nations as an arch-imperialist whose alleged eagerness to intervene in World War I demonstrated his willingness to fight for economic empire. Williams claimed that internationalism "led America into a position" where the nation either had "to abandon" its "determination and destiny to lead the world or go to war."[38] *Tragedy* stated that Wilson chose the latter because he believed America's economy depended on it—after all, 77 percent of all US exports relied upon the allies. Therefore, according to Williams, America's participation in World War I was primarily concerned with preserving and extending the Open Door.

Williams also identified strong undercurrents of imperialism in Wilson's League of Nations Covenant, which he argued reflected the Open Door agenda. According to *Tragedy*, the president's objective was to structure the peace "so that America could provide the intellectual, moral, economic, and military power and leadership to reinvigorate and sustain the liberal way of life throughout the world." Wilson hoped to achieve this by opposing "traditional colonialism and revolutionary nationalism" and proposing a system "under which the Open Door Policy would be used to reform the political and economic life . . . according to American interests." The aim was to assert "the predominance of American power and leadership." Meanwhile, the harmony of interests that the League represented ensured that "every nation could vote, but nothing could be done without prior existence of a concert of power among the big nations," which were inevitably led by the United States.[39] Consequently, America would dominate world markets while smaller nations had no real say in the running of their own economies—thus institutionalizing the United States' economic empire.

In Williams's eyes, US policymakers attempted to consolidate this empire during the 1920s and 1930s, fought to sustain it during World War II, and attempted to assert US economic hegemony in new areas of the globe thereafter. Consequently, *Tragedy* claimed that Franklin Roosevelt's Good Neighbor Policy might have been "infused with the tone and substance of *noblesse oblige* and announced in the rhetoric of America's mission to defend and extend democracy," but in reality "its context was defined by the immediate and specific needs of American businessmen" and "by the long-range objective of a broad integration of the economy of the United States with that of Latin America."[40] The Good Neighbor Policy was therefore nothing more than a subtle plan to extend America's economic hegemony.

The Roosevelt administration was highlighted in *Tragedy* because this period witnessed the consolidation of corporate capitalism and the internationalization of business; Williams believed this was a crucial development in the history of American imperialism. Just like those who had suffered the economic panics of the 1890s, corporate businessmen allegedly believed that US economic expansion was absolutely vital if America was to make a permanent recovery from the Great Depression. Consequently, corporations came to identify "economic welfare with the continued existence and expansion of the American system throughout the world"; this ambition inevitably clashed with the expansionism of the Axis powers and subsequently with Soviet communism. Because "there is no doubt about the final convergence of thought between the Roosevelt administration and the leaders of America's corporate economic system," Williams denied that FDR was an exceptional president and a war hero.[41] Instead, *Tragedy* portrayed him as yet another economic imperialist who demonstrated that the crux of American diplomacy had not changed since the 1890s.

As a result, Williams claimed that US participation in World War II occurred for the same reasons as the intervention in World War I. Americans were faced with a stark choice: war or depression. To illustrate this point he quoted *Fortune*, a journal that expressed corporate opinion at the time: "The US economy has never proved that it can operate without the periodic injection of new and real wealth." Williams pointed out how *Fortune* proposed extending the American frontier to encompass the entire globe; this meant reforming the world into a pro-capitalist order that facilitated American expansion. Williams argued that "the convergence of a sense of economic necessity and a moral calling transformed the traditional concept of Open Door expansion into a vision of an American Century."[42] To achieve this goal, the United States had no option but to fight the Axis. Furthermore, Williams adhered to Beard's theory that Open Door expansion enabled America's corporate elite to consolidate their power and wealth at home. Because the majority of the population believed that economic expansion was necessary for the nation's prosperity (and so willingly supported the strategy), the wealthy came to see imperialism as a means of preventing social upheaval in America itself. Consequently, Williams believed that the Open Door was not only the crux of US economic expansion but also an evasion that helped political and economic elites to avoid radical social domestic reforms.

As was discussed in chapters 2 and 3, the economic interpretation of US diplomatic history was not something that Williams pioneered. His views might have been highly controversial in the early Cold War period, but his emphasis on economic factors was not entirely new. As revealed in chapter 2, Beard had previously attributed US foreign policy to economic triggers; meanwhile, it was Harrington who first promoted the economic interpretation of US diplomacy at the University of Wisconsin. However, what made Williams so controversial in the 1950s and early 1960s was his insistence that US economic expansion was the primary cause of current international tensions; in other words, Williams blamed the United States' historic obsession with economic expansion for causing the Cold War. Furthermore, he also believed that US policymakers could and should have done more to ease Soviet anxieties after 1945. This marked Williams as different from Harrington, who recognized that while Williams followed "the (economic) line taught" at UW during the 1950s, he was also "very much impressed with the point that we ought to get along with the Russians."[43]

Williams's critique therefore turned containment on its head. Rather than seeing containment as a defensive posture, Williams believed that Kennan's doctrine "stressed the traditional Open Door faith in America's overwhelming economic power to force the Soviet Union along a path preferred by the United States." This economic perspective also led Williams to depict the Truman Doctrine and the Marshall Plan as "two sides of the same coin of America's traditional program of open-door expansion." *Tragedy* stated that Truman's underlying concern was to "sustain and expand private enterprise" in order to prevent a sequence of crippling depressions. Meanwhile, George Marshall also defined "expansion as the key to prosperity."[44] Therefore, both men were portrayed as disciples of the old frontier mentality.

Because it was America's decision to extend the Open Door to Eastern Europe after World War II that had caused the Cold War, Williams believed that the death of Franklin Roosevelt was largely irrelevant; all US policymakers (irrespective of which administration they belonged to) were united in their determination "to force the Soviet Union to accept America's traditional conception of itself and the world." In Williams's eyes this represented the transformation of the Open Door policy "from a utopian idea into an ideology, from an intellectual outlook for changing the world into one concerned with preserving it in the traditional mold."[45] After all, expanding the Open Door ultimately required the propping up of old European empires in order to suppress revolutionary socialism in developing regions; this was necessary to hold the door open to US trade and investment in Asia, the Middle East, and Africa—areas where socialists might otherwise establish an alternative economic model not amenable to American interests.

Although Williams believed that American intentions were generally benevolent (albeit misled), he argued that the United States' decision to impose its economic model on developing nations violated the cherished principle of self-determination. He asserted that "the tragedy of American diplomacy is not that it is evil, but that it denies and subverts American ideas and ideals." He beseeched the US government to abandon "the frontier-expansionist explanation of American democracy and prosperity," "stop defining trade as a weapon," and help "other peoples achieve their own aspirations in their own way."[46] The problem, as Williams explained in an interview with the *Daily Cardinal* in May 1966, was that US policymakers believed "other societies" were "incapable" of implementing "positive change" by themselves.[47] Instead, they assumed that US economic expansion (via the Open Door) was the best way to improve the lives of indigenous populations. Unfortunately, however, because the absence of tariffs actually enabled large American companies to profit at the expense of local producers, Williams believed this assertion was flawed.

The Wisconsin scholar interpreted the Vietnam War within this framework. *Tragedy* denied it was simply a fear of communism that prompted US military action in Vietnam; rather, he argued that it was the threat that revolutionary nationalism posed to the Open Door. Williams believed that US policymakers also justified military intervention by assuming that liberal economics would be far better for the Vietnamese than the alternative offered by Ho Chi Minh. Unfortunately, however, by imposing their will on alien cultures, the United States came to be seen by people in developing countries like Vietnam as "the major obstacle to the revolution of rising expectations," while the Open Door only seemed to "confront them with a closed door to their own progress."[48] This was a direct contradiction of the United States' commitment to freedom and democracy, and a perversion of America's better self.

Williams traced this violation of self-determination back to America's imperial turn at the end of the nineteenth century. It was this tendency that made the United States an imperial nation—albeit one that practiced a more subtle form of imperialism than traditional colonialists. "When an advanced industrial nation plays . . . a controlling and one-sided role in the development of a weaker country, then the policy of the more powerful country can with accuracy and candor only be described as imperial. The empire that results may well be *informal* in the sense that the weaker country is not ruled on a day-to-day basis by resident administrators . . . but it is nevertheless an empire." This was Williams's definition of "informal empire." He applied this term whenever the United States enjoyed the fruits of an imperial relationship without the burdens of formal governance. This was not traditional colonialism, because direct authority did not rest in the hands of Washington officials. However, the less developed nation still made its choices "within limits set, either directly or indirectly, by the more powerful society." *Tragedy* therefore depicted the 1890s as the beginning of the "modern American empire," for the US used its overwhelming economic power to "cast the economy and politics of the poorer, weaker, underdeveloped countries," in this case the Philippines, Cuba, and Hawaii, "in a pro-American mold."[49] Furthermore, if military force was needed to assert US authority, officials were more than prepared to sanction violence. Williams believed economic expansion was too important to be restrained.

Williams also claimed that the Spanish-American War enshrined another key aspect of American imperialism: the crusading belief that American values were superior. This trend became particularly pronounced in the early twentieth century during the Theodore Roosevelt and Wilson administrations, when Williams argued that ideological and religious connotations were added to the Open Door. *Tragedy* described this new psychology as "an all-encompassing conception of the world . . . Americans could not only conquer nature, but they could put their self-interest to work to produce the well-being and harmony of the world. Their theory not only held that they could do such things; it asserted the natural necessity of such action. Any other course violated natural law."[50] This somewhat self-righteous zeal was a manifestation of Manifest Destiny and the confident belief that God was on America's side; for example, Wilson thought it was the United States' responsibility to extend its authority over semibarbarous people and regenerate civilizations. The Open Door, therefore, became an all-inclusive policy of economic, ideological, religious, and even racial imperialism.

Interestingly, however, Williams did *not* argue that the rhetoric of the Open Door deliberately masked self-interest—a stance taken by some subsequent dissidents. *Tragedy* maintained that American leaders were mostly well-intentioned and truly believed American values could help less-developed nations. The problem was that US policies were defeated by inherent contradictions; for example, Americans sincerely hoped that the Open Door would improve less-developed societies (after all, trade was seen as the natural way to achieve prosperity, individual freedoms, and ultimately democracy), but they failed to realize that alien cultures did not always want liberal economics, nor were their cultures necessarily compatible with Anglo-Saxon values. Furthermore, although Williams admitted that the United States rarely pushed for direct control over nations, instead preferring absentee authority, he argued that power frequently remained firmly in the hands of Christian white men or local pro-American groups that "were not very democratic in political and social matters." Furthermore, the fruits of America's economic penetration were not always used to "initiate and sustain the balanced development of a poor country"; as a result, many people wondered whether the United States was "a more subtle—and hence more dangerous—imperial power."[51]

Because US policymakers promised to bring democracy and economic development to developing regions, but only succeeded in securing American economic interests, Williams argued that the Open Door was frequently perceived as colonialism under another banner.[52] This was one of the central tragedies of American diplomacy: in its quest to obtain economic security and simultaneously spread the perceived benefits of liberal economics across the globe, the United States, which saw itself as the quintessential anti-imperial nation, had become the world's preeminent imperial power. This was not because of the self-interest or strategic errors of specific policymakers but was caused by the mistaken belief, shared by the majority of the American population, that the United States' economic well-being (and indeed the economic stability of Western Europe) could only be secured by creating a world in which the Open Door could flourish unopposed.

The Sources of US Imperialism

In an interview with two graduate students at the University of Wisconsin in the fall of 1969, Williams explained why he believed empire was "as American as apple pie." He claimed it was because of the way Americans "conceptualized" imperialism, and how the earliest American colonists defined their independence from the British in terms of creating their own empire.[53] Williams argued that Americans began to see expansion as a solution to economic and social problems over time. This began in the eighteenth century, when agricultural communities became reliant on foreign markets for their economic well-being. After the Civil War, metropolitan areas began to adopt the same mindset; consequently, politicians were compelled to listen because a consensus on the desirability of economic expansion had emerged. However, what was it that convinced Americans that expansion was the only solution to their problems? Furthermore, why did Americans think that expansion into foreign lands was morally justified? Williams believed the answer lay in Americans' unique Weltanschauung, or "conception of the world."[54]

Williams defined the American Weltanschauung as the way in which Americans interpreted events according to their political, religious, economic, and cultural values. One of *Tragedy*'s fundamental assertions was that during the 1890s, when the domestic frontier had closed, Americans had an overtly economic conception of their troubles. "They explained difficulties, and likewise advanced solutions and alternatives, by reference to economic phenomena. This did not make them economically motivated in the pocketbook sense, but it did lead them to believe that their objectives in the political and social realms could only be attained through economic means."[55] Williams believed that Americans' assumption that they must secure economic objectives to secure their national well-being had a profound influence on their Weltanschauung. This assumption, or conviction, was made all the more powerful by the psychological impact of Turner's frontier thesis, which convinced many citizens and policymakers that expansion was integral to American freedom and democracy.

Williams believed this combination of economic and emotional triggers gave economic expansion an irresistible momentum on the eve of the Spanish-American War: "Wanting democracy and social peace, they argued that economic depression threatened those objectives, and concluded that overseas economic expansion provided a primary means of ending that danger. They did not want war . . . in order to increase their own personal fortunes. But their own conception of the world ultimately led them into war in order to solve the problems in the way that they considered necessary and best."[56] Consequently, Williams disagreed with liberal scholars like Richard Hofstadter that the sinking of the Maine (the American warship dispatched to Havana that sank in mysterious circumstances) had a large bearing on President McKinley's decision to wage war on Spain. He did not deny that the subsequent public uproar increased pressure on the government to intervene, but overall, Williams concluded that war came "as a consequence of a general outlook that externalized the opportunity and the responsibility for America's domestic welfare; broadly in terms of vigorous overseas economic expansion in Latin America and Asia."[57]

Williams argued in *Tragedy* that US imperialism in the twentieth century was triggered by the same overriding conviction that the nation must find foreign markets or face the prospect of recurring economic crises. It is unlikely that Williams himself subscribed to this theory (as we shall see), but the crucial supposition was that American policymakers believed it was true. *Tragedy* therefore adhered to Beard's hypothesis that a false prophecy (that is, the overriding belief that foreign markets would solve the nation's problem of chronic overproduction) was responsible for driving America's economic expansion. However, Williams took Beard's theory further by fusing his ideas with Turner's emphasis on Americans' frontier mentality. Consequently, in exploring the reasons why US policymakers believed an expansionist economic policy was necessary, *Tragedy* focused on the "relationship between expansion, democracy, and prosperity." Williams believed Americans' perception that freedom and expansion were inexplicably linked was exploited by imperialists like Brooks Adams, Theodore Roosevelt, and John Hay to create "a broad consensus in favor of an expansionist foreign policy as a solution to their existing troubles and as a way to prevent future difficulties."[58]

Williams analyzed the psychological dimensions of US foreign policy more than any of his contemporaries, but he was not the only one to do so. In fact, *Tragedy*'s emphasis on Americans' state of mind was somewhat reminiscent of Hofstadter's essay "Cuba, the Philippines and Manifest Destiny," which argued that a psychic crisis (created by the end of the frontier) was responsible for late nineteenth-century US expansion. However, whereas Hofstadter contextualized national anxieties surrounding the end of continental expansion as short-lived and as part of a greater emotional outcry for war, Williams argued that the end of the domestic frontier had a far more profound effect. He believed that Americans saw overseas economic expansion as a permanent solution to the nation's economic ills, for this would provide the extracontinental frontier that Turner had foreseen.

Of all the dimensions that constituted the American Weltanschauung, Williams claimed the conviction that economic expansion would provide the nation with economic and social well-being was the most important. He argued that Turner's frontier thesis acted as a psychological trigger that led to a universal demand for economic imperialism across every state and social class. The working class wanted expansion to provide markets for manufactured goods and agricultural produce; the industrial elites and the wealthy demanded expansion to extend their wealth and guard against social revolution. Meanwhile, the belief in Manifest Destiny (the notion that God had chosen the United States to civilize the world) overshadowed fears that expansion might violate American principles; expansion was, therefore, perceived as both a moral duty and a national necessity.

Williams's focus on Americans' imperial Weltanschauung provided a new perspective in the study of American empire. *Tragedy* cannot be described as

Marxist because it did not argue that US economic expansion was an inevitable consequence of American capitalism. Neither was the book a mere imitation of Beard. Even though Williams agreed with Beard that US imperialism was a response to rising manufacturing production, his interpretation differed from *The Open Door at Home* because it claimed that the roots of American expansion were agrarian as well as industrial; consequently a consensus on the desirability (and necessity) of foreign markets existed. In summary, *Tragedy* took existing left-wing interpretations of US expansion and added powerful psychological triggers. Furthermore, Williams articulated his concept of US imperialism in more detail by using the term "informal empire," which stressed the differences between American expansion and the traditional colonial empires of Europe. By identifying long-term trends that embraced economic, psychological, and ideological factors, *Tragedy* presented a fascinating critique of American imperialism that embraced over two centuries of national history. However, this is not to say that the book did not have weaknesses. In fact, Williams's seminal work was intriguing for its ambiguities as well as its originality.

A thorough review of *Tragedy* reveals a number of complexities and contradictions concerning the sources of US imperialism. For example, an initial reading of the book can give the impression that Williams was not really sure what the ultimate causes of American imperialism were. There appear to be three trains of thought, which the author seemed to merge and separate somewhat conveniently to support his arguments. The first assertion was that mistaken conviction was the root cause of US imperialism—in other words, the unfounded belief shared by Americans that the nation's domestic well-being depended on expansion overseas. The third edition of *Tragedy* described this "dogmatic belief, that . . . domestic well-being depends upon . . . sustained, ever-increasing overseas economic expansion" as the main driving force behind US policy.[59] Williams suggested that this conviction was a central part of American leaders' Weltanschauung; therefore, their minds defaulted to this mistaken conviction whenever foreign policy decisions were made.

Because this was such a generalized statement, which was difficult, if not impossible, to support, Williams sometimes gave the impression that American institutions did actually require expansion to survive. Although this was out of character, and Williams at no point claimed explicitly that imperialism was an inevitable by-product of capitalism, critics zeroed in on this second hypothesis and denounced the young Wisconsinite as a subversive communist (a characterization that was unfair). A more balanced perspective was the one offered by Robert W. Tucker in *The Radical Left and American Foreign Policy*. Tucker surmised that Williams himself was "never quite clear whether America's institutions necessitated expansion or whether America has been expansionist out of mistaken conviction." However, he concluded that *Tragedy* mostly asserted that mistaken conviction was the villain, because "the argument of necessity appears to have a *prima facie* implausibility when based upon America's *existing* foreign economic involvement."[60] This analysis was more accurate and sophisticated.

Having said that, Tucker believed the relatively small nature of US economic commitments overseas undermined *Tragedy*'s central assertion somewhat. Although Williams tried to preempt critics who dismissed *Tragedy* on these grounds—claiming that as little as "10 percent of any operation is a significant proportion"—few orthodox critics were convinced.[61] Indeed, it is likely that even Williams himself realized that the relatively low level of US foreign economic involvement (compared with domestic operations) undermined *Tragedy* somewhat. This could be why the Wisconsin scholar advocated a third hypothesis about the origins of US imperialism toward the end of the book: he claimed that American capitalism had created a national psyche that demanded expansion. This was not Marxist economic determinism but, rather, a unique breed of psychological determinism.

Williams's oscillation between theories was somewhat confusing at times. However, it is most likely that Williams believed mistaken conviction was the root cause of US imperialism. For example, both the first and third hypothesis emphasized American psychology as the driving force behind expansion. Furthermore, *Tragedy*'s central theme of Weltanschauung was all about a national mind-set and how this impacted on policy formation. Furthermore, Williams held US institutions in high regard; therefore, it is unlikely that he believed US institutions actually required expansion to survive. The young Wisconsin scholar wanted to work within the existing political system to create reform—unlike the radical elements of the New Left who sought revolution to overthrow the government. If Williams believed expansion was necessary to sustain US institutions, he would have called for their abolition rather than their reform.

In a postscript to the third edition of *Tragedy*, Bradford Perkins described *Tragedy* as "inspirational rather than specific."[62] This is still the best way to approach the book today. Although critics highlighted examples of when economic factors appeared not to influence US foreign policy, as if doing so undermined Williams's whole argument, these scholars forgot one major point: that all broad interpretations of history are marred by instances when specific events do not fit an overall pattern. It was unrealistic to expect *Tragedy* to be any different. The story of American expansion was a huge area of historical research; thus it would have been extremely unlikely that every single event in the nation's past would have fitted Williams's framework. What is more, these critics failed to realize that the existence of exceptions does not always disprove a general rule—even though it was possible to criticize *Tragedy* on other grounds.

A fairer criticism of *Tragedy* was the assertion that the book rested on one fundamental assumption; this was Williams's insistence that economics was always at the heart of policymaking at all times (there was no space for political motivations or the weakness and inexperience of some presidents in the Wisconsin scholar's critique). Rather, Williams argued that every single administration acted purposefully to ensure the nation's continued economic expansion. Certainly, this was somewhat inadequate. Even if economic aspirations were primary, it seems unlikely that other factors did not play a crucial role on occasions. Furthermore, if Williams really did believe that mistaken conviction drove US policy, surely it was not inconceivable that other unfounded convictions played a decisive role—for example, who was to say that mistaken convictions about US military security did not influence policy decisively?

Blemishes like these clearly left Williams open to criticism. For example, Richard Melanson berated *Tragedy* for its supposed scientific approach when the author offered "no evidence, apart from his own historical interpretation, that men make decisions and adopt policies according to his model." Williams's cause was not helped by the fact that he used footnotes sparingly—a fact that made *Tragedy* appear polemical. Even when Williams did quote official sources, the evidence was not entirely convincing; consequently, it is hard to disagree with Melanson when he observed that the Wisconsin scholar seized upon "any reference to Open Door expansion, no matter how obscure or problematic," while "statements about power, security, and fear" were "either ignored or dismissed as tactical smokescreens."[63] Many critics also denounced Williams's economics, saying his sums simply did not add up. Alfred Eckes applauded Williams for being the first noneconomist to demonstrate the economic aspects of World War II diplomacy but questioned his premise that the business community saw exports as the best way to create prosperity. Eckes argued that Williams had "oversimplified a complex relationship between trade and employment" and that "government leaders did not agree that . . . in the event of another collapse export expansion was preferable to internal remedies."[64]

Williams's use of definitions also left something to be desired, although an initial reading of *Tragedy* gives the impression that Williams had found a creative solution to the problem of defining US imperialism. Because traditional colonialism was expensive and contradicted the American values of freedom and democracy, a fierce debate raged between imperialists and anti-imperialists about how best to facilitate economic expansion. In 1900 the imperialists argued that the Philippines should be kept as a traditional colony, whereas their opponents preferred quasi-independent nations under US supervision. *Tragedy* asserted that Secretary of State Bryan ultimately chose the latter course because it enabled the United States to reap the economic benefits of the islands without the burdensome responsibility of everyday governance. Williams defined this policy as "imperial anticolonialism," for the strategy was neither "classical colonialism" nor "anti-imperial." The plan was to establish a stable form of government for the Filipinos and then protect the islands from outside interference. Imperial anticolonialism underpinned America's "informal" empire—an empire that enabled the United States to extend its power and influence in the Pacific without actually integrating the Philippines into the US political system.[65]

Despite the creation of new definitions, many critics attacked Williams for the language he used to describe American expansion. For example, one of the criticisms leveled at *Tragedy* was the book's failure to define *imperialism* and *expansion*. It is hard to dismiss this argument, because Williams did indeed fail to provide explicit definitions of these terms—a weakness that, incidentally, also applied to many subsequent radical interpretations of US imperialism. A good example of this criticism was J. A. Thompson's essay "William Appleman Williams and the American Empire." Thompson accused the Wisconsin scholar of deliberately describing "imperialism" and "expansion" in loose terms in order to create a false sense of continuity. He complained that Williams's "Open Door imperialism" was so imprecise that it included "any political action (however weak) designed to promote foreign trade."[66]

Bradford Perkins made a similar observation. Although he believed *Tragedy* was right to highlight how "growth" had played a key role in American development, he believed it was misleading to mingle "territorial expansion to control new areas of production with efforts to dispose of a surplus through expanded trade, to say nothing of a quest for ideological dominion."[67] This is the nub of most critiques of *Tragedy*. Most observers would call expansion an increase in foreign trade, whereas imperialism involves something broader (for example, the economic integration and/or political control of other nations). But Williams did not make such precise definitions. Instead he talked ambiguously about how America's economic expansion became imperial as the Open Door became steadily more exploitative and ideological in nature. This is perhaps the most unsatisfactory aspect of *Tragedy*. After all, the accusation of imperialism is hard to substantiate unless it is accompanied by a precise definition of what the term means.

Another valid criticism was *Tragedy*'s failure to compare the United States with other great powers from the past. Although Williams had demonstrated the difference between old-fashioned colonialism and US "informal" empire, this was not enough on its own; for example, what about moral comparisons? It is likely that Williams neglected these because he believed the United States should aspire to higher standards than other nations. As a result, he judged American conduct in the harshest possible light (and gave little indication that other great empires throughout history acted in an equally or even more repressive manner). Had Williams made basic moral comparisons, he would have stressed how "the method of indirect and informal empire" was not actually "an American invention." For example, Gallagher and Robinson's essay "The Imperialism of Free Trade" (1953), an essay that the Wisconsin scholars knew well, preempted Williams by describing how Great Britain had previously annexed trade "with informal control if possible" and "with rule when necessary."[68] These British scholars also argued that "for purposes of economic analysis it would clearly be unreal to define imperial history exclusively as the history of those colonies colored red on the map."[69] Consequently, American foreign policy might have been tragic, but it was not unprecedented and certainly no more depraved than the imperialism of previous superpowers. Indeed, one might argue that informal empire was far less sinister than the traditional colonialism of old Europe.

From *Tragedy* to *Contours*

Two years after *Tragedy* was published, Williams attempted to enhance his critique of US imperialism (and perhaps redress some of *Tragedy*'s ambiguities) in a new book called *The Contours of American History* (1961). Although *Tragedy* was Williams's best-known text, some observers believe that *Contours* was the Wisconsin scholar's best work. For example, whereas McCormick considers *Tragedy* to be "neo-Beardian" (although *Tragedy* placed Beard's general hypothesis into a larger sociological context with less emphasis on narrow self-interested economic groups), he argued that *Contours* was the better book because it placed more emphasis on exploring "the systematic needs of American capitalism."[70] As the name suggested, *Contours* placed US expansion into the broadest possible historical context, demonstrating how imperialism was rooted in not only the traditional American Weltanschauung but also the nation's capitalist society itself. This gave Williams the chance to investigate whether capitalism had created a national psyche that demanded expansion, the theory he alluded to toward the end of *Tragedy*.

There was only one place that such a broad study could begin—at the very beginning of US history. Williams went right back to the social and ideological precedents established by America's closest cultural cousins, imperialist Great

Britain. Although the Founding Fathers were revolted by the mother country's exploitation of the colonies, Williams demonstrated how America's economic and social origins owed much to British mercantilism. The key assertion was that British mercantilism had sacrificed its soul to imperialist urges just before the War of Independence, and now America was following a similar course because of the rampant individualism of capitalist society. Williams identified three stages in America's development to support his thesis: "The Age of Mercantilism 1740–1828, The Age of Laissez Nous Faire 1819–1896," and finally "The Age of Corporate Capitalism 1882–1961." *Contours*' prime supposition was that the social responsibility inherent in early American mercantilism was gradually eroded over the subsequent two periods until America became what the Founding Fathers had feared most—a benevolent despotism. This troubled Williams greatly, for he believed that Americans had forgotten about domestic social reforms and embarked on an imperialist course instead.

In many ways *Contours* reiterated the points Williams had been making for years: America had never been truly isolationist, the frontier had created an expansionist Weltanschauung, and economic expansion was seen as the solution to the nation's problems. All the familiar arguments from *Tragedy* were there. However, this time Williams added a new twist. Instead of looking at expansion as a theme in isolation, he entwined the history of US expansion with the economic development of America (from eighteenth-century merchants to the industrial revolution). This added a new dimension to Williams's overall critique and helped him explain why imperialism had become institutionalized. At the same time, *Contours* also provided the reader with much more to chew over. For example, Williams's views on society and capitalism appeared to be more Marxian than those presented in *Tragedy*. Furthermore, *Contours* also included some interesting insights into the spiritual role of man. However, perhaps the most significant feature of the book was Williams's impassioned assault on the role of corporations in society, which he blamed for sustaining a culture of imperialism. In doing so, *Contours* presented some fresh perspectives on US expansion and took Williams's arguments further.

Contours began by examining the role of expansion in British mercantilism—the argument being that many of America's imperial tendencies originated across the Atlantic. Williams showed how British mercantilists not only saw empire as essential for agriculture and commerce, but they also saw expansion as the ideal way to create prosperity and stop social unrest. Williams traced this philosophy from prominent thinkers such as John Donne to John Locke and Adam Smith, men who did much to frame the American Weltanschauung. This emphasis on socioeconomic philosophers expanded *Tragedy*'s analysis.

Williams had examined the influence of men like Brooks Adams before, but he had not identified such historical and cultural precedents. For example, he argued that Locke's teachings had a huge impact on the mind-set of early Americans. Locke was presented as an arch-imperialist, who saw wealth as finite; therefore, "the only way to achieve welfare was to take enough away from others to raise the national average."[71] The idea that a nation could not develop without an empire became a central facet of the American Weltanschauung, as did Adam Smith's insistence that market expansion was needed to absorb economic surpluses.

The early chapters of *Contours* revealed Williams's personal socialism in an obvious way. He blamed the subversion of mercantilism into laissez faire on America's well-to-do elites, who he claimed eventually gave up campaigning for the general good in order to extend their own wealth and liberties. Williams believed elites took the philosophies of Locke and Smith and integrated them into a new Weltanschauung to suit their circumstances. The Wisconsin scholar believed this new mind-set perverted Calvinism to provide individuals with a moral justification to follow their egos and accumulate riches. Suddenly, it became God's will to pursue one's own selfish agenda; consequently, the chance to create a truly human community was lost for generations. Williams also highlighted the role played by Social Darwinists, who used the natural sciences and religion to condition Americans into thinking that "competition produced the changes necessary for survival . . . and progress."[72] Williams believed this logic simply clouded the fundamental issue: that the general welfare would never be improved in a society that was based on private property—unless of course, the nation turned to imperialism and took land and wealth from others.

Williams also made a number of interesting observations about British imperialism. He argued that as the British Empire had rested primarily on trade, it constantly attempted to wriggle into foreign markets. Williams therefore acknowledged that the United States was following in the footsteps of Great Britain by preferring informal economic imperialism to outright colonialism. *Contours* continued by stressing how expansion had become central to mercantilism generally; imperialism was seen as both necessary and benevolent, not least because it enabled Britain to spread Christianity and cultural values across the globe. Suggestions that the United States was pursuing the same path as imperial Britain would have been scoffed at by most observers at the time. However, Williams believed that America had emulated Britain's socioeconomic model to a large extent; so he expected US foreign policy to take a similar course.

Although Williams recognized that Americans wanted their empire to be benevolent, he argued that they ultimately failed in this aspiration. *Contours* told the story of how good intentions went awry during a series of economic crises as individualism wreaked havoc on the American economy. Overall, Williams claimed that early US mercantilism had great potential to produce a good society at home and a benevolent empire abroad, but the transformation of the American economy into laissez-faire and corporate capitalism prevented this from happening. Whereas mercantilism placed much emphasis on colonies' welfare, Williams believed the individualism of laissez faire created an economic free-for-all that caused many Americans to demand expansion without a conscience. In times of trouble, the people fell back on their expansionist Weltanschauung, demanding a foreign economic frontier to create enough wealth for the whole nation.

Williams argued that the government's role in society changed too as mercantilism gave way to laissez faire. Instead of fostering the general welfare, Williams believed that Washington officials tried to maintain the existing framework, stop monopolies, and, most importantly, solve the dilemma of private property by expanding the marketplace—even if this meant seizing foreign resources. Furthermore, because freedom was defined as a "release from restriction," Anglo-Saxon Americans believed it was their natural right to seize land and develop it for their own individual interests. Williams was scathing about this lack of morality, claiming that "it provided no basis upon which to deal with evil in a nonviolent way" and that "its solutions were persistently aggressive and acquisitive."[73] He was also scathing about America's insistence on free trade, especially as Adam Smith had warned that removing tariffs would give advanced nations a decisive advantage over developing nations. Williams therefore saw laissez faire as a self-interested system that gave the United States the best possible chance to exploit the opportunities of empire.

The Monroe Doctrine was presented as an important cog in the psychology and execution of American economic expansion during this period. Orthodox histories often depicted the Monroe Doctrine as a defensive document, but Williams argued it was the classic statement of US expansionist intent. *Contours* stated that the Monroe administration was very interested in European markets and designed the doctrine to give America the best of both worlds: in other words, to keep the Europeans out of the US backyard while they sought new opportunities on other peoples' patches. Consequently, Williams called the document the "manifesto of American empire" that subsequent presidents used to further American interests; for example, he claimed that John Quincy Adams and Henry Clay were very concerned with Latin American trade and used the Monroe Doctrine to justify their ambitious plans for the continent.[74] Williams also asserted that there was no limit to America's imperial intent. He claimed that presidents as early as Andrew Jackson had designs on China, Korea, and Asia because they were the keys to global economic predominance. Williams believed this proved "eerily prescient" and confounded the view, argued by Williams's orthodox contemporary Ernest May, that America "had world power thrust upon it."[75]

Although *Contours* argued that an imperialist momentum was established during the nineteenth century, the book's key premise was that economic expansion reached its zenith during the age of corporate capitalism from 1882 to 1961; this was the period when US imperialism intensified as the result of the consolidation of international corporations and the internationalization of business. Williams believed that laissez-faire and corporate capitalism were actually quite similar, but with one crucial difference: the former viewed the economy as a melting pot of separate interests, whereas corporations created a much more organized, "inter-related system." As a result, the advent of corporate capitalism diminished the value of individuals, made people into economic units rather than human beings, and placed great power and influence in the hands of a few corporation leaders whose "approach to organizing and balancing the political economy" remained an "interest-conscious conception."[76] Not surprisingly, Williams thought the arrival of corporations heralded a new breed of expansion, as these vast conglomerates pressured the government into foreign wars to serve their interests. The Wisconsin scholar argued that the Spanish-American War was the early manifestation of this new, assertive America.

Although Williams had not changed his mind about the fundamental characteristics of American imperialism in the two years between writing *Tragedy* and *Contours*, his overall understanding appeared to have evolved somewhat. He placed the same emphasis on the frontier mentality and the conviction that US prosperity depended on expansion, but his social, ideological, and economic thinking went deeper. For instance, he examined the American Weltanschauung in a more specific socioeconomic context, paying particular attention to private property. He saw individual property rights as the crucial factor that unbalanced the US socioeconomic equation; private property cemented wealth in the hands of the few, so the United States was forced into imperialism to provide enough wealth for all its citizens (the alternative was greater inequality and social unrest). This was far more satisfactory than *Tragedy*'s general assertion that domestic conditions and foreign policy were linked.

Furthermore, *Contours* took a closer look at how the ideology of US expansion became a national consensus. Because imperial policies seemed to alleviate economic problems, Americans convinced themselves that expansion was ethical as well as necessary (and they ignored the fact that expansion denied self-government to conquered territories). Williams characterized this aspect of the American Weltanschauung as a perversion of true American values—one that made no sense and was therefore "non-intellectual." His analysis of how religion was twisted to justify expansionism strengthened his argument, as did his examination of how laissez faire created a national psyche that always thirsted for more, whether this was for land or individual wealth. *Contours* also made further revelations about the frontier mentality—insights that enhanced the familiar arguments of *Tragedy*. Williams contended that the frontier created a military definition of the world, especially as Americans viewed it as an area to move into, not a boundary. As a result, the United States simply could not tolerate any other nation in the American hemisphere—an attitude that was "militantly, even aggressively, expansionist."[77]

Overall, *Contours* provided a more convincing exposé of US economic expansion than *Tragedy*. A further example was the extent to which Williams analyzed the specific motives of capitalist leaders: there was much more emphasis on Americans' competitive mindset and their struggle to win a greater share of the global market in individual industries. This was a definite improvement from *Tragedy*'s argument that all Americans at all times were driven by the same general urge to expand. Furthermore, this new analysis demonstrated the relationship between business and government in a more lucid manner. Discussions between politicians and corporation leaders were quoted to support Williams's arguments, giving the reader a much clearer impression of how Americans allegedly viewed the economic world as "a battlefield."[78] Consequently, *Contours* was more persuasive at explaining the dynamics behind US expansion.

Contours also shifted more responsibility for US imperialism onto the American people. Although *Tragedy* pointed out that expansion had the overwhelming support of the public (and was often demanded by both rural and metropolitan populations), *Contours* went further by suggesting that politicians were often responding to political pressure for expansion. Williams even suggested that some presidents were opposed to imperialism but had no choice in the matter—anything else would have been political suicide. For example, *Contours* asserted that Theodore Roosevelt was against territorial expansion yet was forced into seizing the Panama Control Zone from the British in what Williams called one of the most "brazen" bits of "imperial land grabbing in modern history."[79] This was a definite point of departure from *Tragedy*, which highlighted how a national consensus existed concerning the desirability of expansion but often blamed American leaders for driving expansionist adventures. *Contours* also demonstrated how Williams's thinking went beyond Beard (who frequently portrayed the working class as blameless bystanders during the nation's imperial turn).

However, Williams occasionally seemed to imply that decades of falling back on expansion as a solution to economic problems eventually geared the US economy toward imperialism—thus turning what was initially a mistaken conviction into a reality. For example, American businesses established overseas operations that eventually became essential to their profitability. However, it must be pointed out that Williams never made this explicit. Furthermore, it must be stressed that at no stage did Williams claim that the nature of American capitalism made imperialism inevitable. Consequently, *Contours* cannot accurately be described as a Marxist tract, even though Williams frequently gave the impression that US imperialism was caused by the nation's socioeconomic structure. What separated Williams from the Marxists was the question of inevitability. Marx, Lenin, and Nearing (plus several New Left scholars during the 1960s) all asserted that imperialism was an inescapable by-product of capitalism. Williams on the other hand was not so definitive. Although he argued that US capitalism had evolved in a manner that had ultimately produced expansionism, he believed this process could be reversed by domestic socioeconomic reform. This is why Williams should forever be associated with Beard (or described as an independent scholar) rather than being portrayed as a Marxist.

Significantly, neither *Tragedy* nor *Contours* stated that capitalism itself was necessarily to blame for US imperialism—rather it was the specific way in which capitalism had been utilized by Washington officials and business leaders. Both Beard and Williams believed it was possible to reform US capitalism in order to produce a prosperous and equitable domestic society. At the end of *Contours*, Williams emphasized that expansion had been "the easy way out" of economic problems and that "it was possible to build a community—a commonwealth—based on private property without relying on imperial expansion."[80] The Marxists, on the other hand, held no such hope that capitalism could bring anything other than imperialism, war, and inequality.

When considering *Tragedy* it is always best to place it alongside *Contours*. The books were published within the space of two years and the latter elucidated Williams's original assertions. When read in isolation, *Tragedy* can seem vague and polemical, whereas the two books together offer a much more comprehensive interpretation of United States imperialism. Furthermore, the books arrived at the start of a crucial juncture in the history of the American left. The 1960s were the decade when the Vietnam War and the civil rights movement created a groundswell of dissidence on campuses across the nation. When this new breed of radicals looked for inspiration in their assessment of US foreign policy, it was natural for them to look to Williams. Consequently, both *Tragedy* and *Contours*, published as they were in 1959 and 1961, became flagship texts in the historiography of American empire.

Contemporary Critiques

In his interviews for the UW Wisconsin Oral History Program, Harrington argued that Williams "had more to do with shifting American diplomatic history towards being critical and being less pro-State Department than almost anybody else."[81] However, as discussed in chapter 1, Williams was not the only dissident to emerge during the 1950s. C. Wright Mills, a scholar who was once described as "the angry young man of American sociology," also blamed the US socioeconomic structure for US imperialism—albeit in a somewhat contrasting manner.[82] As a sociologist, Mills looked at American expansion from an alternative perspective. He was not a Marxist in the purest sense of the word, because he was a keen advocate of individual freedoms. However, he was very concerned with the social structure of US society, which he claimed centralized power in the hands of a privileged minority.

Mills outlined his unique perspective in *The Power Elite* (1956). This was a radical insight into the structure of American society and it argued that the public had little influence over the nation's course. In a direct challenge to the prevailing view that the United States was run by the people for the people, Mills argued that a power elite actually dominated policy formation—which they shaped to serve their interests and perpetuate their wealth and control. But who exactly belonged to this allegedly all-powerful elite? Mills claimed it was "men whose positions enable them to transcend the ordinary environments of ordinary men." This group included those who "command the major hierarchies and organizations," "rule the corporations," "run the machinery of the state," and "direct the military establishment." This alliance between the government, big business, and the military occupied "the strategic command posts of the social structure," which made it possible for them to loosely coordinate policies that cemented their power and extended their wealth.[83]

Unlike Leninist critiques of capitalist society, *The Power Elite* did not assert that authority resided in the hands of the wealthy because of a class conspiracy against workers. Rather, Mills claimed that the ruling elite in America was not a self-conscious group. In fact, he contended that members were "often uncertain about their roles" and "less acutely aware of [their power] than of the resistance of others to its use." Nevertheless, Mills argued that the issue of whether the elite was aware of its power was largely irrelevant—what really mattered was the fact that "political, economic and military circles" acted as "an overlapping clique" that "shared decisions having at least national consequences." This group was not omnipotent (like the rulers of Stalinist Russia), because they occasionally had to answer to public opinion. However, Mills was forthright in his assertion that the power elite in America by 1957 was more powerful than it had ever been. There were limits to the sway the power elite enjoyed, but "never before had the limits been so broad."[84]

Mills claimed that it was relatively easy for the power elite to manipulate policy to serve its interests because of the crossover of wealthy individuals who worked in both governmental and corporate environments during their careers. He also highlighted how key individuals sat on the boards of several corporations at once, while certain members of the corporate rich also acted as both advisors and donors to political parties. Mills argued that "money allows the economic power of its possessor to be translated directly into political party causes." As a result of this apparent unification between the political and the economic, Mills claimed that the American public had very little power. Although they had the ability to vote, they were more or less incapable of purging the "political directorate" or influencing national policy.[85] Consequently, the young sociologist claimed that the democratic nature of the United States was in actual fact a fallacy. Real power rested in the hands of the power elite; the personnel occupying the top political jobs might change from time to time, but their replacements would possess a similar sociopolitical outlook and represent the same class interests.

On the surface, this social critique may not appear to be directly linked to the issue of US imperialism. However, Mills placed full responsibility for US foreign policy on the shoulders of this privileged, self-interested elite. When it came to domestic economic issues, Mills believed that corporations did their best to influence political decisions. After all, "the success of the corporation today depends to a considerable extent upon minimizing its tax burden, maximizing its speculative projects through mergers, controlling government regulatory bodies, (and) influencing state and national legislatures."[86] The same was true when it came to American foreign policy. Mills claimed that after 1945 (when World War II had revived the US economy), corporations came to realize that their profits often depended on events outside the Western Hemisphere. The corporate-oriented power elite thus began to exert pressure on their government associates to pursue foreign policies that protected and extended their interests abroad.

At the center of Mills's critique of American imperialism lay his conception of what he called the "military-industrial complex." *The Power Elite* stated that the United States was dominated by a triangle of corporate, governmental, and military interests—all of which overlapped in terms of social values and economic interests. Mills argued that the unification of America's political economy during World War II had included "the merger of the corporate economy and the military bureaucracy." Consequently, just as the role of the government in the economy increased during the 1940s, so did the role of the military in both. The very nature of the war had made this inevitable. "The very organization of the economics of war made for the coincidence of interests and the political mingling among economic and military chiefs."[87]

Mills claimed that during the process of reconversion after 1945 (as the American economy adapted to peace), military and corporate chiefs were careful not to destroy the relative prosperity created by the war—especially considering the hardships of the Great Depression. The result was the perpetuation of "a permanent war economy," in which "military demands continued to shape and pace the corporate economy."[88] The military therefore remained at the heart of the political economy as the Cold War began. Mills reflected wryly that this was not because American policymakers feared the possibility of war against the Soviet Union but because the Pentagon was many corporations' best customer.

This hypothesis had not been asserted by left-wing dissidents before. The likes of Beard and Nearing had speculated that wars were sometimes fought to boost the US economy, but prior to Mills, nobody had argued that the military itself was a key player in the formation of expansionist policies. Between the two world wars, dissidents depicted the military as a mere servant of the government. Although they argued that economic interests often pressured politicians into taking military action (for the sake of protecting foreign markets and investments), there was no conception of an economic-military alliance. Mills even claimed in *The Causes of World War Three* (1958) that the health of the US economy was so dependent on military expenditure (and a permanent preparedness for war) that whenever negotiations with the Soviet Union took place, "stocks, by their jitters, reflected what is called a 'peace scare.'"[89]

Mills's work was significant in the historiography of American empire because he took Beard's theory that US imperialism was a product of domestic economic problems but also considered the impact of socioeconomic changes in the United States. In doing this, Mills provided new revelations into the relationships between corporations, government, and the military—insights that provided a different perspective on the formation of US foreign policy. Furthermore, Mills made fresh observations into what he saw as stark differences between US imperialism and that of the Soviet Union. The prime differentiating point was "the economic element." He argued that Soviet expansion after

World War II was motivated by "booty," that is, Russians sought direct political control over Eastern Europe to either accumulate valuable capital goods or extract agricultural surpluses; this followed traditional-style colonialism, which reaped economic benefits and prevented the poorer nation from industrializing. On the other hand, Mills believed that US imperialism was caused by an imbalance or "contradiction" in the nation's capitalist economic system.[90] For America to prosper, Mills claimed, it was necessary to open up foreign markets in backward countries for the export of surplus goods. The countries where markets were found would then be used as producers of raw materials, which US industry required to continue production. The goods manufactured would then be sold back to the poor nations, thus creating a cycle of dependency. Mills argued that American capital accumulated in these foreign markets over time, thus making it necessary for US policymakers to safeguard these investments. This was a risky strategy because it externalized US economic prosperity and made the government vulnerable to pressure from corporations with significant foreign interests.

This aspect of Mills's critique was imitated by New Left historians during the 1960s (particularly Harry Magdoff). It differed somewhat from Williams's perspective because it focused on the reliance of the US economy on foreign operations (rather than emphasizing how economic expansion was an unnecessary evasion) and also cast doubt on whether US policymakers had good intentions. Whereas Williams believed that American intentions were honorable, Mills's *Causes of World War Three* doubted whether economic expansion was anything other than self-interested. "The US elite are doctrinaire capitalists, which means—given present world economic conditions—that they are utopian capitalists as well. I do not believe that they know of any way, in which even *they* really believe, to maintain their capitalist interests and at the same time to industrialize the underdeveloped world. In the economic and political world of today, I do not think that US capitalism is an exportable system." This disparaging interpretation of US Cold War policy depicted American expansion as exploitative, self-interested, and disingenuous. Mills was always quick to find an ulterior motive for alleged US generosity; for example, he argued that Washington gave foreign aid "for military reasons," not humanitarian concerns, while "little or nothing" was offered when neither capitalist nor military benefits would result. Overall, *The Causes of World War Three* stated that "there is no comprehensive plan, no systematic idea [and] no general program for the economic development of India, Latin America, the Middle East, Africa, [and] South-East Asia." Protestations to the contrary were "merely propaganda."[91]

Mills's critique was more reminiscent of Williams when he focused on the intellectual dimensions of US expansion. *Tragedy* asserted that Americans' penchant for economic aggrandizement was the result of a flawed Weltanschauung that convinced policymakers that foreign markets were necessary. Mills's *Power Elite* also explored the intellectual aspects of US diplomacy by claiming that US policymakers were afflicted by "crackpot definitions" of the world.[92] Both Williams and Mills lamented the lack of intelligent, open-minded debate in America during the 1950s. At the beginning of *The Causes of World War Three*, Mills asked, "Is war, today, a matter of blind drift, of overwhelming events of historical destiny—or is it a matter of men making decisions?" As far as the radical sociologist was concerned, "doctrinaire incompetence" was the reason why humanity stood on the brink of mutual destruction.[93] Mills blamed the power elite for this intellectual failure. Because US policymakers had emerged neither from "a civil service that is linked to the world of knowledge and sensibility" nor from "nationally responsible parties that debate openly and clearly," Mills believed they were intellectually blinkered. Hence, when they forced their outlook onto the American people, they only succeeded in "raising irrationality to principle."[94]

Mills's analysis of the intellectual aspects of US imperialism was not as sophisticated as Williams's (for example, he did not explore how the frontier mentality and Americans' belief in Manifest Destiny helped to propel expansion), but his critique did surpass *Tragedy* and *Contours* in one respect: Mills provided readers with a more specific plan to save the United States from catastrophe. This plan involved the abandonment of both NATO and the Warsaw Pact, the cutting of military budgets, the prevention of the use of science for military purposes, plus the prohibition of arms shipments to the Middle East, Latin America, Southeast Asia, and Africa. Furthermore, Mills suggested a United Nations–sponsored Middle Eastern Authority, which could control the region's oil and sell it at a controlled price (the proceeds of which would be used to develop the infrastructure of local countries). This latter proposal was specifically designed to combat imperialism, for "the imperialist claims and actions of the corporations, and of their governments, cannot be maintained today without violence and the threat of violence."[95]

Overall, however, Mills's critique was not as nuanced as Williams's work. Not only did *The Power Elite* and *The Causes of World War Three* present very little evidence to support the radical sociologist's contentions, but Mills's analysis also hinted at unlikely conspiracies for which there was little evidence. It was not surprising, therefore, that contemporary critics were unconvinced by his theories. Writing in the *American Sociological Review*, Leonard Reissman complained that Mills's "outstanding fault" was "the uncritical acceptance of his own position."[96] Meanwhile, Robert Agger dismissed the radical's social model, criticizing a "lack of data . . . at least a lack of relatively systematic, empirical data about the development of the power elite and its dynamics."[97]

Nevertheless, despite the polemical nature of his critique, it cannot be denied that Mills made a significant contribution to the historiography of US imperialism. His work was "widely read and praised by activists"; as a result, it could not have failed to influence the next generation of radicals.[98] In fact, in an article in *Mademoiselle* in 1961, antiwar figurehead Tom Hayden announced that Mills was one of only three figures over thirty years of age still trusted by young people in America.[99] The specific issues Mills raised inspired subsequent scholars to explore similar themes. For example, Magdoff followed Mills's lead by specializing in the consequences of economic strategies like foreign aid. However, whereas Mills was content to make polemical accusations, Magdoff found the evidence to support his theories. He did this by researching statistics from an assortment of official organizations, such as the Agency for International Development and the Directory of International Trade.[100]

Although Richard W. Van Alstyne also argued that the United States had been expansionist throughout its history (his book *The Rising American Empire* attributed America's quest for "an indefinite sphere of influence" to nationalism and a lust for power), Mills and Williams provided the most potent repudiations of orthodox Cold War scholarship.[101] Consequently, their work attained a cult following on the left. This is because they provided what dissidents considered to be a "better" critique of US diplomacy than the interpretations written by "court historians"—in other words, the orthodox scholars affiliated to the State Department who supported America's Cold War strategies and depicted US imperialism as an aberration.[102]

A typical example of what the left called a "court historian" was Ernest May, whose book *Imperial Democracy* (1961) exonerated US policymakers and businessmen from instigating the Spanish-American War and blamed the American people. May's theory was that the United States became expansionist because this was what the overwhelming majority of the public wanted; American leaders were therefore pressured into imperial acts and were simply doing their democratic duty as elected representatives (hence the title *Imperial Democracy*). Although Williams had acknowledged that the public frequently demanded economic expansion, he believed policymakers and businessmen were complicit in the decision to expand economically. After all, both *Tragedy* and *Contours* stated that there was a consensus within America concerning the desirability of exploiting foreign markets. *Imperial Democracy* explored many of the same themes but reached different conclusions. For example, May admitted that America's new-found industrial strength made her more assertive in the 1890s, and he recognized the problem of US surplus production, but he denied the existence of a consistent program to acquire foreign markets, or a continuous pattern of economic expansion. Instead, May looked at events in isolation, considering political and moral factors as well as economics.

When it came to America's imperial turn at the end of the nineteenth century, May asserted that McKinley was initially reluctant to wage war with Spain over Cuba. He claimed that "only after the public had shown where it was willing to go did the executive branch step forth to lead." He also argued that McKinley "capitulated to the jingoes" for the sake of his own political career and a sense of moral duty. The crux of his thesis, however, was his contention that "the sole concern of the president was the mood and whim of public opinion." Unfortunately, there were aspects of May's theory that did not add up. For example, he claimed that McKinley eventually became keen on imperialism after the Spanish-American War without a suitable explanation. May simply informed readers that the war "appeared to change McKinley," who then had no qualms about taking Guam and Puerto Rico; there was little real political or ideological analysis, just the simple assertion that the president "seemed to become an imperialist."[103] At one stage, May tried to explain McKinley's change of heart by claiming he wanted to win the political support of business elites who had interests in Cuba. Unfortunately, this contradicted his earlier assertion that the business community opposed intervention because war could have destabilized the stock market. This line of argument also seemed contradictory because it undermined *Imperial Democracy*'s general depiction of President McKinley as the innocent bystander pressured into war by the American people (if the president intervened in Cuba to appease business elites, he was surely motivated by his own political self-interest). May's interpretation of 1898 was therefore somewhat incongruous.

Even though liberal critics argued that Williams's critique of American imperialism during the 1890s was ambiguous, the same accusation could be leveled at May. Cynical critics might even have surmised that May's urgency to exonerate US leaders of possessing imperialist ambitions could have been the result of his personal affinity to Washington policymakers; May served as an establishment intellectual during the 1960s. Meanwhile, *Imperial Democracy* did not clarify how America's alleged humanitarian urge managed to create an empire that encompassed Hawaii, Cuba, the Philippines, Guam, and Puerto Rico. Could it be that economic desperation had "shaken" the people, along with a conviction that salvation lay in overseas markets?[104] May might have disagreed with Williams's assessment of the 1890s, but at least the Wisconsin scholar made an attempt to explain how a yearning for expansionism developed over several years from all sections of society, rather than acting as an apologist for US expansion.

Out of Tragedy

When a young Williams began reinterpreting the main lines of American history in the 1950s, most of his contemporaries regarded his work as non-history because he did not use the concepts and methods that defined acceptable discourse. But despite this controversial start to his career, Williams's views became increasingly respected, climaxing with his elevation to head of the Organization of American Historians during the 1980s. It was a dramatic turnaround: the deductions he made in the early Cold War period were so radical that few dared to take him seriously; however, by the end of his career, many of those who disagreed with his conclusions grudgingly appreciated the contribution he had made to the debate on US expansion.

Tragedy and *Contours* turned conventional history on its head. Not only did they state that US policymakers followed an imperialistic path because of a nonsensical Weltanschauung, but the books also criticized the ideologies that Americans held dear. The romantic view of the frontier was challenged, as was the notion that capitalism and individualism were inherently linked to freedom. Instead, Williams claimed that the frontier had been an evasion from domestic socioeconomic reform, while the evolution of US capitalism had created a powerful appetite for imperialism. Williams argued that Washington officials had squandered numerous opportunities to reform US domestic institutions and create a good society that served the general welfare. Instead, he claimed that policymakers preferred Open Door expansion—a strategy that favored US businesses but often worked against the economic welfare of developing nations. Furthermore, Williams claimed that expansion had not even worked, for the United States had continued to suffer economic crises even after the establishment of an insular empire.

Although orthodox scholars often baulked at Williams's thesis, they were eventually hard pressed to dismiss all of his observations. For example, America had indeed created an informal empire in the late nineteenth century. Contemporaries might have rejected Williams's claim that economic factors were primordial, but *Contours* demonstrated that US policymakers were at least aware of the economic benefits that expansion would bring. Furthermore, it became hard to dispute Williams's assertion that the United States had (at least occasionally) deviated from the principles it held dear. Williams's critique was also more holistic than critics liked to admit. The American Empire depicted in *Tragedy* was first and foremost an economic empire, but it also possessed powerful ideological and psychological undercurrents. Consequently, when observers such as James Warburg portrayed *Tragedy* as mere "economic determinism," they were being unfair.[105] As we have seen, Williams did not claim that imperialism was an inevitable by-product of capitalism, nor did he focus exclusively on economics.

Having said that, it is easy to see why many critics thought Williams was a Marxist. For example, he asserted that "social alienation was the inevitable outcome of capitalist individualism" and that "the market uprooted communities."[106] Furthermore, he had a "tremendous influence on the development of the New Left." Overall, however, he was a socialist in the progressive mold—much like the former New Dealers that comprised the UW history department during the 1950s.[107] In addition, Williams was usually keen to engage with his orthodox contemporaries and persuade them that his perspective had merit; he did not develop a siege mentality like many New Left Marxists. Unfortunately, however, Williams's reputation as a pariah made this difficult. When he approached a group of liberal scholars (including May) at a conference in Chicago they spurned his offer to socialize, drink whiskey, and discuss his point of view. According to McCormick, "they wouldn't engage with him at all."[108]

What Williams's critics failed to recognize was that although Williams's broad methodology could be described as Marxian, his work was firmly rooted in the Wisconsin tradition. He did not "ride the counterculture to prominence" like many of his New Left contemporaries during the 1960s; rather, "the culture caught up with him." With his midwestern roots, Williams remained a social conservative at heart. He provided 1960s radicals with "a conservative alternative," and when the protests against the Vietnam War at UW turned violent, Williams soon retreated to Oregon.[109] Rather than calling Williams a Marxist, and grouping him together with New Left radicals, historians should criticize his work on different grounds. For example, Williams was arguably too ambitious; after all, it was nigh on impossible to fit over two hundred years of history into a single framework. Furthermore, the fact that Williams has been described as "a romantic" and "an idealist" by those who knew him suggests that he occasionally found it difficult to retain an air of scholarly detachment.[110] Another weakness (or double standard) that characterized Williams's work was his aforementioned propensity to judge the United States by higher standards than other countries. At times it appeared as though Williams was guided by his own version of American exceptionalism—one that expected the United States to behave impeccably without a care for its own interests. This was somewhat unrealistic.

Nevertheless, for all its ambiguities, Williams's work prompted many Americans to reappraise their nation's global role—or at the very least consider the more practical and utilitarian aspects of US diplomacy. Although Williams stretched his framework to its very limits (and perhaps beyond them), many critics eventually conceded that *Tragedy* "framed arguments about its subject" throughout the 1960s.[111] Even if some readers baulked at Williams's emphasis on US imperialism, *Tragedy* demonstrated that "America's humanitarian urge to assist other peoples" was sometimes "undercut—even subverted—by the way" it went "about helping them."[112] Meanwhile, Williams's sympathizers hailed *Tragedy* as "the best possible antidote to the complacency nourished in the American people by a government which seemed almost wholly unaware of the bankruptcy of its foreign policy."[113] As a result, Williams became the best-known Cold War revisionist of his era. His work also inspired subsequent dissidents who emulated the Wisconsin scholar by emphasizing the continuous nature of US expansion from the nineteenth century into the Cold War. The most sophisticated of these were written by men who knew Williams personally. Indeed, they were his students and teaching assistants at the University of Wisconsin.

5

The Wisconsin Interpretation Expanded

> A nation does not become a great global power over a relatively short period of time with officials who are absent-minded or passive.
>
> Walter LaFeber, 1963

The Pivotal Decade

The 1960s have long been identified as one of the most turbulent decades in the history of the United States. It was a period of social turmoil, transition, and uncertainty. The civil rights movement and the war in Vietnam arguably polarized the nation to levels not witnessed since the Civil War. As television, newspapers, and radio bulletins carried news of violence on campuses and on the streets, some policymakers feared the breakdown of US society itself. Given this volatile social environment, it was not surprising that the 1960s emerged as a key period in the intellectual history of the left. This did not seem likely at the beginning of the decade, when orthodox scholarship remained in the ascendancy, but as the Vietnam War escalated into a major conflict during the mid-1960s, the level of dissent grew considerably.

As discussed earlier, orthodox scholarship tended to be patriotic and supportive of the government's foreign policy. Intellectuals often enjoyed a close relationship with political leaders, and some historians even found themselves on the government payroll; as a result, "not since the first administration of Franklin Roosevelt had intellectuals been so close to the seat of power, and not since the Presidency of Woodrow Wilson had they been issued the challenge to define and rationalize a new world order."[1] These "court" intellectuals, who included the likes of Ernest May and Williams's bête noir, Arthur Schlesinger Jr., defined the international environment in black-and-white terms.[2] They portrayed the United States as the defenders of freedom and democracy while the Russians were presented as malevolent imperialists.

Political and academic discourse rarely strayed from this characterization of the Cold War rivals. Even when liberals criticized certain aspects of US foreign policy, such as the pitfalls of containment, they "still pledged allegiance to the anti-communist ideal"; consequently, although some liberals questioned whether the United States was combating communism in the right way, orthodox scholars never questioned the morality of what the United States was trying to achieve. The benevolence of America's national mission seemed unquestionable—and therefore it remained unquestioned. This, above all else, was why Robert Tomes believed the United States began the Vietnam War on the back of "boundless optimism, confidence, and hubris." He believed that the apocalyptic language of the Cold War "was more than just flamboyant rhetoric"; it was "all too often the expression of sincere emotion and self-righteous conviction."[3]

However, as the 1960s progressed, and the war in Vietnam intensified, emotional rhetoric also began to flow from swelling dissident ranks. A growing number of intellectuals were horrified by the violence in Southeast Asia and implored policymakers to end the conflict. One of the most interesting aspects of this dissent was the number of intellectuals who began to question the United States' national mission for the first time. In the words of Novick, these Americans began to ask: "Was the United States, as most historians had said, a traditionally isolationist nation, dedicated to minding its own business; a nation which, despite an aberrant spasm at the turn of the (nineteenth) century, had been overwhelmingly anti-imperialist; a nation which had only slowly, reluctantly, and in self-defense, come to accept 'the responsibilities of world power?' Or had the traditional version gotten it all wrong? Were we, in fact, something very, very different?" Novick argued that during World War II, American scholars had asked, "What should we do?" In other words, should the United States fight Nazi Germany or remain isolationist? During the Vietnam War, he claimed that the debate was much more fundamental. The question became "who are we?"[4] Williams's work provided the left with an answer.

When LaFeber and McCormick began their graduate studies at the University of Wisconsin, they had no idea that Williams's perspective would become so fashionable. Although left-leaning journals like *Monthly Review* and *Studies on the Left* discussed events in Southeast Asia, the conflict in Vietnam remained relatively small (only American advisers and a limited number of

Special Forces were sent to the region during the presidency of John F. Kennedy). However, as the decade wore on and the war escalated, a new generation of UW historians, all of whom had been instructed by Williams or Harrington, launched their careers at a time when dissent became more prevalent. Whereas Williams had been something of a lone voice, warning Americans about the dangers of establishing vital economic interests abroad, McCormick, LaFeber, and Gardner emerged during a decade when the left managed to achieve "a certain legitimacy."[5]

However, while they came to prominence at the same time as other Cold War revisionists, LaFeber, McCormick, and Gardner's interpretations differed from their contemporaries—particularly the Marxist New Left. Rather than aligning themselves with the radicals who confronted the authorities on the streets, the Wisconsin scholars believed they were "path breakers for a new way of looking at things." McCormick recalled how he met "plenty" of Marxists on campus at UW, but "we considered ourselves to be socialists not Marxists"; therefore, they had more in common with Williams and UW's progressive tradition. Although McCormick and LaFeber fought Williams "tooth and nail" during their first year in Madison, they were "slowly convinced by him" during their second year, when Williams was writing *Tragedy*.[6] Even though they did not agree with Williams on every single issue, they worked as his teaching assistants at various times and, in the words of LaFeber, enjoyed "incredible opportunities to talk with him, and at length"; consequently, Williams "greatly influenced" them all.[7]

There has been some debate as to whether the Wisconsin School was broader than the group inspired by Williams. Harrington, for example, suggested that the school could "be defined more broadly" and "should include" those historians who were trained at UW but went on to different universities and emphasized different factors (he cited Wayne Cole and David Healy as examples). Harrington also argued that some of Curti's former graduate students should be included. However, because Curti focused on "the intellectual side of things" rather than economics, his views were distinct from the Wisconsin School of diplomatic history.[8] Williams, LaFeber, and McCormick all promoted a critique of American foreign policy that cited economic and psychological factors as the driving force behind US imperialism. This was a unique interpretation that provided the most insightful radical critique of American diplomacy during the Vietnam War.

As a result, Williams, McCormick, LaFeber, and Gardner should be classified as a unique group. Although they ultimately employed slightly different definitions to describe US imperialism, and emphasized political factors to varying extents, they were all, in the words of McCormick, "on the same wavelength most of the time." Most significantly, they all subscribed to an economic perspective taught by Harrington and the Beardian theory that US policymakers used economic expansion as a solution to the problem of domestic overproduction—even though they often reached this conclusion independently. For example, McCormick claimed that he wasn't swayed by the power of Harrington and Williams's argument alone. "I went through every trade journal myself and all I saw was overproduction, overproduction, overproduction. . . . It was Marx's underconsumption on its head."[9] Meanwhile, LaFeber decided that Pratt's interpretation of the Spanish-American War was erroneous while critiquing a fellow student's paper in one of Harrington's graduate seminars; although Pratt's "non-economic interpretation shaped the views of the textbooks and most scholars" at the time, LaFeber (encouraged by Harrington) "decided it might be well to give the 1898 war's causes another look."[10]

The Wisconsin scholars were also influenced by British historiography. Before taking up his position at UW, Williams had spent time at the London School of Economics, where he pondered Robinson and Gallagher's aforementioned essay "The Imperialism of Free Trade." Indeed, Williams's concept of imperial anticolonialism certainly derived, to a significant extent, from the British scholars' model of "informal empire" (the British preference for reaping the economic benefits of empire without formal political control). LaFeber was also a student of the British Empire. His minor field at UW was in British imperialism; therefore it is no surprise that the Wisconsin scholars adopted an approach to studying US foreign relations that was broader, and less parochial, than orthodox historians across the United States. Their contemporaries soon came to see them as a distinct group, and they stuck together through thick and thin: they socialized together, attended conferences together, and contributed articles to *Studies on the Left*. What is more, they were also extremely confident about the validity of their thesis. McCormick reflected that "we didn't care if we got criticized, we were young and arrogant at that time; we went to see orthodox guys like May and Perkins and we thought 'this is going to be a piece of cake'; we weren't impressed by them at all."[11]

The Wisconsin scholars were decidedly unconvinced by the aberration theory of US imperialism. Neither did they agree with orthodox critiques of the Cold War. However, unlike the New Left scholars who emerged during the 1960s, the Wisconsin revisionists did not turn radical in response to the perceived immorality of the Vietnam War; their hostility to orthodox interpretations of American history was not primarily political. The likes of Williams, LaFeber, McCormick, and Gardner would have composed their radical critiques of US imperialism irrespective of the conflict in Southeast Asia. This is because their interpretations stemmed from the unique intellectual heritage of the University of Wisconsin, the education they received from Harrington, and their enthusiasm for using empire as a conceptual framework for the study of US diplomacy. In the words of LaFeber, "We tried to work out a broader context that attempted to restore the place of economics after the economic themes (associated with Beard) were attacked by Bemis, Pratt and others in the 1940s and 1950s. But we also tried to give a more complete picture, while stressing the economic—after all, when writing about the worst depressions in US history to that time (1873–1897 and especially 1893–1897), it was ludicrous to assume it didn't act as a causation and shape world views in the making of US foreign policy as well as domestic policy."[12]

America's "New Empire"

Four years after the publication of *Tragedy*, and two years before Lyndon Johnson deployed infantry combat units to Vietnam, Walter LaFeber's first book appeared: it was called *The New Empire: An Interpretation of American Expansion, 1860–1898* (1963), a title that hinted at the work's breadth. Although LaFeber focused on US territorial expansion during the 1890s, he claimed this period could only be comprehended by looking at domestic and foreign policy in the previous three decades; consequently, *The New Empire* fitted the Wisconsin mold because it argued that US expansion was a long-term phenomenon rather than an aberration. It was also, according to its author, very much shaped by Harrington's seminars.[13] However, despite the book's similarities to *Tragedy*, *The New Empire* received a warmer reception from orthodox critics and won the coveted Beveridge Prize (which was awarded by the American Historical Association). Although this might seem strange, there were good reasons for this: LaFeber was careful not to make controversial claims, and his tone was also more cautious. As a result, *The New Empire* did not offend orthodox sensibilities to the same extent as *Tragedy*.

LaFeber's book charted the relationship between America's industrial-technological transformation and US foreign relations, and described how that transformation threatened chaos and radicalism in society. Believing this link had been tragically neglected by historians, LaFeber set out to prove that the social and economic turmoil of the late nineteenth century was directly responsible for America's emergence as a world power. He concluded that US expansion was not a "spur of the moment" aberration but a well-planned, "natural culmination" of the nation's economic development.[14] This supported Williams's thesis and refuted contemporary orthodox accounts of American imperialism, such as Robert Osgood's *Ideals and Self-Interest in American Foreign Relations*, which claimed that US policymakers "exerted a major impact upon the world competition for power" at the end of the nineteenth century and acquired a "far-flung" empire "unwittingly."[15]

Two years beforehand, May's *Imperial Democracy* had claimed that US policymakers "had not sought a new role in World Affairs"; rather, by acting to protect the Cubans from Spanish tyranny, the United States "had greatness thrust upon it."[16] May argued that US presidents were innocent representatives pushed into imperialism by public opinion; he specifically denied that McKinley had any aspirations on Cuba and claimed that the president only waged war with Spain as a last resort. *The New Empire* challenged this view. LaFeber depicted McKinley as a strong leader, "the first modern chief executive," who had long planned to take both Cuba and the Philippines as a strategic solution to US overproduction.[17] LaFeber recognized that public opinion did indeed turn in favor of the Spanish War, but he saw events in a larger context, arguing that all US leaders between 1865 and 1898 acted creatively to economic pressures under the influence of their own worldviews (which saw US expansion as necessary, natural, and morally justified).

The New Empire was based on extensive research of the Library of Congress manuscript collection—particularly the papers of Walter Quentin Gresham, who was Grover Cleveland's first secretary of state (between 1893 and 1895). Just like Williams, LaFeber discovered that public officials were very concerned with the overproduction of American farms and factories and believed that overseas markets were a viable solution. Although LaFeber had great respect for these officials and believed they acted with "intelligence, discipline, and courage" in the face of economic turmoil, he agreed with his Wisconsin contemporaries that the drive for foreign markets ultimately led to an "aggressive US policy" in the Western Hemisphere, which unintentionally violated US values.[18]

LaFeber's analysis led him to conclude that the 1890s were a "watershed," not an aberration, since the Spanish-American War and the US annexation of the Philippines and Hawaii would not have happened without decades of economic metamorphosis. He argued that America's descent into imperialism occurred after a painful period of boom and bust between 1860 and 1889, during which the United States became more and more involved in international affairs. Consequently, "it was not accidental that Americans built their new empire at the same time their industrial complex matured." Like Williams, LaFeber asserted that a consensus of politicians, businessmen, and the agricultural community saw overseas markets as a new frontier of opportunity and the only solution to the nation's ills. As a result, it became "impossible to find a single person who did not favor increased commercial entanglements."[19]

The New Empire defined the period between 1860 and 1889 as America's "Years of Preparation," when the "roots of empire" took hold. To support this supposition, LaFeber focused on the imperial aspirations of William H. Seward, who was secretary of state between 1861 and 1869. He called this great American statesman the "prince of players" in America's budding empire and claimed that Seward's imperial vision came to dominate US policy into the twentieth century. LaFeber argued that Seward believed in an "imperial Manifest Destiny" and worked tirelessly to move America toward Asia via the Pacific. To achieve this, he coordinated a carefully constructed "integrated empire" based on cheap labor, raw materials, high tariffs, and the development of domestic canals and railroads.[20] Furthermore, Seward rejected outright colonialism and favored the expansion of the Union through trade—a key tenet of the "informal" empire that Williams had articulated in *Tragedy*.

LaFeber argued that Seward's early model of American empire remained the basis of US expansion into the 1870s. For example, Ulysses S. Grant (president from 1869 to 1877) sought control of the Caribbean islands for raw materials and strategic bases, while pressing for a US-controlled Isthmian Canal. Then, during the 1880s, Chester A. Arthur's administration continued the pursuit of overseas trade by negotiating reciprocity treaties with Mexico, Cuba, Puerto Rico, the British West Indies, Santo Domingo, El Salvador, and Colombia. However, LaFeber argued that Americans' vision for a commercial empire became crystallized at the start of the 1890s under President Benjamin Harrison and Secretary of State James G. Blaine. LaFeber quoted a speech made by Blaine at Waterville, Maine, on 29 August 1890, when the secretary called for the "annexation of trade" rather than the "annexation of territory."[21] These words brought into focus the dream of bringing the Western Hemisphere together through trade, conferences, dispute solving, and peaceful intercourse. LaFeber claimed this was the Monroe Doctrine implemented via energetic commercial expansion instead of belligerent threats. Again the emphasis was similar to Williams's "informal" empire, but LaFeber expanded this concept by giving it a hemispheric context.

Like *Tragedy*, *The New Empire* stressed that trade was the primary means of American expansion. The book also highlighted how the United States was prepared to use force to secure this strategic objective. For example, Harrison was willing to use military power to protect vital shipping routes. According to LaFeber, the United States moved to secure naval bases in Hawaii, Cuba, Puerto Rico, the Danish West Indies, and Peru in order to establish an infrastructure that could protect trade routes to and from Asia. Consequently, there was continuity (and a pattern) to US expansion, because events at the end of the decade would not have been possible without the accomplishments of previous years.

Although LaFeber saw the second administration of Grover Cleveland as a hiatus in the development of the New Empire, he believed the years 1893 to 1897 represented an important link between the imperialism of Harrison and William McKinley. LaFeber believed that Walter Gresham was as committed to economic expansion as Blaine. LaFeber claimed that Gresham may not have wanted to annex Hawaii, but he was equally willing to manipulate the island's affairs for commercial gain. For example, the Cleveland administration insisted that American planters should keep their power and influence in Hawaii, and made it clear that the United States would not tolerate the influence of European powers in the region. LaFeber argued that this effectively extended the Monroe Doctrine to the Pacific.

In addition, *The New Empire* stated that the Venezuelan Boundary Crisis of 1895–96 was a vital event in the history of US imperialism, for it illustrated the importance of economic expansion to US leaders. This dispute erupted when the British claimed disputed territory between Venezuela and British Guiana—strategic land that controlled entry into the Orinoco (a vital waterway for South American trade). LaFeber claimed that US policymakers felt compelled to make a stand against the British because they could not tolerate commercial competition in their sphere; therefore, they invoked the Monroe Doctrine, which claimed that American dominance over the Western Hemisphere was vital to US institutions and welfare (like Williams's *Tragedy*, *The New Empire* stressed how Americans linked expansion with freedom and democracy). Although military conflict was ultimately avoided over Venezuela, LaFeber saw the incident as an indication that Cleveland was willing to risk confrontation with a major power to defend America's new commercial empire.

LaFeber believed that the Venezuelan crisis increased the imperialist momentum within the United States and helped to move the nation toward war with Spain in 1898. However, although LaFeber claimed that each successive administration furthered US economic expansion, it is important to point out that *The New Empire* denied the existence of a specific plan to extend US influence across the globe. Although LaFeber highlighted a general movement toward the expansion of American trade and influence, he stressed that there was no codified grand strategy passed secretly from president to president. Rather, the American empire was built step by step as policymakers confronted the nation's economic problems as best they could. LaFeber argued that because

Americans believed economic expansion was vital, each administration reacted to its own specific crises in a predictable way—that is, by pursuing additional expansion.

Rather than following a Marxist interpretation, *The New Empire* had much in common with *Tragedy*. Both Williams and LaFeber identified what they saw as a prolonged slide into imperialism over a long period of time but denied the existence of a grand conspiracy. Instead, they claimed that the American Weltanschauung prompted US policymakers to pursue economic expansion every time the nation was gripped by an economic panic. American imperialism therefore might have seemed inevitable, but this was only because US policymakers were unable to see that expansion was not the only solution to overproduction (it was not because capitalism always resulted in imperialism per se). Consequently, the Wisconsin scholars argued that the roots of the Spanish-American War lay in approximately half a century of commercial expansion, without resorting to economic determinism.

Because events in Cuba, the Philippines, and Hawaii occurred as a response to America's domestic economic problems, LaFeber argued they could not be separated in US diplomatic history. "Both Cuba and the Far East were different manifestations of the expansion of the New Empire."[22] He contended that Americans were prepared to fight Spain over Cuba because the fabled China market was failing to produce the fruits predicted. Therefore, when William McKinley won the 1896 election promising to restore US prosperity, this meant finding solutions to extracontinental problems. When the war finally started in 1898, LaFeber claimed that the president clearly had one eye on the Pacific; *The New Empire* challenged the orthodox view that Commodore George Dewey's victory at Manila was a coincidence, because the Philippines were critical not just in the context of the war but also as a stepping stone to Asian markets in the future. LaFeber believed that the Pacific and the Caribbean were vital to American interests at the same time because they were both integral to the overseas commercial empire US policymakers craved.

Although LaFeber's account contradicted orthodox interpretations of the Spanish-American War, his analysis was different from the New Left accounts we will examine in chapters 6 and 7—primarily because LaFeber eschewed economic determinism. Unlike the New Left, LaFeber also had some sympathy for American statesmen: he explained that McKinley "did not want war," but eventually succumbed because "he did want what only a war could provide," which was "the disappearance of the terrible uncertainty . . . and a solid basis from which to resume the building of the new American commercial empire."[23] However, the insistence that US policymakers were generally well-intentioned (and only resorted to imperialism because of a flawed worldview) did not stop LaFeber from emphasizing the self-interested nature of American foreign policy during the period. For example, *The New Empire* stressed how McKinley immediately looked to the Pacific after declaring war on Spain. The annexation of Hawaii was proof of this. LaFeber claimed that political stability in Honolulu was essential for US trade; therefore, there was a certain inevitability about America's annexation of the island, which he claimed had been moving toward the US orbit for years.

Furthermore, even though LaFeber was generally reluctant to make controversial claims, he was not totally afraid to highlight some of the more unsavory aspects of American diplomacy. For example, LaFeber claimed that the military interventions in Brazil and Nicaragua between 1894 and 1896 showed that US policymakers were prepared to fight for US economic expansion, regardless of the consequences for other nations. He also highlighted America's willingness to ignore self-determination in Hawaii; he made his point by quoting the US minister to the kingdom of Hawaii John Stevens, who lambasted Queen Liliuokalani for her "extreme notions of sovereign authority." Meanwhile, *The New Empire* also described the negative effect that US expansion had on the Cuban economy, which collapsed in 1894. Although LaFeber was no determinist, he therefore agreed with contemporary radicals that the Monroe Doctrine was "a doctrine of self-interest."[24]

Overall, however, LaFeber's critique was cautious. While he was influenced by Williams, he seemed careful not to imitate every aspect of Williams's critique; for example, *The New Empire* placed much more emphasis on the value of Hawaii and the Philippines as strategic bases and coaling stations, arguing that Dewey's victory at Manila showed Americans that such installations were "essential . . . if the United States hoped to become a dominant force in the Far East."[25] LaFeber was also more sensitive to political factors than Williams. For instance, he acknowledged McKinley's fear that inaction over Cuba might cost him votes in the business community, especially when a group of importers, exporters, bankers, and vessel owners sent him a petition demanding action. *The New Empire* also recognized that the search for foreign markets was not always driven by the same people. During the Harrison administration, the State Department was primarily responsible for economic expansion, whereas under McKinley, business interests played a greater role.

LaFeber's analysis of America's philosophical expansionists also differed somewhat from Williams's interpretation. This is because *The New Empire* went into far more detail and occasionally discussed different personalities. LaFeber examined members of the establishment who preached and popularized a doctrine of imperialism and tried to assess their impact. Although Williams had examined the influence of Turner and Brooks Adams on US policymakers before, LaFeber devoted an entire chapter to America's expansionist cheerleaders. He looked at not only Turner and Adams but also Josiah Strong and Alfred Thayer Mahan. LaFeber claimed these men were responsible for "the intellectual formulation" of US imperialism. He therefore assigned them a key role.[26]

According to *The New Empire*, Strong "blew a clarion call for American expansion" louder than Turner's. Strong was depicted as the champion of a new "missionary frontier" that advocated "a thunderous Protestant missionary charge" to "conquer the American west for Christ and then use this region as the home base for overpowering the world." This was Strong's solution for the spiritual, economic, and political rejuvenation of the United States; he saw expansion as a religious mission that was vital to the nation's future. Strong expressed these ideas in *Our Country* (1885), a book that sold an amazing 175,000 copies within a decade. LaFeber claimed that "in terms of popularity few books of the time could equal it." As a result, Strong became "a national figure, spreading his ideas from innumerable lecture platforms and through other books."[27]

The New Empire also highlighted the important role played by Mahan, who had recognized the disappearance of the American frontier and its implications for the US economy at the same time as Turner. As a navy man, Mahan believed that the solution to chronic overproduction was mastery of the high seas, which could provide Americans with an omnipresent frontier for commerce. He even foresaw the advantages that commercial expansion had over outright colonialism; this led LaFeber to conclude that Mahan "actually supplied the rationale for the open-door philosophy several years before the State Department issued the [Open Door] notes."[28] Rather than seeing the oceans as a barrier against European interference in the Western Hemisphere, Mahan saw them as great highways of opportunity that must be protected. A powerful and intimidating navy was therefore a must.

Because men like Mahan had the ear of prominent policymakers such as Theodore Roosevelt and Hilary Herbert (who became secretary of the navy in Cleveland's second administration), LaFeber believed the philosophical founders of American imperialism had a direct impact on the course of US diplomacy. Similarly, he claimed that the crusading rhetoric of Strong and the advent of Social Darwinism, which justified US expansion as necessary for survival, created a religious and intellectual consensus on the need for expansion; this powerful elixir of ideologies justified this expansion at any cost, even if this meant war. LaFeber argued that "this admiration of force and war offered something new in American history, for with the possible exceptions of some of the inhabitants of the Old South and the pioneer's notions of how to deal with Indians, Americans had generally regarded war as an evil to be avoided."[29] In this way, the American Weltanschauung became corrupted by religious arrogance and confident militarism—both of which triggered imperialism.

This aspect of LaFeber's analysis also contradicted orthodox interpretations of the 1890s. For example, Robert Osgood admitted that men like Mahan and Adams were genuine nationalist imperialists with a plan for US expansion, but he claimed that their influence was minimal. Osgood argued that the intellectual imperialists were very much in a minority and that their rhetoric made imperialism seem unattractive. He claimed that Mahan and Theodore Roosevelt were "motivated by an aggressive national egoism," and actually "hindered the achievement of their objectives by associating them with a kind of egoism not in accord with America's basic hierarchy of values." Because the majority of Americans found their "missionary imperialism" repugnant, the intellectual realists who promoted US expansion could not have had a decisive impact upon the nation's foreign policy. If anything, Osgood believed they created a public backlash that led to "idealistic utopians" replacing realists as the spokesmen for the American mission.[30]

In challenging orthodox critiques of the United States' imperial turn, LaFeber took the economic line taught by Harrington (and amplified by Williams) but added extra dimensions. After identifying a similar link between domestic factors and foreign policy, *The New Empire* claimed that the advent of industrialization exacerbated the imbalance of the US economy and increased the demand for a long-term solution. Owing to their unique Weltanschauung, Americans found salvation in the form of overseas commercial expansion, which was considered to be a new and seemingly infinite frontier. Then, as the crisis of the 1890s deepened, the United States resorted to violence and outright colonialism to sustain its push for foreign commercial opportunities. However, although LaFeber argued that US policymakers created the "New Empire" with "common purpose," he also emphasized that American expansion was undertaken "amid much debate."[31] For example, he highlighted instances when US officials agonized over expansionist policies and pointed out that the lust for foreign adventures was far from unanimous.

LaFeber was therefore more circumspect in his analysis than Williams. This was reflected by his use of definitions. Whereas Williams used audacious expressions such as "imperial anti-colonialism" to describe US expansion during the late nineteenth century, the younger scholar was more hesitant. Indeed,

LaFeber deliberately avoided using the word "imperialism" in relation to American foreign policy. In the preface to the first edition of *The New Empire*, LaFeber was at pains to explain why he had chosen certain words and expressions to define the United States' emergence as a great power. This served two purposes. First, it gave LaFeber the opportunity to justify his critique and appease those who might be hostile to his interpretation. Second, it gave the young scholar a chance to explain a paradox created by the title of his book: LaFeber was reluctant to use the word "imperialism," but he had no problem using the word "empire."

LaFeber claimed that he had avoided the word imperialism "because the connotations given to it in the Cold War make it almost meaningless." This was a reference to the political climate in America during the early 1960s, when the term imperialism became a stick with which to beat the Soviet Union. Instead, LaFeber said he preferred to use the more innocuous term "expansion," which was not so politically loaded. However, it is difficult to accept this explanation in light of his refusal to use the word "colonialism" in regard to Hawaii and the Philippines. By his own definition, LaFeber described colonialism as "a policy which attempted to obtain both formal political and economic control of a given area and which especially aimed to use this area as a source of direct economic benefits."[32] Surely the US annexation of Hawaii and the conquest of the Philippines therefore amounted to colonialism? After all, even Julius Pratt had admitted in *America's Colonial Experiment* that the US acted like a colonial power in the late nineteenth century by creating "a protected market for its own manufactures and a source of needed raw materials."[33]

In *The New Empire*, LaFeber claimed he had avoided the term "colonialism" because American policymakers did not want Hawaii and the Philippines "primarily in order to obtain direct economic returns"; rather "the United States annexed these areas to develop interests in Asia and, in the case of Hawaii, to safeguard the commercial passageway which Americans hoped to build in Central America." LaFeber therefore asserted that the term "expansion," which he defined as "attempts to find trade and investment opportunities in areas where the United States did not want to exert formal political control," was more suitable.[34] However, there must be doubts as to whether the term "expansion" was appropriate in regard to Hawaii and the Philippines. This is because (a) the United States did eventually seek control over the islands' political destiny, and (b) both territories were taken to extend commercial horizons (as vital strategic bases and coaling stations); as a result one might argue it was irrelevant whether the economic benefits came from the islands directly or not. LaFeber's use of definitions therefore seemed somewhat illogical at times.

However, when one considers the intellectual environment of the early 1960s, it is understandable why the Wisconsin scholar went to great lengths to avoid using controversial terms—even if his rationale for doing so did not always seem watertight. Indeed, when I asked LaFeber about his use of definitions, he argued that "the early 1960s" (before the Vietnam War) posed "difficulties for critical analyses of US history that are too easily forgotten." He recalled his very real concern that mentioning "imperialism" and American diplomacy in the same breath would lead critics to "instantly downgrade" his manuscript—particularly ones who "couldn't deal with" his argument and might "dismiss any use of imperialism" as a way of "avoiding the research itself" and the conclusions reached.[35] Perhaps, therefore, one should forgive LaFeber's ambiguity regarding definitions. This was the young scholar's first book and he had a reputation to build. Antagonizing orthodox contemporaries was unwise; his contention that US expansion was a long-term phenomenon was controversial enough. Whereas Williams was never one for understatement, LaFeber did not want *The New Empire* to be too provocative. Furthermore, it must not be forgotten that *The New Empire* was a more moderate critique than *Tragedy*: the book recognized that American expansion did not always have an unstoppable momentum and "could not be hurried."[36] This was why, according to LaFeber, Harrison was unable to annex Hawaii in 1893; public opinion simply would not sanction such a move at the time. A more cautious use of definitions was therefore understandable and appropriate.

Overall, LaFeber stressed Americans' reluctance to assume direct political control over new territories to a greater extent than Williams. In fact, LaFeber described US expansion as a cautious compromise between imperialists and anti-imperialists. "Few Americans believed that the Latin American and Asian markets were of little importance to the expansive American industrial complex," but on the other hand, "few agreed that . . . the United States should claim and occupy every piece of available land in the Pacific."[37] However, by stressing the long-term nature of US expansion as a solution to overproduction, LaFeber's critique firmly belonged to the Wisconsin School of diplomatic history. In fact, one could argue that LaFeber's decision to adopt a more moderate tone than Williams, and make more of an attempt to eradicate generalizations and false continuities, actually improved the Wisconsin critique—even though, as LaFeber recalls, Williams did not believe that his work went far enough.[38] Although Williams teased LaFeber about this until his death in 1990, the fact that *The New Empire* was less antagonistic than *Tragedy* (and contained considerably more footnotes) meant that orthodox contemporaries were prepared to take LaFeber's book more seriously. This did much to promote the Wisconsin interpretation of US expansion and give it more credibility.

The Imperialism of Anti-Imperialism

By the early 1960s, the key tenets of the Wisconsin interpretation of American empire had been established. Williams and LaFeber argued that US expansion was essentially a quest for new economic frontiers—in other words, the foreign markets that policymakers believed were necessary to alleviate the nation's chronic overproduction. This perspective was entrenched by Lloyd Gardner's *Economic Aspects of New Deal Diplomacy* (1964), which claimed that Franklin Roosevelt was similarly influenced by past administrations' emphasis on the Open Door.[39] However, whereas LaFeber's *The New Empire* primarily focused on the Western Hemisphere, the ultimate economic frontier promised to be the Far East, where millions of Chinese customers seemed poised to absorb American surpluses. Indeed, LaFeber had argued that the United States annexed Hawaii because the island was "absolutely essential as a coaling station and naval base if the United States hoped to become a dominant force in the Far East." He also claimed the same was true of the Philippines, which was not directly valuable as a territory but was "key" as a "way station to the Orient."[40] Because Americans were fascinated by China, believing this vast and mysterious land could solve the imbalance that blighted the US economy, McCormick focused much of his research on US relations with this distant colossus. He outlined his conclusions in *China Market: America's Quest for Informal Empire, 1893–1901* (1967).

China Market charted the interplay between America, China, and European powers that led to the Open Door negotiations at the end of the nineteenth century. McCormick argued that China represented the ultimate test of US "neocolonialism" and whether the policy could propel American economic expansion throughout the world. In many ways, McCormick's critique was similar to that of Williams and LaFeber. For example, he made the familiar assertion that "expansionists like McKinley were amazingly consistent and conscious in their efforts to create a workable, tactical blend of informal empire," a reality "quite at odds" with orthodox portrayals of US "irrationality or innocence." McCormick similarly believed that economic problems, specifically the Panic of 1893, were responsible for "bridging the very real gap between expansionist tendencies and expansionist fulfillment," a hypothesis he admitted was "an economic interpretation" similar to that of his Madison contemporaries.[41] However, because McCormick concentrated specifically on the China market, his interpretation of American policy in the 1890s provided fresh insights. Although he emphasized the same Open Door paradigm, he also questioned whether US policymakers were as bold and ambitious in their quest for expansion as Williams implied. Consequently, McCormick was very much aware that his "critique was different"; his research, after all, had unearthed "evidence that Bill [Williams] hadn't had the opportunity to see."[42]

China Market agreed with *Tragedy*'s assertion that Americans regarded trade with China as the solution to their economic woes—and he agreed that US policymakers prioritized economic expansion above all other diplomatic aims. However, rather than implying that US policymakers pursued a consistent and large-scale imperial strategy, McCormick argued that McKinley tried to tap the China market through a foreign policy of "pragmatic expansionism," that is, practical responses to German and Russian commercial gains in the region. He claimed this approach entailed a series of interrelated moves that extended the United States' control over Hawaii, the Philippines, Wake, and Guam. The aim was to "construct a system of coaling, cable, and naval stations for an integrated trade route which could help realize America's overriding ambition in the Pacific—the penetration and ultimate domination of the fabled China market."[43]

McCormick's work demonstrated the way in which US economic expansion in different parts of the world were inextricably linked. For example, *China Market* stressed how the timing of the Sino-Japanese War of 1894–95 had a crucial bearing on US policymakers, for it focused minds on the need to exploit Chinese trade before other countries secured important concessions. McCormick argued that when the war ended, many Americans believed the Chinese "colossus" was ready to wake up; therefore, the United States was compelled to seek possessions in the Pacific as a matter of urgency, lest other powers capitalize on commercial opportunities in the Far East before America was ready. McCormick claimed that the Sino-Japanese War did not start interest in China, but it "redefined the myth in terms of nascent reality, to give it both the credibility and immediacy necessary to provoke a broad-gauged intensive effort to translate fantasy into fact." The desire to exploit China was augmented by the Panic of 1893, which also created an appetite for overseas expansion. Together, he claimed these forces were "the propellants for American expansion across the Pacific."[44]

However, because McCormick denied that the United States annexed territories for their direct economic worth or reasons of Manifest Destiny, *China Market* repudiated the notion that US policy represented "large policy imperialism." Instead he promoted a new definition called "insular imperialism," which meant the possession of small island territories to further grand economic objectives. Like Williams, McCormick recognized America's preference for "commercial Open Doors over closed colonies or spheres of influence," but *China Market* placed more emphasis on "the government's responsibility" in this process "to act energetically to open new doors and prevent old ones from being closed." During the late nineteenth century, McCormick believed the government had adopted "a more non-ideological, pragmatic approach" to economic expansion, which was characterized by "more utilitarian, business-like methods of doing a necessary job efficiently, but at least possible cost." This was typical of "pragmatic expansionism," a type of imperialism that was more practical and less concerned with Manifest Destiny than Williams's broader critique.[45]

Chapter 4 discussed how *Tragedy* attributed US expansionism to a powerful elixir of ideology and perceived economic necessity. Men like Brooks Adams helped to convince American policymakers that expansion was the natural solution to overproduction, not only because it made economic sense but because it was God's will. McCormick disagreed with this assessment. Although he admitted that ideology did play some role, he argued that its impact was limited because "there was a striking disparity between the grandiose rhetoric of Manifest Destiny and the simpler reality of a consciously self-limited imperialism." In McCormick's opinion, America would have sought greater prizes than small island possessions if ideology had been the prime inspiration for US expansion. Instead he emphasized the pragmatic nature of US imperialism, which "generally sought to impose limits and lighten the burdens and responsibilities of expansionism."[46] *China Market* therefore depicted US expansion as a constrained and practical phenomenon that evolved as a response to economic setbacks.

Because McCormick's economic line was somewhat different from his Wisconsin contemporaries, he was more explicit in defining his approach. He also wanted to differentiate his work from the numerous New Left critiques of US diplomacy that had emerged by the time *China Market* was published in 1967; McCormick claimed his interpretation was not a "narrow economic interpretation" or a "pocketbook determinism" that centered "on special interest groups and efforts to shape policy according to special needs." Although McCormick conceded that interest groups were important, he argued it was dangerous to overstate their influence because interest groups were not monolithic. Instead, McCormick asserted his conviction that American leaders were much more likely to respond to national urges and the need to save the US system from "stresses and strains."[47] This was obviously similar to Williams's theory that US expansion was triggered by the American Weltanschauung, but McCormick's position was more specific.

In *Contours*, Williams had argued that the overriding concern of US policymakers was their assumption that America's socioeconomic fabric would collapse without continued commercial expansion, but he did not satisfactorily explain how corporations and powerful interest groups influenced policy within this framework. For example, he claimed that McKinley went to war against Spain "on the grounds that specific and general American interests could not be satisfied by any other course."[48] This was typical of *Contours*' failure to separate the wishes of individual business interests from those of the business community at large; Williams had seemed to argue that all corporations supported economic expansion, which in turn consolidated America's propensity for commercial imperialism; unfortunately, this oversimplified the complex network of corporate business interests and created an ambiguity as to whether individual business interests drove US foreign policy or whether the national Weltanschauung remained ascendant. *China Market* made McCormick's position unambiguous: business interests were important but not as significant as the overriding requirement of politicians to establish a healthy economy for the whole country.

McCormick was also interested in the role of "power elites," the concept introduced by C. Wright Mills. *China Market* defined power elites as "social elements with the most *direct power* to influence national decisions and alter events." This consisted of men who had power to control social relationships through property ownership, plus the business community at large and its intellectual allies. McCormick recognized that this approach had weaknesses for it failed to show "how non-elite groups such as farmers and industrial workers limited the freedom of choice and action" available to policymakers. Nevertheless, he believed that an examination of property owners and the business community as a whole offered the best insight into US expansion. After all, he believed these were the men who thirsted for new commercial horizons to offset "the frightful specter" of socioeconomic upheaval.[49]

Furthermore, *China Market* also defined these proponents of US overseas expansion in a different way than Williams. McCormick described Americans who sought "the economic fruits of expansion without the burdens and risks of governmental force and a formal empire" as "free-trade imperialists" (a definition previously used by Beard). This expression was a more potent way to portray US expansionists, because it encapsulated how Americans intended to use the nation's "economic supremacy" to further its expansion; this was, after all, the United States' "most potent weapon." The term "free-trade imperialism" also reflected the primary means of US commercial expansion in China, namely the Open Door, which emphasized free trade throughout the region.[50]

As the Open Door was central to US commercial ambitions in the Far East, *China Market* considered the policy in great detail. This included a dissection of its strengths and weaknesses, plus analysis of whether the policy was imperial or not. This last question was particularly interesting, for it questioned Williams's assertion that the Open Door was "imperial in nature."[51] Like Williams, McCormick saw the Open Door as "America's basic response to the methodological question of how to expand."[52] However, whereas Williams believed the policy distilled "motivations, pressures, and theories into a classic program of imperial expansion," *China Market* preferred to characterize the Open Door as "a most interesting hybrid of anticolonialism and economic imperialism."[53] The difference was small but significant. Williams did not believe that the economic nature of the US expansion made its aspirations any less imperial, whereas McCormick was keen to stress that commercial expansion was a more pragmatic and limited approach than "classic" imperialism. Once again ideology was at the heart of this distinction. Williams argued that the Open Door was fused with an "industrial Manifest Destiny" that sought to "cast the economy and the politics of the weaker, under-developed countries in a pro-American mould."[54] *China Market* on the other hand was less concerned with ideology and simply portrayed the Open Door as a pragmatic means of grasping commercial opportunities.

Nevertheless, *China Market* did not deny that American policy toward China ultimately led to imperial behavior. US intentions might have been limited compared with classic European colonialism, but McCormick argued they still exhibited imperialist tendencies. For example, he admitted that the United States was thoroughly self-interested and treated China as a "passive object." He also asserted that China's sovereignty was just an illusion because the Chinese had little control over their own destiny and remained "not an actor but something to be acted upon." Meanwhile, McCormick emphasized that China was unable to develop a balanced economy because the United States prevented the country from industrializing. He claimed that US policymakers restricted China to agriculture and light industry so that the Chinese could not compete with American factories; this approach was "more than mildly reminiscent of Europe's eighteenth-century policies towards her colonies." Overall, McCormick concluded that "while the US wanted an independent China, it did not wish one too independent—at least not independent enough to close the door." He defined this approach as "neo-colonial," for the US sought to "perpetuate China's economic dependency" for her own benefit.[55] This was similar to Williams's original description of "informal" empire, but McCormick emphasized the pragmatic nature of US expansion, whereas Williams had a broader vision of US imperialism in which moral, ideological, and religious factors played a greater role.

Consequently, *China Market* demonstrated a gradual mellowing of the Wisconsin interpretation of US imperialism over time. Although McCormick had used the words "informal empire" in the title of his book (an intriguing choice considering that the neo-colonialism identified by McCormick was milder than Williams's informal empire), the Wisconsin critique became more moderate just as New Left scholars began to propose increasingly radical interpretations during the Vietnam War. *China Market* continued in the same vein as LaFeber's *New Empire* by describing US imperialism as occasionally hesitant and pragmatic. This might have been radical compared with orthodox liberal interpretations of American expansion, which described the nation's imperial turn at the end of the nineteenth century as an aberration, but it was far more restrained than contemporary Marxist interpretations, which frequently depicted US imperialism as part of a grand imperial strategy stemming from the fundamental imbalances of capitalism.

This mellowing of the Wisconsin critique was nowhere more apparent than in McCormick's analysis of the Open Door, which contrasted with Williams's assessment. Whereas Williams had passionately refuted orthodox evaluations that described the policy as "a futile and naïve gesture" (instead he argued that the Open Door was "a brilliant strategic stroke which led to the gradual extension of American economic and political power throughout the world"), McCormick was not so sure.[56] Consequently, *China Market* placed the strategy in a whole new context, arguing that Hay's strategy reflected a contradiction at the heart of US power: Americans had great economic strength (and confidence in their ability to dominate markets on a level playing field), but politically the United States was impotent.

McCormick claimed that the Open Door was chosen as the means of US economic expansion because it was the only way Americans could access Far Eastern markets; after all, the United States had little political weight in China at the time and had been completely unable to stop European powers from creating spheres of influence in the region. As US policymakers were largely unable to control political events in the Pacific, they had no choice but to try and persuade economic rivals to adhere to the Open Door; the only other option was the partition of China, which would have been wholly unacceptable to the American public. McCormick also claimed that this strategy demonstrated the United States' financial weakness—which was why the Open Door was only defined in commercial terms. McCormick concluded that "given America's commitment to economic penetration in China, given the peculiar combination of American strengths and weaknesses, the Open Door policy was the most realistic one at hand."[57] This reinforced his assertion that US economic imperialism was characterized by pragmatic responses to strategic problems.

Because it focused on the limitations of American power, and US policymakers' pragmatic attempts to extend US influence in difficult circumstances,

China Market made the Wisconsin interpretation of US expansion seem less radical. McCormick's analysis also accentuated the gulf between the Wisconsin School and the New Left, who frequently portrayed US imperialism as limitless and insatiable. However, because he followed the same economic line as Williams, and because he accentuated how US expansion violated self-determination, McCormick's view still contradicted orthodox perspectives. Furthermore, McCormick had many positive things to say about the Open Door. He argued that historians had usually expected too much from the policy, seeing it as either "everything or nothing" (i.e., a total success or a complete failure). McCormick also claimed that the Open Door should not be judged as an end in itself: "It was simply an effort to structure a framework within which the more traditional dynamics of diplomacy could operate."[58]

China Market stated that scholars should focus on the Open Door's individual successes rather than judging the policy on whether it secured the China market for US producers (something it ultimately failed to do). While McCormick admitted that these successes were small, the Open Door still gave the US more leverage to open markets and made it more difficult for Europeans to justify their individual spheres. Furthermore, *China Market* stated that the moral language used in Hay's Open Door Notes was a useful public relations exercise because it made American intentions appear benevolent. Consequently, McCormick concluded that the Open Door was moderately successful because it forced its opponents "to employ more indirect and less effective means for fulfilling their ends, thus limiting their freedom of choice and action" while offering a more "peaceful substitute to the imperial rat race."[59]

By looking at American policy in China in detail, McCormick was able to provide a more realistic appraisal of US imperialism in the Pacific. He concluded that the pragmatic and often cautious manner in which America extended her influence into Hawaii, Wake, Guam, and Manila did not qualify as "imperial—in the narrow sense of the word." Rather, *China Market* identified a paradox in US foreign policy, because "American expansion was designed in part to serve an anti-imperial purpose of preventing the colonization of China and preserving the Open Door." McCormick defined this strategy as "the imperialism of anti-imperialism," a concept that rivaled Williams's "imperial anti-colonialism."[60] The difference between the definitions was subtle but revealing: although Williams was prepared to recognize US anti-colonialism, he was reluctant to acknowledge American anti-imperialism.

Like Walter LaFeber in *The New Empire*, McCormick recognized that the Wisconsin interpretation of US imperialism had weaknesses and wanted to tackle them. For example, he agreed with Williams that orthodox definitions of

US expansion were inadequate because they were "too narrow" and "only equated colonialism with imperialism," but he believed that *Tragedy* and *Contours* were also "a little inconsistent" in their "use of definitions." McCormick doubted whether "imperial anti-colonialism" was appropriate, because on the surface it could be confused with the anticolonial stance of American anti-imperialists in the late nineteenth century. Consequently, although McCormick admitted that he coined the phrase "the imperialism of anti-imperialism" somewhat snidely, he was genuinely attempting to define the complex and often contradictory elements of US expansion more accurately.[61] This demonstrates that the Wisconsin School critique of American imperialism was far from static. It evolved throughout the 1960s and in many ways surpassed Williams's more emotive and rather sweeping interpretation.

By analyzing US policy toward Hawaii, the Philippines, and China in more detail, both *China Market* and *The New Empire* demonstrated that the history of US imperialism was actually more complicated than *Tragedy* and *Contours* had suggested. They agreed with Williams that the 1890s witnessed "a pressing need for a new frontier in new markets," and they concurred that "it was nearly impossible to find any prominent members of the power structure who did not, by 1889 think and act within such a conceptual framework." But they started to question exactly who belonged to this "power structure," and they stressed that US policy did not always move in an expansionist direction at all times—for example, LaFeber's assertion that public opinion occasionally restrained US imperialism (which was why the annexation of Hawaii was unfeasible in 1893), plus McCormick's emphasis that the "US did not want to plant the stars and stripes on every ocean-bound rock and pebble."[62] Even though Williams recognized that US policy was not characterized by outright colonialism, his attempt to identify broad trends over a number of decades led him to ignore instances when US expansion was actually quite restrained. This created a false impression that America's entire history was characterized by imperialism. By eradicating these false continuities, McCormick and LaFeber made the Wisconsin concept of economic empire more accurate and sophisticated; they ultimately made it more acceptable to orthodox contemporaries too.

The Agrarian Roots of US Imperialism

Ten years after *Tragedy* was published, and with the antiwar movement in full swing, Williams updated his critique with a fresh examination of American expansion. The book was called *The Roots of the Modern American Empire: A Study of the Growth and Shaping of Social Consciousness in a Marketplace Society* (1969). *Roots* explored similar themes as *Tragedy* and *Contours*, but this time the Wisconsin scholar's emphasis was somewhat different: he still explored the link between economic interests and US foreign policy, but this time he focused on agricultural interests rather than the influence of industrial elites; his premise was that rural communities had been calling for expansion (economic if possible, territorial if necessary) a hundred years before the imperial turn of the 1890s. Consequently, while the Marxist-Leninist scholars associated with the New Left and the antiwar movement were concentrating on the link between imperialism and the maturation of industrial capitalism, Williams's research took him in a different direction.

Because agricultural folk constituted the majority of the American population during the late nineteenth century, Williams believed they played a crucial role in the evolution of US imperialism. Agriculturalists were therefore depicted as arch-imperialists in *Roots*, whereas the metropolitan regions were attributed a secondary role. Williams argued that calls for foreign markets reached a crescendo in the 1880s and 1890s, when Americans faced a crippling agricultural surplus and a fully occupied frontier; the agricultural majority believed they had little option but to call for new markets because they were impoverished and needed exports to survive. Williams argued that over time urban politicians began to realize the political benefits of giving the agricultural majority what they wanted. Industry also slowly began to recognize the advantages of expansion. As a result, a consensus emerged that ultimately took the nation to war with Spain in 1898.

Roots depicted the nineteenth century as a long sequence of economic crises—the solution to which was invariably seen as economic expansion. Williams argued that as agriculturalists were the poorest members of society, they called for this expansion more vociferously than any other group. He claimed that by 1873 they had become militant and organized into groups such as the Grange, which deliberately functioned as a voice for marketplace entrepreneurs and as a political pressure group to advocate expansion. Although the Grange ultimately failed to improve the lot of agriculturalists (they campaigned for the remonetization of silver and a fairer deal for farmers over railroads and canals), Williams believed the organization was an important forerunner to more successful organizations such as the Southern Farmers Alliance, the Farmers National Congress, and the Farmers Mutual Benefit Association, all of which demanded the vigorous pursuit of foreign markets for American surpluses. The growth of these groups demonstrated how the agricultural community became overtly imperialist as the nineteenth century progressed.

The crux of Williams's argument concerned the electoral importance of the agricultural community. He contended that since agriculturalists represented vital sections of the voting population, urban politicians eventually found their cries hard to resist. This was illustrated by the case of James G. Blaine, who advocated expansion in order to win western and southern votes, plus the election campaign of Grover Cleveland, who appealed to farmers by targeting Cuba and the Philippines as lands ripe for new economic frontiers. The election of 1896 was presented by Williams as the classic example of how expansion became the vital political issue by the end of the century. He claimed that the question was not *whether* the US should expand or not (that was a given) but *how* this expansion should take place. Therefore, the election was fought entirely on the basis of tactics, with William J. Bryan proposing remonetization of silver and McKinley promoting bimetallism and reciprocity.

Although Williams was a little vague as to why urban businessmen eventually adopted the rural mindset, he claimed that a national consensus on the necessity of expansion emerged during the final two decades of the nineteenth century. As evidence, he pointed to the National Association of Manufacturers, which mimicked rural organizations by calling for immediate expansion overseas as early as 1885. Consequently, when Hawaii became a focal point for US imperialism in 1893, Williams argued that both the rural and metropolitan majority favored annexation.[63] By highlighting that imperial urges came from the American people, Williams reiterated one of the central hallmarks of his critique. He also repeated the familiar ideological factors that drove US expansion. However, just as *Contours* elaborated on the ideas set forth in *Tragedy*, *Roots* now took his analysis one step further. For example, Williams explored the influence of Adam Smith on the American Weltanschauung. The Wisconsin scholar argued that Smith's *Inquiry into the Nature and Causes of the Wealth of Nations* was well known in rural America in the late nineteenth century. Therefore, the book gradually emerged as a "grand thesis and statement of the principles of the political economy," while Smith himself emerged as "America's philosopher-king."[64]

Because Adam Smith called for an integrated world marketplace, Williams claimed that US farmers complained bitterly when foreign countries set tariffs that hindered Americans' freedom to trade globally. This in turn led them to demand retaliatory action by their government. As foreign markets were seen as the solution to US economic problems and the hardships that farmers endured, Americans saw the economic spheres of interest established by other nations as threats to US prosperity. Furthermore, they refused to tolerate economic competitors within the Western Hemisphere. This made US policymakers extend their conception of the American security sphere to extracontinental areas. This inevitably had imperial connotations.

Roots also made new insights into the way expansion as a policy became entrenched. Starting with the depression of 1837, Williams claimed that economic expansion as a solution to domestic ills worked so well that Americans assumed it would be the natural answer to future economic problems too (no matter how simplistic this view seemed). This assumption was sealed in 1862, 1873, and 1880, when exports again played a central role in the nations' economic recovery. On the latter occasion, Williams argued it was actually the failure of European crops that provided an unprecedented boost in US agricultural exports. Therefore, when European crops recovered and the sorry cycle of depressions resumed, Americans were perplexed. However, rather than reassessing their general outlook, Williams claimed that US policymakers continually fell back on the dogmatic belief that economic expansion would be *the* solution to fresh crises. Other reasons (or extenuating circumstances) for past economic recoveries were consequently ignored. The frontier mentality (which linked constant expansion with prosperity) was too powerful for Americans to overcome.

Despite these new observations, *Roots* continued in the same vein as *Tragedy* and *Contours* in terms of language and rhetoric. For example, Williams contended that the Spanish-American War of 1898 could only be justified in terms of the US right to expand. He believed that the Cuban issue displayed "all the classic problems of imperialism," for the US "placed greater importance on the freedom of Americans to penetrate the market than upon the freedom of Cubans to govern their own marketplace."[65] Although the other Wisconsin scholars would have agreed with this sentiment, their language was not as strident. LaFeber's *New Empire* did not mention the term imperialism at all, whereas McCormick's *China Market* was always keen to stress the limited and pragmatic nature of US imperialism. Williams on the other hand had no problem advocating that US policy displayed the classic hallmarks of imperialism. Even though America only grasped a territorial empire at the end of 1890s, *Roots* claimed that the Cuban and Filipino excursions were more militant expressions of the traditional expansionist outlook that the agricultural community had been advocating for years.

As was the case with his previous work, Williams's provocative thesis received a critical response from more orthodox contemporaries. For example, Carl Degler complained in the *American Historical Review* that Williams's approach was too one dimensional. "Is there no place in an explanation of the coming Spanish-American War, for example, for humanitarianism, a sense of mission, a foolish sentimentality, or a prideful nationalism? Must the whole complicated business be reduced, as I fear Mr. Williams does reduce it, to a desire for Cuban markets?"[66] Although it is hard to disregard this criticism completely, Degler's characterization of *Roots* was an exaggeration; economics might have been Williams's primary thrust, but *Roots* also embraced nationalism, Manifest

Destiny, and psychological factors. Furthermore, although it would be fair to say that both *Tragedy* and *Contours* played down America's humanitarian urges, *Roots* actually addressed the desire of US policymakers to help other peoples. This included discussion of specific occasions when humanitarian concerns were at the forefront of US policy.

Another intriguing addition to Williams's analysis was his depiction of a neocolonial situation within America itself. As Williams wrestled with the contradictions of American society, he concluded that the relationship between north and south displayed hallmarks of an imperial affiliation. He argued that the north's urban leaders had deliberately kept southern farmers poor, an issue that ultimately caused the Civil War. He even claimed that the antislavery movement in the northwest was only secondarily concerned with freeing slaves; it was more about stopping the south from benefiting from the new trans-Mississippi empire. Williams claimed that when the south threatened to leave the Union, it was pacified in much the same way as the Hawaiians and Filipinos. This was because the north believed southern states were essential for access to foreign markets.

Although *Roots* covered familiar ground, the book remains an important landmark in the historiography of US imperialism. Two years beforehand, in 1967, McCormick had lamented how his own book, *China Market*, had failed "to show in any adequate way how such non-elite groups such as farmers and industrial workers limited the freedom and action available" to those in power.[67] *Roots* not only provided this new perspective, but it also added humanitarian considerations to the Wisconsin model (and was more sensitive to political factors than Williams's previous books). Furthermore, *Roots* was significant because Williams had obviously had a change of heart concerning footnotes. In *Tragedy* and *Contours*, citations and other references were conspicuous by their absence. Williams had even attempted to justify his lack of cross-references by arguing that footnotes could be manipulated unless they were provided in their full context. However, by 1969 Williams seemed to have moderated his view; *Roots* was supported by a vast array of citations from speeches, pamphlets, journals, and agricultural magazines (indeed, Edmund Ions conceded that "it cannot be charged that the thesis lacks scholarly apparatus"[68]).

Having said that, one drawback of *Roots* was Williams's continued unwillingness to define "imperialism." Furthermore, he could not explain how or when urban workers joined the agricultural majority to form a consensus on the need for expansion. These weaknesses led some reviewers to dismiss *Roots* as mere economic determinism, even though Williams explicitly argued that imperialism could have been avoided had Americans followed the lead of socialist reformers like Eugene Debs. Meanwhile, David Pletcher complained that the book didn't explain the origins of US imperialism in enough detail, claiming it was more "a survey of internal economic-social history," this despite initially praising *Roots*' "provocative, even brilliant thesis."[69]

In retrospect, much of the criticism leveled at *Roots* appeared to arise from a misinterpretation of the book's purpose. If taken literally, the title can imply an all-embracing study of every aspect of American imperialism, whereas it is more likely that Williams chose "The Roots of the Modern American Empire" as mere wordplay to emphasize the book's agricultural focus. If the title is taken literally, then *Roots* undoubtedly provided too narrow an interpretation of the causes of US imperialism. However, critics like Degler who attacked the book's economic emphasis were guilty of treating *Roots* in isolation. When considering Williams's work it is always best to consider *Tragedy*, *Contours*, and *Roots* as a package. The first book explored the American Weltanschauung as the primary cause of US imperialism, the second delved into socioeconomic triggers, while the third provided a valuable insight into the previously underplayed rural majority. Similarly, when historians assess the Wisconsin critique of American empire they should focus on the work of LaFeber and McCormick as well as Williams. Although their interpretations all had weaknesses individually, their overall critique was more holistic and enlightening when considered as a collective.

The Wisconsin Critique and Cold War Revisionism

During the mid-1960s it became clear to many observers that a swift and decisive victory in Southeast Asia was unlikely. The deployment of thousands of troops to Vietnam had brought little success, and many critics began to feel uneasy about America's Cold War strategy. These frustrations led to the dissemination of several dissenting interpretations of US foreign policy—many of which blamed the United States for provoking not only the Vietnam War but also the Cold War itself. The Wisconsin scholars wrote some of the most prominent of these revisionist critiques. Indeed, *Tragedy*'s assertion that US economic expansion "crystallized the Cold War" (because US policymakers refused to offer Stalin any alternative to their "Open Door world") became a hallmark of revisionist literature.[70]

Because orthodox observers like Irwin Unger and Willard Hogeboom believed that "a revisionist approach to the origins of the Cold War" was the singular most important feature of New Left scholarship, Williams himself was frequently described as either "a senior member of the New Left" or "a New Left historian."[71] This characterization was inaccurate. Although it is understandable why critics of Cold War revisionism made this mistake—even Harrington admitted that his former pupils were "pretty far over" to the New Left because they were not critical enough of the Russians—the Wisconsin critique of US imperialism was unique.[72] Consequently, the Wisconsin scholars should be distinguished not only from the Marxist New Left but also from other Cold War revisionists such as Gar Alperovitz, whose book *Atomic Diplomacy: Hiroshima and Potsdam* (1965) claimed that US policymakers used nuclear weapons against Japan to intimidate the Russians and gain the ascendancy in postwar negotiations.

Alongside *Tragedy*, LaFeber's *America, Russia and the Cold War* (1967) was the most prominent example of Cold War revisionism written by a Wisconsin scholar. Like *Tragedy*, LaFeber's critique placed American diplomacy since World War II in the broad context of US economic expansion since the nineteenth century. However, LaFeber also took into account the ideological antagonism between America and the Soviet Union, as well as reiterating the familiar argument that containment served the strategic economic needs of the nation. He argued at the outset that American-Soviet rivalry was not new; it went back to the 1890s when the two competitors faced each other on the plains of northern China and Manchuria. LaFeber claimed that the United States was determined to apply the Open Door policy to the region, a goal that was at odds with Russia's imperialist plans. "Since becoming a major world power in the 1890s, the United States had viewed anything in the world resembling Stalin's iron fence as incompatible with American objectives. An open, free world had no such division."[73] This argument was clearly reminiscent of *Tragedy*: it highlighted the United States' intolerance of any sphere that might restrict US economic expansion. LaFeber claimed that any nation that restrained Americans' perceived right to expand was automatically seen as an enemy. However, rather than simply concentrating on the American point of view, the younger Wisconsin scholar also drew attention to Russian concerns, most notably the country's fears of capitalist encirclement.

In *America, Russia and the Cold War*, LaFeber empathized with Russia without ever excusing Stalin's imperial ambitions. For example, the book argued that Soviet security concerns post–World War II were legitimate, but it did not exonerate Russia's political repression in Eastern Europe. LaFeber pointed out that Russia had been invaded twice during the twentieth century and was economically crippled in 1945. He also drew attention to Stalin's fear that the "imperialist struggle" would recommence after Hitler was defeated—an anxiety that made the Soviets seek an Eastern European security zone. To support his argument, he quoted Churchill's famous "Iron Curtain" speech at Fulton, Missouri, which contained references to a "fraternal association of English-speaking peoples" ordained by God to reorder the world. LaFeber believed this constituted a "direct threat to Soviet power."[74]

LaFeber argued that US policy was driven by Americans' belief that their prosperity and security depended on the health of international trade. As the Soviet bloc was an obstacle to US plans for the global economy (and threatened to close the door in Eastern Europe) the Russians had to be contained. The Marshall Plan therefore played a key role. The strategy involved using financial aid to "maintain demand for US exports" and "preserve US and European control over Middle East oil supplies." By protecting and extending America's Open Door world, the plan would simultaneously "eliminate the threat of spreading nationalism (and) socialism." Consequently, it became "an all-purpose weapon for Truman's foreign policy." Like Williams, LaFeber depicted the Truman Doctrine, which publicly committed the United States to fight global communism, and the Marshall Plan as "two halves of the same walnut."[75]

In a similar manner to LaFeber's interpretation of the 1890s, *America, Russia and the Cold War* attributed American belligerence to the perceived needs of the US economy. The book argued that "American open-world diplomacy crashed against Stalin's iron curtain" as first Poland and then East Germany were pulled into the Soviet orbit. The question confronting US policymakers was this: how could "the world's most powerful nation respond to these frustrations of its dream for the post-war world?"[76] The difference between LaFeber and Williams, however, was that LaFeber did not blame US policymakers for the Cold War exclusively. Instead, he believed international tensions were caused by an unfortunate clash between two totally diametrically opposed worldviews. For example, LaFeber argued that the Soviets withdrew behind the iron curtain because they were suspicious of US intentions. On the other hand, America regarded the Soviet refusal to cooperate with the World Bank and IMF with equal suspicion. This led to a breakdown in understanding, albeit one that the United States could have prevented; because America was economically stronger than the Soviet Union at the end of World War II, and possessed a nuclear monopoly, LaFeber claimed that US policymakers should have been more appreciative of Stalin's security concerns. Therefore, although LaFeber did not blame the United States for causing the Cold War per se, he agreed with his friend Lloyd Gardner that America was "more responsible for the way in which the Cold War developed."[77]

LaFeber also believed that intellectual failures played an important role, since Americans were incapable of separating their economic security from that of the free world generally. Believing that the Soviet Union was determined to accumulate satellites across the globe, satellites that would undermine the Open Door world, US policymakers committed the nation to "assume unilaterally the defense of the free world at a tremendous price with no hesitation."[78] LaFeber claimed that in reality, the Soviet Union was defensively minded during the early stages of the Cold War, and only sought a limited sphere of interest in Eastern Europe to guarantee its own security. However, American insecurities and an unrealistic perception of the nation's security perimeter led the United States to fight revolutions across the entire planet. He believed this was an unrealistic goal that led inexorably to Vietnam.

Like Williams, LaFeber claimed that US policymakers' attempt to sustain and extend the Open Door across the globe had imperialistic connotations. After all, this strategy required the manipulation of events in distant lands and often sacrificed the aspirations of the individual countries involved. In addition, LaFeber highlighted how America's Cold War strategy seemed to stretch the concept of traditional imperialism to an unprecedented extent: empires throughout history had always sought control and influence over specific regions or a particular sphere of interest, but in this case the United States seemed to have defined its sphere as the entire world. However, once again LaFeber tempered his argument by portraying the Cold War as a tussle between two competing superpowers—outlining how both the United States *and* the Soviet Union had been "expansive forces" in many areas "since at least the nineteenth century." He concluded that both superpowers would have competed for influence in the developing world with or without the Cold War, although American-Soviet diplomatic clashes since World War II certainly "sharpened these drives" and allowed "each side to intensify its dynamic, historical expansion with the defensive terms anti-communism or anti-imperialism."[79]

Nevertheless, while LaFeber recognized the imperial tendencies of both the United States and Russia, more attention was paid to US expansionism. In particular, LaFeber was quick to point out an apparent contradiction in America's approach to spheres of influence. Official accounts of the Cold War blamed Soviet incursions into sovereign Eastern European nations for causing international tensions, but *America, Russia and the Cold War* highlighted how the Western Hemisphere had long been "a laboratory of United States policies." The hypocrisy was therefore clear: if the United States was permitted a sphere of interest near its own borders, surely the Soviet Union was entitled to the same? LaFeber therefore contended that America wanted "exclusive power in the new" world "and the right to exert American influence in the old."[80]

Although *America, Russia and the Cold War* was a revisionist text that criticized the United States more than the Soviet Union, its tone was less radical than

Tragedy. LaFeber also provided a more detailed account of the political entanglements that consolidated American economic hegemony over Europe: he stated that the North Atlantic Treaty Organization (NATO) was created not only to "encourage military development" but also to "compel the western world to accept new political alignments." LaFeber believed that American policymakers regarded NATO as an opportunity to "strengthen its ties with, and influence over, Europe by creating military ties which would provide fresh channels for American aid and policies." To support his argument, he quoted Senator Tom Connally, who remarked that "the Atlantic Pact is but the logical extension of the principle of the Monroe Doctrine."[81]

America, Russia and the Cold War also explored how US policymakers adopted a hard line with Russia for political advantage at home; LaFeber frequently identified differences of opinion within the White House and Congress, a development that proved that US diplomacy did not always move in the same direction. This avoided Williams's mistake of assuming that all Americans prioritized economic expansion at all times. LaFeber also discussed the dwindling of US power for the first time; this was a subject that became increasingly prevalent in studies of American imperialism during the post-Vietnam era. Although the book was only written in 1967, LaFeber was all too aware that US power was waning somewhat—and not just because the war in Southeast Asia was rumbling on without decisive victory. For example, *America, Russia and the Cold War* claimed that the emergence of the European Economic Community (EEC) had widened the split within NATO and threatened an independent economic bloc. LaFeber argued that this was a clear challenge to US economic dominance, for the EEC decreased Europe's dependence on America, tied West Germany to Western Europe, and "created a middle bloc between the US and the Soviet Union."[82] Meanwhile, LaFeber also examined how the Vietnam War itself caused a rift between America and its allies. Although the United States had military treaties with forty nations, only Australia, New Zealand, and South Korea sent troops to help the American forces. This implied that US authority over Western Europe was no longer absolute.

America, Russia and the Cold War's analysis of SEATO (South East Asian Treaty Organization) also highlighted the political dimensions of LaFeber's critique. The author claimed that SEATO was similar to NATO but with one important difference: it committed America not only to resist armed attack but also to guard against subversion. LaFeber argued that this was an open-ended commitment similar to the US policy toward the Western Hemisphere; consequently, he believed that just as the Monroe Doctrine "had warned the Holy Alliance to keep 'hands-off' Latin America . . . now the United States, in

Dulles's words, 'declared that an intrusion [in the Far East] would be dangerous to [America's] peace and security.'" According to LaFeber, the US commitment to SEATO went a long way to explaining America's escalation of the Vietnam War. However, unlike the orthodox liberal position, which argued that the United States fought the war to protect SEATO members from communist aggression, LaFeber claimed that America's decision to stand and fight in Vietnam was symptomatic of the "fundamental assumption that America's internal political, economic and psychological needs dictated such commitments."[83]

The Wisconsin Critique Enhanced

The work of the Wisconsin scholars during the 1960s played a pivotal role in the historiography of US imperialism. Although their central thesis was similar to *Tragedy*, and LaFeber has modestly claimed that he "couldn't by any means 'enhance' Williams's critique" (he instead described his contribution as "reinforcing" his friend's work), LaFeber and McCormick certainly added something new to the debate.[84] For example, LaFeber shared Williams's conviction that the seeds of America's empire were sown long before the 1890s, but he provided more political analysis and made a greater effort to define key terms. Meanwhile, McCormick specifically looked at economic opportunities in China and stressed the pragmatic aspects of American imperialism. Furthermore, Williams's *Roots* explored the agrarian origins of American expansion at precisely the time that contemporary Marxist critiques were focusing on US industry. The Wisconsin scholars therefore remained pioneers in their field.

Williams, LaFeber, and McCormick undoubtedly expanded the Wisconsin interpretation by embracing new factors and writing critiques with greater analytical rigor. However, not everybody was convinced by their conclusions. Their most ruthless critic was James A. Field, whose essay "American Imperialism: The Worst Chapter in Almost Any Book" described the Wisconsin critique as "a backward approach to history" that transformed America's "record of almost total lack of accomplishment . . . into evidence of an overwhelming wave of imperialism." Field argued that "the claimed impact of the so-called 'imperialist' tracts on either the American people or important figures in government tends to dissolve upon inspection," not least because there was an absence of "identifiably influential persons or pressure groups" that favored expansion.[85] Unfortunately, Field's line of argument was too extreme to be taken seriously. After all, a sequence of interventions in Hawaii, Cuba, the Philippines, Brazil, Venezuela, Guam, and Samoa hardly seems insignificant. Meanwhile, LaFeber and McCormick had shown that prominent Americans like Brooks Adams, plus important industrial and agricultural groups such as the National Union of Manufacturers, were keen to capitalize on the potential benefits of economic expansion.

The main problem with Field's essay, like many other critical appraisals of the Wisconsin critique since the 1960s, was his constant misrepresentation and simplification of the Wisconsin scholars' core thesis. For example, he implied that *The New Empire* and *China Market* told a tale of ceaseless "island-grabbing" that depicted the 1890s as "years of burgeoning sentiment for imperialism."[86] Unfortunately, this analysis simply demonstrated that Field had missed the point. *The New Empire* constantly emphasized "the crucial anti-annexationist argument that the constitution and traditional American society would be ruined by expanding into non-contiguous areas," but the book also highlighted the fact that this was "irrelevant granted the common assumption of the need for commercial expansion."[87] The crucial factor was what LaFeber saw as an inextricable link between foreign policy and domestic conditions. *The New Empire* and *China Market* never claimed that the majority of Americans were frenzied imperialists. Instead they emphasized that the public gradually and reluctantly followed an expansionist course because they believed economic expansion was the only way to solve the nation's economic ills. As a result, American imperialism evolved as a sequence of pragmatic steps to ease economic crises rather than as a burgeoning thirst for imperial conquest.

What Field failed to realize was that LaFeber and McCormick did not outline a grand imperial master plan. They simply advocated that in times of economic crisis, Americans had a propensity to look overseas for new economic frontiers. This was not a preplanned conspiracy to achieve global domination but a gradual process that involved economic expansion as a pragmatic response to the nation's problems. This process was not wanton, nor did the whole country unite vociferously to demand expansion at every turn. Rather, Williams's former pupils believed that foreign markets were so important to Americans that US policymakers ultimately made the search for them a priority. Therefore, despite the influence of crusading imperialists like Mahan and Brooks Adams, American imperialism was generally reluctant in character; US expansion responded to necessity rather than jingoism, although it was not afraid to use force to secure its objectives. This was a definite improvement from Williams's *Tragedy* that downplayed anti-imperialist sentiment to emphasize the long-standing tendency of the United States to expand.

In misinterpreting LaFeber and McCormick's work, Field returned to the familiar argument that US imperialism at the end of the nineteenth century was an accident. For example, he argued that Dewey's victory at Manila was purely to "gain leverage with Spain" and that America only decided to annex the Philippines as an afterthought when it became necessary to keep troops on the islands. Field's essay had some merit because it introduced readers to the importance of telegraph cables during the 1890s (and how the need for ocean cables influenced foreign policy). However, by concluding that America's Pacific acquisitions were nothing more than "historical accidents," "The Worst Chapter" actually regressed the debate surrounding US imperialism to the days of the 1930s and 1950s.[88]

Even though elements of LaFeber's and McCormick's work remained controversial, and orthodox scholars like May continued to promote critiques of US expansion that were overly sympathetic to US policymakers, the Wisconsin interpretations written during the 1960s certainly expanded debate about their subject. They did this by emphasizing political factors, introducing new definitions such as "pragmatic expansion" and "insular imperialism," and emphasizing the occasionally restrained nature of US expansion. In doing so, they tacitly admitted that *Tragedy* and *Contours* were marred by occasional generalizations and false continuities. However, by redressing many of *Tragedy*'s faults, the Wisconsin texts that emerged after *Tragedy* presented a less polemical (and altogether more satisfying) portrayal of American imperialism from the nineteenth century to the Vietnam War. Furthermore, their perspective was far more sophisticated than the Marxist interpretations written by their New Left contemporaries—particularly those accounts promoted by radical student groups like SDS. It is these Marxist critiques, which were "too narrow" in the eyes of the Wisconsin scholars and often written to serve a political purpose rather than a scholarly one, that we shall turn to next.[89]

6

The Student Radicals

Stopping Dow will not end corporate imperialism. It is merely a first step in that direction. Like those fighting tyranny throughout the world, we must build as we resist.

Evan Stark, leader of the student protests at the University of Wisconsin, 1967

Imperialism in Its Simplest Form

In his essay "How New Was the New Left?," Andrew Hunt reiterated the problem that has faced all historians studying the American left during the Vietnam War: "The task of developing a deeper understanding of the New Left and its place in American cultural history has been impeded by the lack of consensus on exactly how to define the New Left."[1] This uncertainty about who and what the New Left actually was has led to several different theories concerning the rise and fall of the movement. David Caute identified three "phases" in its history.[2] Staughton Lynd, who was one of the period's most prominent radical historians, claimed that the New Left originated from a group of leftists who eschewed orthodox Marxist-Leninist dogma in the decade preceding World War II.[3] Meanwhile, several intellectuals, including James Miller and Todd Gitlin, have defined the New Left more narrowly as "a small clique" associated with Students for a Democratic Society.[4]

Arguably the best definition, however, was the one provided by John McMillian in his introduction to *The New Left Revisited* (2003), which described the New Left as "a loosely organized, mostly white student movement that promoted participatory democracy, crusaded for Civil Rights and various types of university reforms, and protested against the Vietnam War." He argued that the movement began to "crystallize in the early 1960s and then "picked up steam towards the middle of the decade" following the escalation of Vietnam.[5] Whereas some definitions have traced the origins of the movement to the first half of the twentieth century, and attempted to draw complex parallels with the Old Left, these accounts have split scholarly opinion: leftist radicalism had its roots in the 1930s, but the parallels were not exact (for example, the New Left emerged during a period of relative prosperity and its members considered themselves to be unique).

Consequently, McMillian's articulation is the least contentious. Although it could have emphasized student radicals' penchant for direct action a little more, it at least avoided the pitfalls that have befallen other definitions. For example, some accounts have ascribed the origins of the New Left to Madison, which Hunt described as "a cauldron of progressive thought and experimentation for decades before the 1960s."[6] Of course, Hunt was correct to describe the University of Wisconsin as a sanctuary of progressivism for many years, but the suggestion that the New Left originated in Madison because of, or partly because, UW had a progressive heritage is hard to substantiate. The fact that radical thought was tolerated at UW more than other American universities certainly attracted inquiring minds to Madison (and therefore led to a higher proportion of dissidents on campus), but the New Left at UW during the Vietnam War ultimately came to shun progressive thought.

The decision by UW student radicals to reject the progressive conception of US foreign relations and embrace Marxism (and a Leninist approach to instigating social reform) differentiated them from UW historians like Williams, McCormick, and LaFeber (who adopted a Beardian approach to studying American imperialism). Despite the university's progressive heritage, and the presence of Williams on campus until 1968, UW students ultimately rejected the best traditions of the UW history department and instead emulated their New Left contemporaries across the United States who, according to Barbara Ehrenreich, considered themselves to be "a radical break from the socialist and communist traditions that for so long defined leftism."[7] Although the New Left ultimately failed to live up to this tag—their intellectual approach and their critiques of US imperialism betrayed traditional Marxist-Leninist leanings—they at least succeeded in separating themselves from leftists with more conservative social values. This is because they concluded that US expansion could only be stopped by destroying both American capitalism and the nation's political institutions. They attempted to do this by inciting revolution on the streets; this set them on a collision course with the police, the government, and eventually the university as well.

It is one of the period's ironies that the New Left at UW revered Williams but ultimately turned their backs on his intellectual approach and his critique of US imperialism. Whereas the Wisconsin scholars wanted to change America (and US foreign policy) democratically by educating fellow citizens about the need for reform, the radical New Left attempted to end the Vietnam War by confrontation and direct action. This chapter will discuss how radical students saw US imperialism as a product of the social-economic structures they aimed to destroy. It will also explain the basic Marxist New Left critique of American empire and begin to demonstrate how this differed from the Wisconsin scholars' interpretation. Furthermore, it will elucidate how the students' understanding of imperialism stemmed from their contrasting intellectual approach (which was based on Marxist-Leninist dogma).

The discussion will focus on Madison (rather than any other university) because the UW dissidents' decision to repudiate their university's progressive heritage and embrace a Marxist-Leninist interpretation underlines the differences between the Wisconsin critique and the New Left most effectively. After all, while McCormick and LaFeber were refining the Wisconsin critique of US imperialism, and Williams's thoughts were turning to *Roots*, a book that argued that the triggers of American expansion were agrarian, the New Left in Madison sought to end the imperialist war in Vietnam by destroying industrial capitalism. The difference was therefore stark. Student radicals at UW were also typical of the New Left nationwide: they were at the forefront of the antiwar movement and (alongside other hotbeds of dissent like the University of California, Berkeley) standard bearers for student protestors elsewhere. Indeed, radicals in Madison very much saw themselves as part of a national movement that shared common goals. For example, many UW students were members of nationwide organizations such as the Young Socialist Alliance, an arm of the Socialist Workers Party, and of course, SDS, which was highly visible in Madison. In a flyer titled "What Is SDS?" UW student radicals outlined their aims, which included activism to "stop the (Vietnam) war," "stop racism," and "identify with workers against corps."[8] Local radicals also showed solidarity with the civil rights movement as well as national antiwar campaigners. The radical left in Madison was therefore a microcosm of the New Left elsewhere in America.

As aspiring Marxists, the UW student radicals emulated their Marxist-Leninist contemporaries at home and abroad by embracing economic determinism—which explained imperialism as an inevitable consequence of the expansive nature of capitalism. All their analysis stemmed from this; therefore, they believed, quite simply, that the United States created an empire to sustain and nourish its capitalist economy. Because they were devoted to this perspective, they claimed that containment was essentially a tactic to preserve and extend US economic expansion. The student radicals even argued that US "military and economic expansion" during World War II showed that Western powers were no better than Stalin: "Everyone imposes their own system as far as their armies will reach." Because the United States had expanded its hegemony over Western Europe and then Asia, they claimed that US policymakers were then compelled "to repress the revolutionary forces" that had been "unleashed" by the conflict. It was necessary to fight the Vietnam War because US policymakers wanted to send a message that all social revolutions in the developing world (uprisings that challenged the American Empire) would fail. Therefore the UW radicals argued that the United States had clearly become an imperial nation; in the case of Vietnam, America allegedly replaced France as a "colonial power."[9]

Of course, it was the Vietnam War that gave student radicals the opportunity to popularize their Marxist critique. The Madison chapter of SDS organized conferences to educate students about US imperialism; the lectures included "Who Really Pays for US imperialism?" and "Empire-Building: A History of the Development of Imperialism" (the latter illustrated how the New Left saw US imperialism as part of a historical trend). Flyers for the event, which used the headline "There Is No Moratorium on the Struggle against US Imperialism," highlighted how "the people of the third world" were "struggling against the pillage America inflicts upon them."[10] Madison's radical magazines also displayed an acute awareness of the United States' alleged suppression of revolutions in the developing world (which they saw as irrefutable evidence of US imperialism). For example, *Connections* argued that American foreign policy had "three traditional themes": "economic and military expansion, obsessive anti-communism, and counter-revolution." In an article called "Twenty Years of Counter-Revolution," the magazine described how US expansion was "spreading from the confines of the Western Hemisphere" and had reached "a peak of destructive intensity in Vietnam."[11]

In typical Marxist style, *Connections* argued that US imperialism was designed to suppress the global left. This was a tragedy because they believed the Greek communists after World War II, and the communists in Vietnam in the 1960s, were the only ones who could "challenge the chronic problems of economic under-development." Like many contemporary New Left scholars, *Connections'* writers believed that US policymakers were prepared to sacrifice self-determination in order to establish a pro-American capitalist world economic order. When it came to Greece, "American hegemony was the price" the Greeks paid "to join the Free World."[12] In many ways, the Madison radicals saw themselves as part of a movement that was fighting US imperialism. In 1968 Evan Stark (the leader of the student protestors) gave an address that asked students to fight against US corporate imperialism. Because this was a pejorative term, the students eagerly connected imperialism and US foreign policy to accentuate the morality of their struggle. Rallying against imperialism also gave a disparate movement a sense of togetherness. For example, the UW Committee to End the War in Vietnam participated in worldwide demonstrations on the anniversary of the Hiroshima bomb. The leaflets they distributed on campus to promote the event depicted the United States as the main threat to world peace and accused US policymakers of waging a "brutal war" that violated self-determination.[13]

As the war in Vietnam intensified, and the prospect of a negotiated settlement diminished, US imperialism became one of the national left's favorite topics. *Monthly Review*, for example, frequently raised the issue of imperialism in relation to US policy in the Western Hemisphere as well as Southeast Asia. The editors set the tone at the beginning of the decade by publishing an inflammatory contribution by socialist revolutionary talisman Che Guevara called "Cuba: Exceptional Case?," which claimed that the Cuban revolution was part of a broad Latin American struggle against "great imperialist consortia." Guevara accused American "monopolists" of being cruel "oppressors," who "proletarianized" Cubans in an attempt to "strengthen their hold on their colonies."[14] The New Left eagerly digested this simplistic Marxist interpretation and made it their own.

The student radicals at UW were particularly aware of this contemporary Marxist literature. For example, an SDS booklet distributed on campus imitated Harry Magdoff (the Marxist intellectual who became an editor of *Monthly Review*) by exploring the roles played by financial aid, the IMF, and the World Bank—institutions that "may appear benevolent" but really "use the leverage of whether or not to reschedule" the "large indebtedness" of developing nations "to ensure conservative monetary and fiscal policies." The SDS booklet described how investment in Latin America restricted nations to one or two dominant industries (such as sugar), a strategy that allegedly "fattened a tiny elite" and "did nothing" for the standard of living of "the rural masses." The authors also claimed that US policymakers' manipulation of tariffs and tax privileges were designed to benefit US corporations rather than the indigenous populations; the overall aim was to establish a "good business climate"—something that required "the preservation of conservative, anti-popular regimes." As a result, SDS was "pessimistic" that poor countries could break "the political control of the oligarchic governments." A "neo-colonial social structure," therefore, became entrenched.[15] This perspective was typical of Marxists at home and abroad; indeed, it echoed the aforementioned literature by Guevara.

Although other radical groups on campus also campaigned against US imperialism—for example, the Young Socialist Alliance also asserted that their goal was to "defeat imperialism in South East Asia and pave the way for social change" in America—SDS made the cause their own.[16] In fact, by 1969 *Kaleidoscope* claimed that SDS had become "an anti-imperialism movement."[17] That very year, SDS grew frustrated at less radical dissident groups for failing to see how imperialism was at the heart of US foreign policy. For example, an edition of *New Left Notes* (the SDS newsletter) criticized the UW Vietnam Moratorium Committee, which included the Wisconsin Student Association and the Committee to End the War in Vietnam, for "diverting attention away from the only real solution—a movement that clarifies the nature of the war and fights to get the US out of Vietnam now." SDS argued that the Moratorium Committee portrayed Vietnam as a "tragic blunder" rather than what it really was: a "necessary and inevitable" part of "the system of US imperialism" that had been "carefully planned for years." *New Left Notes* claimed that control of Vietnam would give US imperialism a base throughout Asia and strike a blow against indigenous revolutions across the region; this would perpetuate the side effects of US imperialism, which allegedly included "lousy wages, miserable conditions, starvation for the people of Vietnam and huge profits for US firms and their allies." The student radicals, then, saw American foreign policy as part of a broader class war against the poor: they believed the conflict in Vietnam "not only" kept "the Vietnamese in poverty" but also allowed "US management to keep the wages of American working people down."[18]

However, because student radicals were primarily drawn to New Left critiques of US imperialism for their political relevance (and only partially concerned with their analytical value), they tended to adopt a most simplistic Marxist interpretation of American diplomacy—one that simply emphasized that imperialist wars were an inevitable consequence of capitalism. Their critiques were also laced with conspiracy theories, implying that US foreign policy was part of a devious plot by the wealthy to suppress the modern proletariat. Indeed, their analysis often left little room for anything other than Marxist clichés and frequently neglected the more structuralist approach adopted by some of the radical left's most cerebral intellectuals like Gabriel Kolko (whose critiques we shall examine in chapter 7). Therefore, the student radicals at UW and their contemporaries across America simply saw the Vietnam War as a by-product of the United States' capitalist economy; destroy American capitalism and there would be no need for a war. As a result, the New Left ignored the more measured, progressive interpretation of Williams, McCormick, and LaFeber.

Former New Leftists like Paul Buhle have since acknowledged that this approach was too narrow. Admitting that "the American Left and radical reforms movements" in general "have never been especially cerebral," Buhle traced how the New Left, much like the Old Left, were heavily influenced by the simplistic methodology asserted by international Marxists.[19] He also stressed how student radicals craved histories that served a political purpose; therefore, they oversimplified historical events in an attempt to convince others to their way of thinking. Thomas McCormick has also criticized the student radicals' historical methods. In words that further indicated the distance between the Wisconsin scholars and the New Left, McCormick complained how, with the notable exception of "serious scholars" like Kolko, the New Left failed to "engage with the term imperialism" and used it merely as a "political stick" to support their politically motivated analysis.[20]

Different Intellectual Approach, Different Critique

Even though the Wisconsin scholars' critique of US imperialism was more sophisticated than the Marxist interpretation outlined earlier, well-regarded historians like John Lewis Gaddis have still described Williams's work as "one of the most influential examples of New Left historiography."[21] Although this characterization might seem incongruous, there were understandable reasons for this misconception. One of the main problems was contrasting definitions of the term "New Left." For example, even Fred Harvey Harrington, when asked about his influence on the Wisconsin scholars, described them as "New Left scholars"—although it must be pointed out that he did so begrudgingly, arguing that he was "a New Left scholar too" according to the critics' definition. Of course, orthodox scholars found it expedient to label all critical appraisals of US diplomacy as "New Left."[22] Portraying Williams as a rogue history professor who was in cahoots with student revolutionaries was preferable to engaging with his ideas (which challenged the altruistic image of the United States that orthodox scholars liked to project).

However, it is also likely that Williams's initial relationship with the antiwar movement convinced many observers to bracket the Wisconsin scholars and the New Left together. During the early 1960s, Williams played an active role in the Committee to End the War in Vietnam and even accompanied protestors on a march up Bascom Hill; at one point he praised them as "the consciousness of the university."[23] Furthermore, one must not underestimate Williams's popularity as a radical lecturer and an outspoken critic of US foreign policy. Even though he was more progressive than Marxist, his work had "an America-centeredness that was attractive to the New Left."[24] Williams's views must have helped to "incite students," to some extent as well, even if "he wanted to hold short of violence."[25] Meanwhile, Williams and the Wisconsin scholars empathized with the New Left's goals (even if they disapproved of the means they employed). McCormick, for example, explained: "I wasn't hostile to the New Left, even though they were a little anti-intellectual; they were morally right, and like me, they were against the war."[26] Consequently, it is easy to see why those who did not analyze the New Left closely enough believed that the Wisconsin scholars belonged to the same group.

The rhetoric of the New Left was also somewhat reminiscent of the Wisconsin scholars, except when it called for aggressive political activism. For example, *Connections* accused the United States of "exterminating the Vietnamese people" and reiterated Williams's belief that "the conflict in Vietnam, like the conflict within the United States itself, will not be resolved until . . . we build a truly classless society."[27] *Connections* also highlighted many of the same issues as Williams. In September 1967 an article called "Terrorism Lives" lamented how citizens were "not able to ask the political questions as to whether our socio-economic institutions are valid, democratic [and] egalitarian." The article also argued that intellectual failures had led US foreign policy astray—a situation that was exacerbated by leading orthodox academics who, because they often had close links to the government, usually attempted to "demonstrate the 'researchable' rightness" of predetermined strategies. As a result, *Connections* agreed with Williams that although the United States "speaks for peace, freedom, political democracy and equality, . . . a transcendent analysis shows that these concepts as they are used are inside out, inverted." In addition, the radicals occasionally claimed that US policymakers were guided by "a certain view of the world."[28] This obviously had parallels with Williams's emphasis on the American Weltanschauung.

The University of Wisconsin's left-leaning student newspaper, the *Daily Cardinal*, which was not strictly a voice of the New Left but printed increasingly radical views by the end of the 1960s, also expressed views similar to Williams's.[29] For example, the paper echoed Williams's plea for domestic reform. "Only a few years ago we were beginning to educate ourselves to the needs of our cities and our people, but now all that is recent past or distant future. Our glorious assumptions of last year are in a shambles, . . . our priorities are all upside down, . . . the fabric of American society and a generation of young men is at stake. Vietnam is worth none of this."[30] As with Williams and the Wisconsin scholars, the *Daily Cardinal* should not be classified as New Left simply because it admonished US policymakers for expansionism and supporting "authoritarian dictatorships." The paper was in fact extremely critical of the student radicals' "fickle desire for confrontational politics."[31] However, conservatives and liberals outside UW might have missed this distinction. *Connections*, which very much belonged to the New Left, and the *Daily Cardinal* were, after all, united in their criticism of the Vietnam War and the US government.

The key point, however, is that although radical students admired Williams, they ultimately abandoned the Wisconsin critique of US imperialism (and progressivism) in favor of a more Marxist-Leninist interpretation. This is because their intellectual approach was fundamentally different: as Marxist-Leninists, they saw US imperialism as an inevitable consequence of capitalism, and (because of their dedication to a Marxist-Leninist view of social change) they believed destroying capitalism was the only way to stop expansionist wars like Vietnam. As a result, the student radicals shunned the model for social change initially promoted by Williams and *Studies on the Left*. During the early 1960s, the original editors of *Studies* echoed Williams by advocating an intellectual approach to instigating socioeconomic reform (which aimed to create class consciousness). However, just like the New Left nationwide, the dissidents in Madison grew tired of this philosophy during the latter half of the decade and followed the example of Tom Hayden, the former president of SDS, who encouraged students to adopt a more confrontational and activist outlook. As the Vietnam War escalated, the New Left even became disparaging of the intellectual influences that had shaped Williams's critique; although most of the radicals' anger was directed at orthodox liberals (men they believed were not doing enough to stop the Vietnam War), they also frequently turned on progressives too. *Connections*, for example, argued that both liberals and progressives were too comfortable and did not have the stomach to fight for meaningful change. Furthermore, the New Left dissidents often saw Williams and scholars over thirty years old as "intellectual monuments" irrelevant to the current struggle. Paul Buhle's *History and the New Left* described how "students talked in a reverential but distanced sense about the 'historic role' of figures such as Williams, even while attending their lectures."[32]

The history of *Studies on the Left* demonstrates the disparity between the intellectual approach of the Wisconsin scholars and the New Left. When the journal was founded in 1959, the editors (which included Lloyd Gardner) wanted the radical left to follow the example of the old American socialist party. The journal enjoyed a close relationship with Williams—the first edition claimed that *Tragedy* would help those who read it "contribute toward the survival and salvation" of humankind—and it was aimed at an academic audience rather than the general populace. Indeed, when the very first edition of *Studies* declared the journal's aims, the editors claimed they wanted to create a radical academic forum that would transcend "the paralyzing effect of forcefully maintained academic standards." There was no talk of radicalizing the masses and creating a revolution. Instead, the editors merely emphasized their commitment "to the humanization of society" and expressed a desire to "work harmoniously and creatively toward the future."[33]

The original editors of *Studies* agreed with Williams that exposing liberalism's flaws would not necessarily bring about the socioeconomic reforms radicals wanted. Instead, they recognized what Williams called "the visceral importance for the left of creating a general social consciousness"; this was a "creative break with the Old Left and its reliance on a crudely deterministic equation between the business cycle and the transition to socialism."[34] Consequently, the original *Studies* board members were not idealistic revolutionaries like the New Left activists during the late 1960s. Although they sympathized with the aims of SDS and other radical groups, the journal was pessimistic about the prospects of achieving political reform through direct action. Instead, they remained sympathetic to traditional socialism and (like Williams) wanted to work through the existing political system; they hoped they could create a mass movement for change by educating Americans about the potential benefits of reform and making it politically impossible for the government to ignore their wishes.

Unfortunately, however, *Studies* eventually lost its original identity when it moved to New York and the board became divided and unclear about the journal's goals. Hayden and Staughton Lynd wanted to focus on the antiwar movement and report on the activist activities of the New Left, whereas James Weinstein, who had been with the journal since it was created, remained faithful to *Studies*' original aims. As a result, two "factions" emerged at *Studies*: a "New Left" faction, which wanted to force change through protests and the destruction of the current system, and a more progressive camp, which stayed true to its Madison roots and subscribed to Williams's model for achieving socioeconomic reform.[35] Although both factions agreed that radicalism should not be co-opted by liberalism, the divisions ultimately contributed to the journal's demise.

Because the original editors of *Studies* and revolutionaries like Hayden believed in different methods to achieve reform and end the war, they naturally adopted different interpretations of US imperialism. The New Left clique saw the Vietnam War as an inexorable by-product of capitalism; therefore, smashing America's economic and political structures was the only way to end the war. The more progressive clique, on the other hand, wanted to preserve American institutions and reform capitalism; they believed the Vietnam War (and US imperialism in general) was tragic precisely because it was not inexorable. Like Williams, the Madison editors believed that redistributing wealth within the United States would increase domestic demand and make foreign markets and imperialism unnecessary.

Given this underlying disparity it is no surprise that the relationship between Williams and the student radicals broke down. Before 1967, UW students were actually more responsive to Williams and his interpretation of US foreign policy. However, as the students abandoned a peaceful program for domestic reform, they looked for more extreme critiques of imperialism that reflected their increasing belligerence; after all, an interpretation of US expansion that merely called for the redistribution of wealth within society (and the preservation of America's political institutions) seemed relatively tame. The students were impatient. Educating the public about the need for reform would take too long. The carnage in Vietnam had to end immediately; there was no time, ironically, to bring peace to Southeast Asia by peaceful means.

As David Maraniss, the prominent chronicler of radical protests at UW, has highlighted, the students subscribed to Henry David Thoreau's philosophy of civil disobedience, which argued that the law of conscience was higher than the law of the land. They were also influenced by the abolitionist William Lloyd Garrison's argument that one must be "an irritant" and call for "immediate change rather than gradualism" when fighting for a moral cause.[36] Williams, however, could not abide lawlessness. This produced a schism between the Wisconsin scholar and the radical New Left. Williams promoted an intellectual approach, whereas the student radicals focused on confrontation; therefore, although the Wisconsin scholars and the New Left agreed on the existence of an American empire, they advocated very contrasting plans to stop it. This is because they believed the roots of US imperialism were different. The key distinction, of course, was the student radicals' devotion to economic determinism.

The story of student dissidence at UW has been chronicled many times—most recently by Matthew Levin in *Cold War University*. Consequently, a detailed account of the escalating unrest in Madison is not needed here. What is important to note, however, is how the relationship between Williams and the New Left disintegrated as the students' tactics became more extreme. During the mid-1960s, student protests at UW focused on the university's compliance with the Selective Service Committee, which drafted students according to their academic performance; the war itself was still an issue, but it remained in the background. The tactics of dissent were also more restrained; the Young Socialist Alliance, for example, initially advocated peaceful, nonobstructive educational demonstrations, as this would avoid confrontation with the police. In 1966, sit-ins at UW were therefore similar to those held by students in Chicago and New York, although the ones in Madison were occasionally more vociferous (for example, UW protestors went as far as occupying administration buildings). However, dissent in Madison became altogether more extreme after the Dow protests of 1967 when a clash between police and students (who were obstructing Dow Chemical's attempts to conduct interviews on campus) ended in violence.

Students initially responded to what they perceived as police brutality (and the faculty's alleged complicity with this barbarity) by organizing a wave of strikes. Although these strikes ultimately fizzled out, there was a marked increase in the volume and intensity of radical rhetoric on campus, and an escalation of support for confrontational and aggressive tactics. For example, whereas the Young Socialist Alliance had previously called for nonobstructive protests, they now called for a "counter-attack" in the form of "sustained, militant, mass action" and "mass revolutionary struggle."[37] Meanwhile, *Connections* argued that the escalation of the Vietnam War and the black revolts in the summer of 1967 had created "an atmosphere of real militancy and determination." The radicals argued that "obstruction was a viable tactic"; "direct confrontation" that would "physically stop" companies like Dow was also justified, because the company was "integral" to "the continuation of the war."[38]

Nothing demonstrated the escalating radicalism of UW students in late 1967 more than the confrontational attitude of *Connections*, which was described by Maraniss as "the epicenter of the New Left in Madison." Indeed, Maraniss argued that the Dow protests were "in many respects a *Connections* production"; for example, prominent protestors such as Stuart Ewen, who was one of Stark's deputies, actually wrote for the magazine.[39] On one level, *Connections* shared Williams's desire to build "a massive democratic movement" in America with "a vision of a truly peaceful, truly free and truly human society."[40] However, the editors of *Connections* abandoned the Wisconsin scholars' approach when they began advocating nonpeaceful means of achieving their revolutionary aims. In September 1967 the magazine called for its readers to criticize society "in explosive terms" and overthrow the government and "social mechanics" of what they called the US "system." *Connections* also warned students that "if one does not advocate revolution" then one "adds a share to the maintenance of [society's] stability."[41]

After the Dow violence, *Connections* began to use the slogan "from protest to resistance." This message resonated with many students who, having witnessed what they saw as police brutality, no longer believed that peaceful marches could be effective; consequently, they turned their attentions to smashing "the war machine," as they thought this was the only way to stop the war.[42] Furthermore, many *Connections* readers considered the post-Dow strikes to be a distraction from the real issue: the need to destroy the US power structure and society. Fellow radicals at SDS propagated a similar message. SDS's newsletter, *The Call*, beseeched students to move from "draft dodging to resistance." They argued that any attempt to instigate socioeconomic reforms via existing electoral politics was futile, since politicians were restricted by "the limits laid down by society."[43] As a result, they asked students to use all means necessary to destroy the government.

In embracing this confrontational posture, the radicals clearly linked US imperialism with the quest for domestic reforms. In doing so they revealed their allegiance to Marxism-Leninism: because they regarded imperialism as the inevitable consequence of capitalism—and because they blamed the US government for sustaining the status quo—they believed the only way to end the Vietnam War was to destroy capitalism and the government. However, this ambitious revolution had to start somewhere. The most obvious place, in the student radicals' eyes, was to attack the university administrators; after all, they were responsible for allowing corporations like Dow to recruit on campus. Furthermore, because UW's administrators had allegedly sided with the police in the aftermath of the protests, the student radicals believed the university had revealed itself as a tool of corporate America, an accomplice of the US government, and therefore an accessory to American imperialism.

The student radicals' decision to turn on the university itself underlined just how different the New Left's intellectual approach was to that of the Wisconsin scholars; after all, Fred Harvey Harrington, the early pioneer of the Wisconsin critique of imperialism, was the university's president while Williams was on the payroll. In the weeks following the Dow violence, a *Connections* article accused the university of "prostituting" the idea of education; the magazine also argued that UW had become "a house of ill-repute" that repressed students.[44] Even the tone of the *Daily Cardinal* ultimately turned indignant: an editorial claimed that the university's ethics were "upside down" and accused the faculty of being "aloof from the questions of the day." Students also began to accuse the university of putting corporate interests ahead of its academic integrity. The *Daily Cardinal*, for example, emulated *Kaleidoscope* by arguing that "the profit motive" was UW's "guiding ethic."[45] Meanwhile, in November the University Community Action Party called UW a "multiversity" because it was "enmeshed" in the US "corporate, military, (and) government structure."[46] The student radicals' logic was simplistic but powerful: because UW-trained young men and women went to work for corporations, the university was seen as "an instrument of US capitalism" and "an instrument of US imperialism." Consequently, the students vowed to operate outside the university's laws to build "an anti-imperialist student movement."[47]

By criticizing and opposing the faculty, the students believed they were fighting US imperialism on campus. This sense was heightened by the fact that UW was home to institutions that ostensibly played a direct role in American imperialism. The most notable of these were the Army Math Center and the Land Tenure Center; the latter was commissioned by the Agency for International Development, which SDS claimed was "a moneyed arm of the State Department" responsible for thwarting economic growth in the Third World.[48] Because these centers were based on campus (and the university received federal funds), SDS argued that UW was "complicit" in the decision to wage war in Southeast Asia.[49] Like *Connections*, which also saw the university as one of the institutions that "perpetuated the American empire abroad," SDS soon went from opposing the war, to opposing UW complicity in the war, to attacking the university itself.[50] As a result, student radicals attempted to remove the existing administrators and make the university more accountable.

To Williams, the idea of confronting the university was abhorrent. Instead, the Wisconsin scholar hoped to establish a student-faculty alliance. However, even the Committee to End the War in Vietnam, an organization with which Williams was affiliated in the early 1960s, seemed to turn away from his intellectual approach; for example, it demonstrated its escalating radicalism (and its shift toward more violent activism) in November 1968 when it encouraged students to take matters into their own hands and "use whatever tactics are necessary," including "direct action."[51] Most significantly, however, SDS announced its intention to "delegitimize the professor as an authority figure"—a goal that clearly indicated the distance between Williams and the increasingly radical New Left.[52]

Within a year and a half of the Dow protests, Williams left Madison to teach at Oregon State University. Although David Cronon, the history department chairman, told the *Daily Cardinal* that "the campus situation in Madison did not precipitate" Williams's decision, it must have played some role.[53] After all, Williams always felt more comfortable in the relative tranquility of small communities; when he left for Oregon he moved to a place (a small town with a population of just over one thousand) that was a world apart from the tensions and antagonisms of UW. It seemed fitting that in March 1969, the same month that Williams's departure from Madison was announced, UW's history students turned on the history department itself: after being barred from departmental meetings for unruly behavior, the students claimed that the department had adopted an "ahistorical view of social change" by resisting "the flow" of opinion.[54] Madison was clearly no longer a place for a social conservative who sought a student-faculty alliance to educate Americans about the need for reform.

The student radicals' devotion to a Marxist-Leninist intellectual approach—one that promoted direct action and embraced an economic determinist view of US imperialism—ultimately made Williams and the New Left incompatible. The Wisconsin scholars worried about what McCormick called the "strain of anti-intellectualism" that characterized the New Left's approach; even Williams, as a man who "had a tremendous influence" on the initial development of the New Left, became concerned by their failure to "engage with Americans intellectually."[55] When students in Madison began to protest against the Vietnam War, Williams and other UW radical scholars such as George Mosse (an inspirational lecturer who taught modern history) initially found the demonstrators inspiring. However, as the tactics of the New Left became more confrontational and violent, and their patience with peaceful methods wore thin, Williams and Mosse came to think of the student radicals as mindless and anarchic. Williams became particularly frustrated by their insistence that "the only way an academic can be an honest radical" was to be "consistently and persistently activist"; instead Williams argued it was equally vital to write "damned important books."[56]

Williams attempted to persuade the New Left hierarchy to change their approach in an interview with the *Daily Cardinal* in April 1970. Although he had already left Madison, he was concerned by events at UW and hoped the article would reduce "the increasingly militant activism of younger radicals." The bulk of his interview, which was conducted by unnamed graduate students, focused on the tactics of dissent and the ways in which Williams believed it was possible to bring about meaningful reform in America via peaceful means. He argued that "there is no point going onto the streets when you're going to get isolated, . . . then politically broken up and destroyed." The problem with the student radicals' strategy was that US society "at this point" was "not that sick"; consequently, "it's not going to be rolled over by a few people in a few cities going into the streets" and confronting the authorities. Furthermore, Williams added that not "everybody wants to fight"—a reminder that moderate Americans who would otherwise welcome socioeconomic reform might be repelled by a lawless minority. Instead, Williams urged the radicals to "come together," stop fighting the faculty, use the university for its primary purpose (which was "intellectual development"), and find creative solutions to transform America.[57]

One of Williams's main problems with the New Left was its inability to broaden its approach. He also criticized "its slowness in undertaking political organization of an opposition that includes non-students." Therefore, although he "positively identified" himself with "their concerns" and "shared their frustrations," Williams believed the New Left was wasting the opportunity that the Vietnam War and the civil rights movement (which demonstrated to many Americans the need for fundamental reform) had presented. However, Williams's frustration at the New Left's strategic frailties was matched by his contempt, as a social conservative, for the behavior of the "small group" of New Left "extremists" who had hijacked the antiwar movement and given the broader left in the United States a bad name. Williams believed the violent radicals displayed a "narrow, ego-centered selfishness" that was "neither radical nor socialist." He compared these student activists to the "laissez-faire capitalists of the late nineteenth century" and condemned their "demand for I power" and their "assertive, devil-takes-what's-left individualism." The Wisconsin scholar believed these demonstrators were "destructive rather than creative" and as much an obstacle to "a moral meaningful radical alternative to the existing system" as the government itself.[58] These strong words demonstrate the incongruity of classifying the Wisconsin scholars and the New Left under the same banner. Their intellectual approaches were clearly different—and consequently their critiques of US imperialism were underpinned by contrasting methodologies and convictions.

The Students with Much to Learn

As the 1960s drew to a close, *Kaleidoscope* published a revealing article titled "Notes on a Decade Ready for the Dustbin."[59] The author was none other than Carl Oglesby, the former president of SDS. Oglesby complained that the New Left chose social revolution because, quite simply, there was no alternative philosophy of revolution other than Marxism-Leninism for student radicals to embrace. The fact that Williams taught at UW until 1968, and that Madison was the birthplace of *Studies on the Left*, seemed irrelevant—the student radicals' determination to delegitimize professors prevented them from seeing the viable alternative that was in front of them. Meanwhile, their attachment to economic determinism prevented them from developing a more sophisticated critique of American imperialism.

Because student radicals in the Vietnam War came to embrace a Marxist-Leninist intellectual approach, they ultimately promoted a Marxist-Leninist interpretation of American expansion. They argued vociferously that US imperialism was a ploy to safeguard the prosperity of the wealthy while suppressing the aspirations of the working class. At the Dow protests, which were seen as an "insurrection" by UW administrators, poems were read in honor of Che Guevara.[60] Meanwhile, radical student literature portrayed American policymakers' attempts to suppress social revolutions in the developing world as an inevitable by-product of US imperialism; they believed imperial wars were necessary to secure access to raw materials and protect the delicate balance of the global capitalist economy. Indeed, the Young Socialist Alliance positively identified itself with Lenin's interpretation of imperialism: "Lenin's characterization of our historical period as the epoch of imperialism remains true. Today US aggression against the Vietnamese people is the most overt and criminal manifestation of that imperialism. . . . This makes opposition to this war the central feature of political life for revolutionaries."[61] This extract, which was typical of radical student literature during the 1960s, clearly demonstrates how the dissidents were devoted to Marxism-Leninism and saw themselves as revolutionaries in the Russian mold.

Like their New Left contemporaries nationwide, the dissidents at UW condemned US capitalism and the society it created. The very first issue of *Kaleidoscope*, for example, argued that capitalism "strips" man of his "essential humanity." As an alternative, the radical magazine called for the "Marxism of everyday life" and a new culture.[62] Meanwhile, SDS criticized the "small elite" that make "life and death decisions" and called for a revolutionary movement that could overhaul the US socioeconomic structure. "Karl Marx said that to be radical is to get to the root, and that is what we want to do; get to the root of the problems that affect our lives. . . . [We want] to build a movement that will give us the power to make these crucial decisions" and institutions "relevant to our lives" and "needs," "not the needs of a murderous corporate system."[63] *Kaleidoscope* echoed this call by arguing that capitalism had failed; they, too, demanded "a movement which flows from our lives."[64]

The student radicals were prepared to use all means necessary to end the war. As they subscribed to the determinist view that imperialism was an inevitable consequence of capitalism, they believed the destruction of America's existing socioeconomic structures was essential. Clearly, this was not the case with the Wisconsin scholars, who argued that US imperialism stemmed from policymakers' mistaken conviction that American prosperity required economic expansion. Williams believed that US foreign policy could be reversed by redistributing wealth within the United States and educating Americans about the need for change; he wanted to reform the United States socioeconomic structure, not destroy it. The Wisconsin scholars' critique was therefore more measured. It was also more holistic in its analysis of the origins of US imperialism—emphasizing a blend of cultural, psychological, and political triggers as opposed to hard economic determinism. This reflected Williams's more enlightened intellectual approach.

When Harrington claimed that Williams was clearly "not the leader of the protest movement," he was unquestionably correct.[65] The Wisconsin scholars were not Marxists with a capital "M." McCormick, for example, claimed: "I did not consider myself to be part of the New Left. . . . I was only part of it in the sense that I was also against the war." Crucially, McCormick also underscored the misconceptions that surrounded the Wisconsin scholars. "I considered myself to be more radical than the others, but I didn't think of myself as an economic determinist—even though some orthodox scholars thought I was."[66] By indulging in militant tactics, and trying to inspire revolution on the streets, the New Left radicals attempted to differentiate themselves from the Old Left and impose their will on American society. However, in trying to reject "both the practical experience and socialist ideology of their elders," they ultimately failed to achieve their objectives.[67] Williams argued that the radicals "substituted a moral determinism" for "economic determinism"; therefore, the establishment was able to deal with the protestors by "co-opting the moral issue" as well as "the economic issue" in the same manner as it had in the 1930s.[68] Meanwhile, the radical students' adherence to economic determinism prevented them from promoting a critique of US imperialism that was substantially different from that of pre–Cold War Marxists like Scott Nearing.

The student radicals, then, failed to escape the clichés of Marxism. Williams, on the other hand, was familiar with Marx, but he "cared most about Marx's insights into quality of life, and what socialism could do to liberate the spirit and creativity." The Wisconsin scholar therefore subscribed to "a more romantic version of Marx" rather than any set of rigid theories—in other words, he took from Marx "what he wanted." Significantly, the student radicals' anti-intellectualism also hindered the fundamental reappraisal of US foreign policy that seemed possible in the mid-1960s. During the Vietnam War, a surge of radical literature promised to revolutionize the writing of US diplomatic history. In the end, however, the hopes of the Wisconsin scholars were dashed. The problem, in McCormick's opinion, was that the New Left activists did not take the study of US imperialism seriously enough. "They weren't really diplomatic scholars at all—they were just radicals; the issue with the New Left was personal rather than systemic."[69] Indeed, once the Vietnam War was no longer a key political issue, many dissidents simply abandoned the field of diplomatic history. As a result, the student radicals' critiques of US imperialism do not bear close scrutiny.

Because many serious New Left intellectuals grew out of the antiwar movement, or were at least given a platform to popularize their views by the protestors, it would be wrong to ignore student critiques entirely (even if they were somewhat crude). Furthermore, the antiwar movement did much to promote the concept of US imperialism. Scholars like Williams and Kolko were not well known outside the intellectual community; therefore, the interpretations promoted by groups like SDS were the only critiques many Americans were aware of. Despite their prevalence though, the students' conception of US imperialism was frequently too conspiratorial and simplistic. They often attributed events to a single causal factor; for example, they argued that America intervened in countries like the Dominican Republic simply because a particular policymaker had personal interests there. The student radicals' analysis was always stuck on this "simplistic" level. McCormick claimed "there was no systematic analysis. . . . They'd say Vietnam has tin and rubber, so that's why America was there, without realizing that plenty of other places have those materials too." Consequently, their argument "made no damn sense at all."[70]

It must be stressed, however, that student critiques of American empire were not the best the New Left had to offer; in the next chapter, we will look at more sophisticated New Left interpretations of US imperialism—critiques written by serious scholars who were dedicated to exploring the subject. Although these histories also had their flaws, they at least adopted a more structured approach. The problem with the students, in the words of McCormick, was that they "passed up the opportunity to understand things in a systematic way." Furthermore, although they called themselves "Marxist," McCormick doubted whether "they had even read Marx sufficiently" enough. "They wanted to be political in goals, so there was no room for serious study; they didn't ask 'What is imperialism?' 'Is this imperialism?' 'Is this empire the same as past empires?' 'Has it changed?' They didn't ask questions because the answers were not important to them. They simply wanted to be a social voice."[71] The difference between the student radicals and the Wisconsin scholars was that the latter used imperialism as an analytical framework for the study of American foreign policy. The former, on the other hand, were not interested in analysis; they took an existing methodology (no matter how out of date) and simply adopted it, with its preconceived conclusions, as their own. This was unfortunate. By embracing Marxism-Leninism (because it was the obvious radical ideology at hand), UW students accepted a simplistic critique of US imperialism and repudiated the far more sophisticated interpretation that emerged from their very own history department.

7

The New Left Intellectuals

> The Vietnam War represents . . . the magnified expression of a real historical trend, . . . the historical experience of counter-revolutionary interventions by the imperialist powers and their inevitable continuing commitment to the social status quo.
>
> David Horowitz, 1969

The Jungle of Dissent

Although the Wisconsin critique of imperialism was the most nuanced interpretation of US expansion during the 1960s, Williams, LaFeber, and McCormick were not the only scholars to promote the concept of American empire. The New Left, for example, contained several serious intellectuals who discussed US imperialism during the Vietnam War. At the start of the decade, domestic dissent against American expansion was rare—and when it did surface, it was restricted to radical left journals with a small readership (such as *Monthly Review*). The topic of American imperialism was therefore not discussed in mainstream political discourse. However, as the war in Vietnam escalated and casualties mounted, this trickle of dissent swelled into a torrent of righteous anger. With the antiwar movement growing and a diplomatic settlement improbable, many Americans began to wonder whether the war was a mistake. New Left critiques of US foreign policy reflected these doubts—and as their authors attempted to rationalize the violence, many of them contextualized the Vietnam War as part of a broader history of international imperialism.

New Left critiques of US diplomacy during the 1960s were the antithesis of the orthodox liberal view typified by Arthur Schlesinger Jr. in his well-known essay "The Origins of the Cold War." Schlesinger argued that the Soviet Union was to blame for international tensions because Stalin's paranoia and the anti-capitalist nature of Marxist-Leninist dogma made accommodation with Russia impossible. Indeed, he claimed that even the "most rational of American policies could hardly have averted the Cold War."[1] New Left scholars, on the other hand, believed that US policymakers were to blame; this is because they believed the United States' determination to establish a pro-American capitalist world order after World War II antagonized the Soviet Union. In what became a hallmark of Cold War revisionism, they emphasized that US ambitions were incompatible with Stalin's desire for a defensive sphere of interest in Eastern Europe. This was similar to the argument expressed by Williams and LaFeber, but New Left scholars were even more radical: they argued that US foreign policy was a slave to the structural needs of American capitalism, questioned the integrity of US policymakers, and occasionally contextualized the Vietnam War as part of a broader conspiracy against the global proletariat.

Although these New Left perspectives might seem extreme, the Vietnam War created an atmosphere in which radical views thrived. As the war dragged on and the government's initial optimism proved unfounded, many disenchanted citizens found it increasingly difficult to trust US officials; therefore, an audience for radical literature was established. For example, David Horowitz, a scholar whose radicalism in the 1960s was a stark contrast to the crusading conservatism of his later years, wrote his first book, *The Free World Colossus*, in 1962 but was unable to find a publisher until 1965 (the same year Lyndon Johnson committed the regular army to Vietnam). Horowitz believed this delay was caused by a "frigid" intellectual consensus that regarded the Cold War as "America's holy crusade to save the world from communist totalitarianism"; as a result, "it was not easy to find a publisher in the United States ready to print" views like his. However, the "mass anti-war movement" proved to be a turning point, for it "created a new climate in which dissenting theory and analysis could begin to develop with some self-confidence."[2]

As the war in Southeast Asia intensified, several intellectuals joined Horowitz and denounced US foreign policy. Some left-leaning liberals even embarked on short-lived radical phases. Consequently, a host of dissenting literature emerged during a relatively short period of time. For example, the *New York Review of Books* attracted disaffected liberals and began to publish increasingly radical perspectives. After 1966 the journal perpetuated a general "mood of insurgency" and promoted revolutionary and anarchist perspectives.[3] Soon it became somewhat fashionable to hold dissenting views. This was reflected by the prominence of writers such as Norman Mailer, Mary McCarthy, Noam Chomsky, plus "radical hipsters" such as Charles Reich and Theodore Roszak, who all published radical commentaries on either US foreign policy, American society, or both.

Although intellectuals like Mailer expressed views on American foreign policy (including references to expansion or imperialism), their work has largely been ignored in this study. This is because these publicly visible intellectuals were associated with the counterculture and did not use empire as an analytical framework to study US foreign policy; consequently, they contributed little to the historiography of American imperialism. These figures will always be regarded as important members of the New Left social movement, since they typified the "universal sense of rebellion" that characterized the period; however, their views had more "to do with style and attitude" than "coherent policy."[4] For example, Mailer's *Armies of the Night* (1968), his personal account of the antiwar march to the Pentagon in 1967, compared the United States to the Egyptian empire by describing the Pentagon as "a giant mudpie on the banks of America's Nile."[5] However, this was nothing more than an isolated reference to imperialism. Meanwhile, Mailer's grisly novel *Why Are We in Vietnam?* (1967) was an anarchic tale of American masculinity gone mad rather than a commentary on imperialism in particular; the story described two wealthy teenagers, "each as separated from social convention as any two rich boys could be," hunting bears (a metaphor for the Soviet Union) in the Alaskan wilderness.[6] Although *Why Are We in Vietnam?* was a statement on the psychology of the American military (the central character, D.J., was about to fight in Vietnam), and also a comment on America's frontier mentality, Mailer exploited these themes for literary impact. *Why Are We in Vietnam?* was therefore a cryptic commentary on US foreign policy, not a key text in the historiography of American empire.

Unfortunately, however, many liberal and conservative observers at the time failed to see this distinction. Instead they frequently classified diverse intellectuals such as Mailer, Horowitz, and Williams in the same "New Left" category. In many ways, therefore, the term "New Left" was inadequate. The radical left in America during the 1960s was an incredibly eclectic group. By categorizing intellectually and culturally diverse personalities under the same banner, historians failed to emphasize the substantial disparities between the various radical voices; as a result, a false sense of homogeneity was created. This generalization might have been expedient for critics of the radical left, who were able to discredit scholars like Williams by bracketing them alongside culturally subversive dissidents, but it did a disservice to serious historians of US diplomatic history. As this chapter will demonstrate, there were significant differences between the radicals. The New Left, for instance, adopted a contrasting ideological outlook to the Wisconsin scholars and promoted a very different model for socioeconomic reform. The counterculture, meanwhile, was a separate phenomenon altogether (often promoting anarchy as opposed to genuine political and economic solutions).

The work of Irwin Unger, the Pulitzer Prize–winning scholar, illustrated how contemporaries either misunderstood or misrepresented the subtle but noteworthy disparities between the radical intellectuals. In an essay published in the *American Historical Review* in 1967, Unger asserted that "dissensions within the New Left history are as general and intense as disagreements among the socialists, anarchists, pacifists, existentialists and neo-populists who composed the New Left movement"; the only thing that united the radical left, according to Unger, was what they disliked, that is, US policy in Vietnam, inequalities in American society, and, of course, orthodox liberal intellectuals. However, having identified the discrepancies between different scholars, Unger still classified these diverse intellectuals under the same banner—that is, he defined both the Marxist radicals and the Wisconsin scholars as "New Left historians."[7]

Unger's decision to categorize the UW historians alongside the rest of the radical left was particularly unfortunate because he began to recognize, more than other contemporary critics, that Williams, LaFeber, and McCormick attributed US foreign policy to different factors. For example, he highlighted how some New Left radicals were embarrassed by Williams's insistence that "ideas, not interests, are what counts" in America's past.[8] Although this was a slightly misleading analysis of *Contours*, as the book often highlighted the influence of specific economic factors as well, Unger was quite right to point out the centrality of ideas in Williams's interpretation of American history. Unfortunately though, he did not discuss the more substantive disparities between the Wisconsin scholars and the New Left. Throughout *Contours* and *Tragedy*, Williams continually blamed US expansion on policymakers' belief that only an increase in foreign trade could solve the imbalances of the domestic economy. On the other hand, New Left scholars such as David Horowitz and Gabriel Kolko were economic determinists in a Marxist mold; therefore, they portrayed US imperialism as an inevitable consequence of American capitalism (anything else was superfluous and detracted from the main issue).

Unfortunately Unger was not alone in failing to emphasize key discrepancies. Orthodox liberals in general failed to see the difference between the Wisconsin scholars and their New Left counterparts. It is hard to know exactly why this was the case (it could have been a matter of political expedience or lazy scholarship), but whenever a radical scholar emphasized economic factors to a significant degree, orthodox scholars tended to denounce their work as a Marxian tract that forced "evidence to fit pre-conceived opinions."[9] Although this judgment was often premature, critics did not hesitate to project "Marxism's supposed sins onto all sorts of radical scholarship."[10] For example, as we saw in chapter 4, *Tragedy* was often condemned as a Marxist tract even though this appraisal was flawed.

While it is true that both the New Left scholars and the UW historians explained the Vietnam War as a manifestation of American expansion, and agreed that the conflict was "an outgrowth of American politics, economy and society all of which they hoped to change," the Wisconsin scholars advocated a different strategy to combat US imperialism.[11] Like Beard, Williams and his devotees argued that US policymakers could reform American capitalism (and thereby evade imperialism) by redistributing wealth within the United States and ending the nation's reliance on foreign markets. The Wisconsin scholars also strived to convince policymakers and the public that expansion was not strictly necessary; by creating an intellectual revolution, rather than a physical one, they hoped to dispel the fallacy that American institutions and the economy were dependent on continuous expansion. The New Left, on the other hand, believed that more fundamental reform was needed: they argued that revolution and the toppling of capitalism was the only solution, since they believed that imperialism was an inevitable consequence of any capitalist economy. This was the main point of differentiation. Both groups emphasized economic factors as the root cause of US imperialism, but the New Left subscribed to a purer Marxist-Leninist theory.

Although the UW historians were concerned about inequalities in American society, they never advocated the kind of revolutionary solutions proposed by the New Left. Whereas Williams disapproved of confrontational activism and violent protest, many New Left scholars openly encouraged students and the working class to rise up against the status quo. New Left literature was correspondingly more extreme. For example, Horowitz asserted on many occasions that US policymakers were part of a global conspiracy against the world's poor; consequently, he had no qualms about declaring the total depravity of US diplomacy. The Wisconsin scholars never went this far. Rather, they claimed that they were often "profoundly impressed" with US policymakers, who they saw as "responsible, conscientious men who accepted the economic and social realities of their day." Even though they conceded that "the decisions of these men" often resulted in "unfortunate consequences," they believed US statesmen attempted to "create what they sincerely hoped would be a better nation and a better world."[12]

As a result, when John Lewis Gaddis (arguably the foremost post-revisionist scholar of the Cold War) labeled Williams's work "one of the most influential examples of New Left historiography," he was wrong. Williams's work might have been an influential example of what was commonly (but incorrectly) referred to as "New Left" literature, but the Wisconsin scholars were different.[13] The New Left were Marxist economic determinists who advocated a political activism that Williams could never accept. Unlike many radical antiwar protestors, the Wisconsin scholars did not reject America's socioeconomic structure outright. Like the progressives, they wanted to reform American political institutions rather than abolish them. The New Left meanwhile considered "the progressive movement a fraud"; progressivism and socialism did not go far enough for radicals like Horowitz. In fact, many supporters of the New Left preferred "anarchism to socialism."[14]

This chapter will explore in detail how New Left interpretations of US imperialism differed from the Wisconsin alternative. It will also discuss the relative merits and drawbacks of New Left critiques (which in many ways reflect the strengths and weaknesses of economic determinism in general). Once again, it should be pointed out that these New Left scholars were by no means monolithic, but they shared two fundamental characteristics: (a) they remained faithful to Marx and Lenin's assertion that imperialism was an inevitable result of capitalism, and (b) they used history as a political weapon to criticize the US government and attack America's socioeconomic structure. This will reinforce and expand the discussion in the previous chapter, which demonstrated the disparity between Williams's "neo-progressive" approach and the Marxist intellectual approach of the New Left in Madison.[15]

The Common Misconception

As this discussion develops, the differences between the New Left and the Wisconsin interpretation of US imperialism will become increasingly apparent. However, it must first be stressed that these contrasting critiques also had outward similarities (which go some way to explaining why so many observers have bracketed them together). For example, the New Left agreed with Williams that the United States intervened in World War II primarily for economic reasons; although US policymakers were worried by the humanitarian consequences of a Nazi victory, they were allegedly more concerned about the potential economic costs of a fascist-occupied Europe. It is no surprise that these similarities existed. The New Left scholars were admirers of *Tragedy*. Even though they were economic determinists (and believed US imperialism was a consequence of American capitalism rather than intellectual failures), they still saw Williams's work as one of "the best accounts" of US foreign relations.[16]

Furthermore, although the Wisconsin scholars and the New Left believed that different factors triggered US expansion, they agreed that American imperialism manifested itself in similar ways. For example, having argued that US policymakers prioritized economic expansion after World War II (albeit for different reasons), it was inevitable that the New Left would concur with Williams that the United States caused the Cold War.

Both the New Left radicals and the Wisconsin scholars criticized the United States on similar grounds. For example, both schools highlighted how the United States' objection to a Soviet security perimeter in Eastern Europe seemed unreasonable in light of the Truman Doctrine and the Marshall Plan. They also claimed that US foreign policy during the Cold War violated the values that the United States ostensibly stood for. For example, they wondered how a global campaign against indigenous revolutions was compatible with the principle of self-determination. Because the United States dictated "to small nations, friends and foes alike, the form of internal social and political system" they should adopt, both the New Left and the Wisconsin scholars concluded that the Atlantic Charter was obviously less important to US officials than the promotion of free trade across the world.[17]

Both sets of radicals also concurred that the United States intervened in World War II to play a decisive role in settling the peace. They claimed that American officials had "a series of immediate objectives, centered first of all around the desire to win battles and defeat the Axis," but also possessed "an elaborate and highly sophisticated set of economic and political goals it defined as urgently desirable war aims." These goals included the containment of left-wing revolutionary movements across the globe, which allegedly threatened "the momentary collapse of European capitalism and, in the Far East, colonialism or oligarchy." They also claimed that the US plans for the postwar world were designed to obtain American "military security via bases," and to secure the nation's "growing spheres of interests elsewhere." When it came to US goals after the fall of Nazi Germany, the Wisconsin scholars and the New Left historians were in agreement: they believed that American officials' ultimate objective was the establishment of a stable pro-American capitalist world order (based on the principles of the Open Door) that would "shift the locus of world power from Europe to the United States."[18]

Given their assumptions about American war aims, it was not surprising that both the Wisconsin scholars and the New Left intellectuals believed US Cold War foreign policy was designed to expand global capitalism. They denied that containment was a defensive response to Russian imperialism; instead, they argued it was US economic expansion that "set the United States . . .

against the Soviet Union" and "against the tide of the left." The radicals interpreted the Vietnam War within this framework, arguing that the conflict was created by US policymakers' determination to keep Southeast Asia within the capitalist orbit. This repudiated the orthodox liberal view that the war was an intellectual mistake. Indeed, the New Left intellectuals characterized the argument that "there was something accidental or unintended about the American response to the world" as nothing more than "a comforting reassurance to those who wish to confuse the American rhetoric and descriptions of intentions with the realities and purposes of operational power."[19]

The New Left scholars believed the war in Southeast Asia was "the most important single embodiment of the power and purposes of American foreign policy since the Second World War." In the radicals' eyes, not only did the conflict demonstrate America's opposition to left-leaning revolutionary movements and Third World nationalism, but it also revealed "the nature of America's internal political process" and its "decision-making structure."[20] Williams and the Wisconsin scholars generally concurred with this sentiment. For example, they argued that US policymakers entered the war to prevent an Asian nation from falling out of the capitalist orbit (a move that might ultimately close the door to American trade in that region). After all, not only would the fall of Vietnam to communism jeopardize the Japanese economy, but it might also inspire other nations in the region to follow the Vietnamese's example (an eventuality that would be a catastrophic blow to US plans for the global economy).

It is also important to note at this juncture that both the Wisconsin historians and the more sophisticated of the New Left scholars rejected what Harry Magdoff called "the pocketbook" theory of the Vietnam War (and of US imperialism in general). They argued that "attempts to explain isolated actions in book-keeping terms" made "no sense" because the economic benefits of American foreign policy were not obvious. They contended that the United States did not send troops to Vietnam to make an immediate profit; rather, the economic and strategic benefits were more subtle and long term. For example, Magdoff asserted that the intervention was not about the specific economic value of Vietnamese markets; it was all about keeping Southeast Asia free for capitalist penetration (this was a broader and more important economic concern). Therefore, "the reality of imperialism" went "far beyond the immediate interest of this or that investor." The "underlying purpose" was "nothing less than keeping as much as possible of the world open for trade and investment" by American businesses.[21]

Finally, both sets of radicals believed the United States' willingness to wage war to protect global capitalism qualified the nation as imperial. They asserted that US internationalism really meant "economic hegemony over the world economy," while America's political wrangling during and after World War II was nothing more than a means of "preserving and expanding America's unprecedented power" over Europe and beyond.[22] Like the Wisconsin scholars, the New Left were not afraid to use the terms "empire" and "imperialism." Although LaFeber had been hesitant to apply the word "imperialism" to US foreign policy in *The New Empire* (which was published in 1963), the increasing volume of radical literature during the Vietnam War made it easier for the radicals to describe the United States as imperial in the second half of the decade. Consequently, the 1960s radicals were united in their belief that the United States possessed an empire.

However, these outward similarities masked vital methodological and ideological divergences. Indeed, these divergences were somewhat typical of the broader historiography of international imperialism during the twentieth century. Although international scholars all had somewhat contrasting views of empire (attributing the origins and manifestations of imperialism to different factors), it is possible to divide them into two broad camps: those who believed imperialism was a necessary by-product of industrial capitalism, and those who did not. These camps became entrenched at the beginning of the twentieth century when Hobson and Lenin, two hugely influential figures, established contrasting perspectives on Western imperialism. Hobson believed that the reform of capitalism could prevent imperialism, while Lenin (despite making "extensive use of Hobson's data") ultimately concluded that imperialism was inevitable.[23]

Although Lenin's *Imperialism, the Highest Stage of Capitalism* can be seen as "a polemical document of limited theoretical value" (after all, Lenin's prediction that imperialism simply delayed the collapse of capitalism proved hollow when the British and French economies survived the demise of their colonial empires), a new form of neo-Marxism that derived from Lenin bloomed after World War II. Adapting to the new international environment, writers like Tom Kemp and Kwame Nkrumah continued to argue that imperialism was an inevitable consequence of capitalism. These neo-Marxists believed state monopoly capitalism provoked a competition among industrial states for raw materials and access to foreign markets; this contest resulted in the exploitation of developing nations—a process that Nkrumah labeled "neo-colonialism."[24] Although this exploitation was not always direct (it was often driven by multinational corporations rather than policymakers), the neo-Marxists argued that unequal trade relations benefited industrialized nations and stalled economic growth in the developing world. This perspective eventually evolved into dependency theory, which argued that developing areas were unable to escape their ties to core industrialized nations because the natural functioning of the integrated world marketplace prevented it. A prominent example was the work of the German American scholar André Gunder Frank, who argued that resources flowed from Latin America to the United States in a manner that was only advantageous to the latter. As we shall see, the New Left provided a similar analysis; therefore, their critiques reflected international trends to a significant extent.

The alternative international interpretation of imperialism after World War II (which repudiated economic determinism) was typified by the British economist John Maynard Keynes, who developed Hobson's analysis by concluding that "a democratic state could direct the economy of a western industrial society in such a way as to enable it to completely reject imperialism."[25] Robinson and Gallagher, who promoted the concept of "informal empire," also belonged to this second group. They argued that Great Britain shunned traditional imperialism because economic benefits could be accrued without the burdens of colonialism; therefore, British imperialism was driven by expediency rather than economic necessity. Of course, Williams's concept of imperial anticolonialism was reminiscent of this approach (although he applied it exclusively to US foreign policy—particularly in the late nineteenth century). Thus, the Wisconsin interpretation also imitated international scholarship to a notable degree.

However, while it must be noted that the New Left scholars' interpretation also echoed the work of American Marxists like Scott Nearing (who advocated an economic determinist view of US expansion in the early twentieth century), the ideological and methodological underpinnings of their critique possessed a stronger international flavor. The work of the Wisconsin scholars, on the other hand, was primarily influenced by existing US scholarship; after all, Williams's critique emphasized the crucial role played by the American Weltanschauung (which was shaped by the United States' unique historical experience). Even though Williams's interpretation was similar to that of Robinson and Gallagher, and the Wisconsin scholar spent time with European scholars at the London School of Economics at the beginning of his career, Williams was primarily inspired by Charles Beard and the progressive view that US foreign policy could be changed by redistributing wealth within American society. In short, the Wisconsin critique was more Anglo-Saxon in nature than its New Left equivalent.

Consequently, although the New Left scholars agreed with Williams that the Spanish-American War could only be seen as an isolated incident if imperialism was solely equated with colonialism—"the fact that the United States may have found a noncolonial form more congenial to its purposes" was no reason to deny the existence of an American empire—the New Left and Wisconsin critiques should be treated separately.[26] The New Left's tendency to contextualize US foreign policy within the broader history of international imperialism was one of the best illustrations of their disparity; this was very much a hallmark of Marxist-Leninist historiography, which placed international events within the context of universal and irresistible historical movements. Conversely, Williams argued that American imperialism was exceptional; it might have resembled British imperialism because US policymakers preferred informal empire to colonialism, but its psychological triggers were unique. Furthermore, because the Wisconsin scholars attributed US expansion to a particular mindset that was peculiarly American, it was impossible for them to contextualize US foreign policy as part of broader international and historical trends (although they did see events like the Spanish-American War within the context of long-term US expansion).

Because of their conflicting approaches, it was inevitable that the New Left intellectuals and the Wisconsin scholars would contextualize the Vietnam War somewhat differently. Kolko and Horowitz, for example, predictably described the Vietnam War as part of "a real historical trend"; because they adopted a Marxist-Leninist approach to the study of empire in general, they argued that Vietnam was part of "the cumulative historical experience of counterrevolutionary intervention by imperial powers and their inevitable continuing commitment to the social status quo."[27] The Wisconsin scholars, on the other hand, contextualized Vietnam as part of the broader history of US expansionism, but they were reluctant to compare the United States to other empires. Therefore, only the New Left historians depicted the United States as an archetypal imperial power that used its economic, political, and military might like previous hegemons to control large swaths of the earth.

Magdoff's critique, which we shall examine in more detail later, particularly demonstrated this difference. Initially, his interpretation seemed to imitate *Tragedy* by emphasizing how colonialism had given way to informal economic imperialism during the nineteenth century. However, Magdoff clearly discussed US expansion in a broader historical context, arguing that the control of raw materials was as important in 1969 as it had been during the height of the British Empire. The New Left scholar therefore argued that the United States' exploitation of underdeveloped countries was anything but unique—indeed, it was a common feature of imperialism since the Industrial Revolution. Because American factories, like those of the European empires, required essential resources such as oil, steel, and industrial chemicals, Magdoff claimed it was only natural that the United States should seek to control its supply of raw materials. The United States was therefore depicted as one of many "rapidly advancing countries rushing for their place in the sun."[28]

Another important point of differentiation was that the Wisconsin scholars concentrated on the intellectual and psychological dimensions of US foreign policy, while the New Left historians tended to focus on the actual functioning of the American empire—that is, explaining how the United States physically extended its economic influence across the globe. For example, Magdoff claimed that the International Monetary Fund (IMF) ensured that the dollar became the key currency in global trade relations; because capitalist nations kept their reserves in dollars, and used US currency as a substitute for gold, the dollar became the key international medium of payments, credits, and reserves (therefore the dollar itself became an "instrument of control").[29] Whereas traditional imperialism had been based on spheres of interest, Magdoff argued that the modern American empire was based on US control over the IMF, the United Nations, and the World Bank. As a result, American power became inseparable from the global capitalist economy at large.

Finally, although both the Wisconsin scholars and the New Left believed that the foreign activities of US corporations were important to an understanding of modern American imperialism, Horowitz, Kolko, and Magdoff contextualized the rise of multinationals within a neo-Marxist framework: they emphasized how the natural functioning of international markets enabled American firms to secure raw materials at advantageous prices (while preventing businesses from developing nations becoming competitors). While Williams simply discussed the burgeoning foreign operations of US corporations with reference to Americans' "frontier-expansionist outlook," Horowitz described how corporate tentacles extended throughout the world, competing for finite resources and making global conflicts inevitable: "The unchecked concentration of financial and corporate power and its expansion beyond local and national boundaries are the very cornerstone of free enterprise capitalism. . . . Within capitalism there is no way to avoid the toils of imperialist rivalry and competition, no way to elude the political and military conflicts that the imperialist struggle entails." Because international corporations were monopolistic, Horowitz claimed that it was essential for the United States to "repress revolutions" across the globe and "weaken and retard the development of the existing socialist states." If wars were necessary, then so be it. It was vital for America to control markets, access raw materials, and raise demand within the domestic economy. As a result, the United States was depicted as an aggressive military industrial complex that deliberately provoked military conflicts to compensate for the imbalances of capitalism and to sustain a "corporatist fascist" system.[30]

The key point of differentiation here was that the New Left scholars did not believe it was a matter of choice for the United States to control international markets and secure cheap raw materials—the capitalist nature of its economy actually necessitated it. Williams, by contrast, discussed Americans' perceived need for economic expansion during the 1890s in relation to the nation's psychological dependence on the frontier; he did not believe that economic expansion was actually necessary (although unfortunately US policymakers mistakenly thought it was). The New Left played down the significance of the frontier experience because their economic determinism rendered any argument extraneous to the expansionist nature of capitalism irrelevant. When the New Left did occasionally refer to the frontier, it was merely in passing (rather than forming a central part of their critique). For example, Horowitz agreed with Williams that US leaders saw "the solution to the domestic economic problems not in terms of internal structural changes, but in terms of staking out ever new, externally situated frontiers," but Horowitz saw the frontier as simply an outlet for US trade, rather than as a national experience that had entrenched an expansionist mind-set.[31]

What is more, the New Left scholars rarely asserted that intellectual failures (including flawed assumptions) were a cause of American expansion. After all, why should they? The dogmatic belief that imperialism was an inevitable consequence of capitalism was the only rationale they required. Of all the New Left scholars, Kolko's interpretation was the broadest and most sophisticated, but even his critique left little room for anything other than determinist logic. For example, *The Politics of War* examined US policymakers' assumption that the Russians were bent on territorial expansion and discussed how this assumption shaped American foreign policy (it did, after all, mean that US officials misconstrued Soviet behavior), but this was the only intellectual failure that Kolko considered. Although his interpretation perceptively highlighted how the US government failed to "seriously consider" alternative perspectives, and "much less assimilated" different views "into functional decision-making," Kolko himself did not consider how factors other than the expansive nature of capitalism could have driven US imperialism.[32]

The Evolution of New Left Interpretations

By the end of the 1960s, New Left scholars had developed intricate neo-Marxist studies that attempted to expose the causes and manifestations of US expansion. Although these critiques were handicapped somewhat by the simplicity of determinist dogma (which attributed complex historical changes to a single factor), scholars like Kolko and Magdoff went further than previous Marxists to demonstrate that US foreign policy was motivated by self-interest rather than philanthropy. However, it was not always thus. At the beginning of the decade, some New Left scholars echoed the leaders of SDS and other antiwar organizations by merely promoting a polemical interpretation of American imperialism—critiques that presented Marxist-Leninist theories as historical truths and produced scant evidence to support their radical assertions.

Despite being one of the New Left's most prized intellectuals, David Horowitz was one such example. Horowitz's analysis often made contentious claims about the self-serving nature of US foreign policy without employing the scholarly apparatus one might expect in a serious work of history. As a result it is impossible to escape the feeling that, just like the student radicals, his critique was designed to serve a political purpose rather than make a contribution of analytical importance. Indeed, his work often betrayed a penchant for Marxist-Leninist rebellion. Horowitz's first book on American interventionism, *The Free World Colossus*, demonstrated this polemical style. Written during the early 1960s, it represented something of a starting point from which New Left critiques evolved over the course of the decade.

The Free World Colossus predictably claimed that US Cold War policy was designed to preserve the prewar status quo (which allegedly served American interests rather conveniently). Horowitz argued that containment was not a "counter-expansionary" reaction to Soviet ambitions; rather, it was a "counter-revolutionary" strategy to destroy all challenges to the pro-American world order.[33] In Horowitz's eyes, the United States was hostile to the Soviet Union because Russia represented the biggest single threat to America's vision for the world. US policymakers were not only concerned with Russia as a military threat, but they were also worried that third world revolutionaries would be inspired by the alternative socioeconomic model that Russian communism provided. Horowitz also claimed that US policymakers expected their nuclear monopoly would force the Soviets to abandon hopes for a sphere of influence in Eastern Europe. American leaders therefore felt no need to accommodate Russian wishes.

Although this interpretation was similar to that of the Wisconsin scholars—for example, Horowitz also portrayed the Marshall Plan as the economic side of the Truman Doctrine, a strategy that was "perhaps the major document in America's Cold War offensive"—Horowitz's critique was more radical and speculative. For example, he argued that the United States was only too willing to offer Marshall aid to the Soviet Union if they compelled Eastern Europe to relinquish aspirations of industrialization; this was allegedly part of an imperialistic plan to maintain Eastern European nations as agricultural dependencies of the West—a goal that was obviously incompatible with Stalin's security agenda. Horowitz argued that American policymakers knew the plan would be unacceptable to the USSR but took great care to "provide the plan with a rhetoric that did not betray the more partisan intentions reflected in its structure."[34]

Horowitz's radicalism was also apparent in his claim that American military spending after 1945 was unnecessary and aggressive. He asserted that the massive program of militarization was really undertaken to boost the US economy ("as the economy began to sag the government sought a solution in additional arms spending") rather than to defeat communism. America's postwar arms boom reflected what Horowitz saw as the "over-militarization" of US policy. He argued that containment itself was "a military and not a diplomatic doctrine" that "would have justified a campaign to eliminate threats to peace all the way to Moscow." Hence *The Free World Colossus* claimed that containment was actually a strategy of constant aggression designed to prevent Soviet expansionism. America's approach, therefore, possessed imperial dimensions, for "the best defense, under a military definition of reality, is always offense." Rather than being a defensive policy of self-preservation, Horowitz believed containment was a proactive strategy to eliminate any threat to US global hegemony. The central question was this: "Where does security end short of domination of the whole earth?"[35]

Horowitz's polemic claimed that US military interventions in Guatemala, Vietnam, and Korea proved that "domination of the whole earth" was indeed the ambition of US policymakers. According to *The Free World Colossus*, the democratic will of indigenous populations counted for little. The book highlighted how the United States had armed a number of repressive dictators around the world in the name of anticommunism—a strategy Horowitz claimed was an excuse to deny poor populations the right to self-determination. The young radical saw these puppets as "guarantors of economic and social stability" who shared US policymakers' desire to preserve the status quo and protect America's procapitalist world order. Whenever these "guarantors" were unable to keep the peace, or safeguard specific businesses' interests, the United States would intervene using military force or the subtler wiles of the CIA—in other words, subversion. Horowitz implied that the CIA overthrew Iranian Prime Minister Mohammad Mossaddegh because the Iranian leader had nationalized the Anglo-American Oil Company against the wishes of the Dulles family. He also claimed that America's intervention in Guatemala was taken "in view of the Dulles brothers' interests" in the United Fruit Company, which had land expropriated by the Guatemalan government in the early 1950s. As a result, Horowitz portrayed the United States as "a worldwide policeman standing guard over vested interests."[36]

Even though the Wisconsin critique also emphasized the US commitment to protect conservative regimes (as this helped to facilitate economic expansion), the Wisconsin scholars never accused individual policymakers of deliberately subverting government policy to serve their personal interests; Williams criticized the worldviews of US statesmen, but rarely questioned their integrity. Horowitz on the other hand suggested that American officials were not afraid to pursue selfish interests—something that implied a conspiracy at the heart of government. *The Free World Colossus* also stated that the United States deliberately placed its economic self-interest above the aspirations of developing nations. Horowitz claimed that the loans advanced to South American countries during Kennedy's Alliance for Progress program perpetuated the region's financial dependency on the United States and did little to foster economic growth. Whereas the Wisconsin scholars believed that US policy was generally well intentioned (and only subverted by intellectual failures), Horowitz saw the Alliance for Progress as a sham that pretended to promote regional security and development but was actually a means of "counter-revolutionary containment" designed to stave off socialism and preserve US hegemony.[37]

It must be pointed out that while Horowitz rarely used the word "imperialism," *The Free World Colossus* still emphasized the "prodigious scale" of US "expansion" and described the techniques policymakers employed to sustain America's global power.[38] For example, foreign aid and military interventions were depicted as means by which the United States extended and consolidated its international dominance. Meanwhile, organizations such as the United Nations (which US officials allegedly manipulated by deciding which nations were able to join the General Assembly) and regional military organizations such as SEATO (which protected the status quo by guarding against communist infiltration) were also portrayed as instruments of American power. The end result was a critique of international relations that presented the United States as a thoroughly self-interested imperial hegemon.

While the Wisconsin scholars also portrayed the United States as imperial, their tone was frequently more measured. For example, LaFeber's *New Empire* and McCormick's *China Market* highlighted when American expansion was cautious, limited, and pragmatic. Horowitz, on the other hand, portrayed US foreign policy as relentlessly expansionist and self-serving. Whereas Williams and his friends believed American officials were essentially well-meaning souls who pursued imperialist wars because of their flawed worldview, Horowitz frequently argued they were motivated by personal wealth and a lust for world power. Quite clearly, therefore, the New Left radical portrayed US policy as decidedly immoral. This difference of opinion led Horowitz to construct an altogether more cynical and angry critique.

Because Williams did not apportion blame on specific individuals—rather he bemoaned a tragic mind-set that had unintentionally diverted the nation from its benevolent course—his analysis implied that the United States was indeed an exceptional nation (albeit one that had lost its way). Horowitz portrayed a very different country: a self-serving "leader of a worldwide anti-revolutionary movement" that acted purely to extend its hegemony and safeguard the personal wealth of its policymakers. Horowitz's analysis also betrayed his Marxist-Leninist leanings. He claimed that since the world's "poor were more numerous than the rich," the United States transformed itself from "a light and hope to oppressed peoples" into "one of the great and hated oppressor nations."[39] The Wisconsin scholars agreed that US foreign policy frustrated the aspirations of the developing world, but they argued that policymakers did this somewhat inadvertently, mistakenly believing that the extension of American power abroad served the general welfare.

When reviewing *The Free World Colossus* for *International Affairs*, H. G. Nicholas described its author as "polemical" and its articulation of "a grand American design for world oppression" as "rather exorbitant" and unconvincing. It is hard to disagree with Nicholas's assessment.[40] Whereas the Wisconsin scholars attempted to articulate the psychological, ideological, and economic dimensions of US imperialism, Horowitz's analysis remained at a very basic level; he simply made speculative and controversial assertions without supporting evidence. Consequently, orthodox scholars were right to dismiss *The Free World Colossus* as a mere exposé of the more unfortunate side effects of US expansion rather than a serious scholarly study. When the book tried to explain the forces that drove American imperialism, it ultimately fell short. This is because Horowitz seemed to use his book merely as a platform to criticize the policies and statesmen he found unpalatable. In many ways, therefore, his critique was hardly more sophisticated than those of the UW student radicals after the Dow protests.

Although *The Free World Colossus* set a precedent for subsequent New Left critiques by describing some of the means US policymakers used to extend American power (such as the use of foreign aid), the book left important questions unanswered. For example, Horowitz argued that American security depended on a stable pro-US capitalist world order but never really explained why. Unlike the Wisconsin scholars, who argued that US foreign policy was driven by a false conviction that new economic frontiers overseas were necessary, Horowitz failed to explain what the underlying causes of US imperialism were. Indeed, he occasionally seemed to argue that the United States was needlessly aggressive, as if the US government was only motivated by power and prestige. On the other hand, his analysis of the Alliance for Progress suggested that America's priority was to safeguard specific business interests and create favorable conditions for private investment overseas, in other words, to "forestall any radical land or tax reform aimed at US corporations abroad."[41] The problem with this assessment was that it merely scratched the surface of the forces that drove American imperialism. Were activities abroad designed to line the pockets of specific individuals or did the United States seek prosperity to fund the military and bolster its security? Unfortunately, *The Free World Colossus* did not provide a definitive answer.

Thankfully, however, more comprehensive New Left accounts of US imperialism emerged as the 1960s progressed. By the end of the decade, writers such as Kolko and Magdoff provided more scholarly and analytical interpretations. These critiques considered political, social, and economic factors before making speculative assertions, and they explored the sources of American expansion without attributing US foreign policy to the personal greed and power lust of specific policymakers. In fact, Magdoff, the former economic advisor of Henry Wallace who eventually became coeditor of *Monthly Review*, seemed determined to find statistical evidence to support his contentions. This demonstrated that not all New Left history was indignant and polemical. Magdoff and Kolko were serious scholars who went to great lengths to demonstrate the validity of their work (even if their allegiance to the radical political left was still very evident).

Furthermore, these more sophisticated New Left writers often pushed the boundaries of Marxist thought. For example, Magdoff's critique conformed to "the traditional Marxist-Leninist model in so far as he regarded imperialism as a necessary stage of capitalism," but he actually rejected "certain basic features of traditional Marxist theory"—such as the fallacy that "imperialist expansion is caused by an excessive supply of surplus capital," and that "overseas investments are sought in order to evade the law of falling rates of profit." This was a valuable development because it explained why Lenin's prediction that capitalism could not survive without colonialism proved incorrect. Magdoff concluded that the experience of colonialism had adapted "the social and economic institutions of the dependent countries to metropolitan needs"; therefore, even when direct political control had been relinquished, the colonial relationship (in economic terms) persisted "thanks to the informal economic, financial and social structures previously created."[42] This demonstrated that some New Left writers were prepared to think creatively and escape some of the Marxist parameters that restricted Horowitz and the radical students.

Kolko was another New Left scholar who attempted to study US imperialism in an analytical manner. Indeed, he bemoaned the paucity of contemporary studies that made "a serious effort to scratch beneath the ideology of US expansion to define its larger needs, imperatives, and functions as a system." Complaining that the study of US imperialism had become a "dry-as-dust topic,"

Kolko set out to provide the answers that Horowitz and the radical students had thus far failed to provide.[43] Although his books *The Politics of War* (1968) and *The Roots of American Foreign Policy* (1969) were somewhat reminiscent of *The Free World Colossus* (for example, Kolko also emphasized the self-interested aspects of American diplomacy and blamed the United States for causing the Cold War), Kolko's critique was less polemical and more nuanced. Rather than simply using imperialism as a political stick with which to beat US policymakers, Kolko was determined to explain the forces that drove American expansion. In the process he became a pioneer of Cold War revisionism alongside the likes of Williams and Gar Alperovitz.

Although Kolko emulated other New Left scholars by placing economics at the heart of his interpretation, observers like Steven Hurst have acknowledged that "no other Marxist has produced a body of work on American Cold War foreign policy that is remotely comparable in scale."[44] This is because Kolko, to an even greater extent than Magdoff, explained what he believed the needs of global capitalism were and described how the United States acted within this framework, intervening to protect and sustain the system when necessary. American foreign policy was therefore portrayed as a means by which US policymakers served the structural needs of domestic and international capitalism. In his early work, Kolko argued that the Vietnam War served these needs directly. However, he subsequently changed tack somewhat by arguing that the war in Southeast Asia was waged to prevent other nations from challenging the status quo (and potentially falling out of the capitalist orbit); therefore, the war served the needs of the US economy indirectly rather than providing immediate gains.

As an economic determinist, Kolko believed that imperialist wars like Vietnam were inevitable. However, while Kolko was a productive force determinist—that is, he believed that the capitalist class (who owned the means of production) used foreign policy as a mechanism to safeguard their wealth at home—his analysis went beyond Horowitz's tendency to point the finger at specific policymakers and criticize their role in determining specific foreign interventions. After all, Kolko's analysis of the US and global economies (which were inextricably linked) suggested that American officials had little freedom of action; they had no choice but to follow an imperialist course because the vitality of the US and global economies required it. Broader discussion of socioeconomic structures was therefore more appropriate than narrow exposés and recriminations.

Kolko's and Magdoff's emphasis on the integrated nature of global capitalism as well as the link between US prosperity and world capitalism in general became a hallmark of their critiques. They also demonstrated how the more sophisticated New Left writers adapted Marxism and economic determinism to modern realities. Magdoff, for example, stressed that US imperialism in the Cold War was more holistic than traditional colonialism (even though it was often indirect and informal). He contended that the American empire displayed "an underlying unity of the domestic economy, the foreign economic activity of industry and finance," and "the military and international diplomacy" of the US government—all of which flowed "from the normal functioning of a capitalist economy." In other words, US imperialism was a wide-ranging phenomenon that fused economic, political, and military power to secure and extend corporate profits across the world. This was allegedly driven forward by both the American government and US business interests, for the post-1945 world had witnessed "a general intertwining of trade and flag."[45]

However, although US imperialism was different from old-style colonialism, both Magdoff and Kolko did see some similarities. For example, as the United States was an industrial power, it still needed to control the supply of key raw materials. Kolko argued that the United States' determination to promote the Open Door throughout the world "functionally meant American economic predominance, often monopoly control, over many of the critical raw materials on which modern industrial power was based." Kolko believed that US policymakers "wished to see the markets and resources of the world available to all on equal terms, but most assuredly to the United States." If American policymakers wanted to establish a "Pax Americana," and an economic empire that "could exist as the pre-eminent factor in the world . . . without the formal political ties of traditional colonialism," control of raw materials was essential.[46] The radical scholars stressed that any interruption in their supply could have a catastrophic effect on the American economy and affect the ability of the US army to function.

Overall though, Magdoff's and Kolko's critiques were significant because they adapted Marxist thought to the modern international environment (even if they emphasized the centrality of raw materials and emulated the Old Left by remaining defiantly determinist). Indeed, it could be argued that Magdoff's critique brought Scott Nearing's *Dollar Diplomacy* up to date. To briefly recap, Nearing argued that US diplomacy was designed to meet the requirements of an evolving capitalist society after World War I. Magdoff performed a comparable task by considering US diplomacy during the Cold War, which heralded a new stage of capitalism: the era of an internationalized global economy. The methodology of both authors was similar. After all, both Marxists quoted a plethora of statistics from government and industry sources to support key suppositions. Furthermore, Magdoff emulated *Dollar Diplomacy* by arguing that the control of raw materials, plus the use of military force to protect overseas investments, markets, and property, was a key characteristic of American imperialism. Most interesting, however, was the way that Magdoff described the network of US financial imperialism in an analogous manner. In *Dollar Diplomacy*, Nearing described how the series of US loans extended to Europe after World War I had established "the economic structure of American imperialism."[47] Magdoff believed that the loans issued by the IMF since World War II served the same purpose. Consequently, the 1960s radical was clearly influenced by the scholarship of the Old Left.

The Trouble with Marxism

Even though Kolko and Magdoff made brave attempts to examine the structural roots of US imperialism in a changing international environment, there was one thing that, more than any other, held even the most dedicated and scholarly New Left historians back (something that imposed limits on Magdoff's critique as much as it had hindered Nearing's interpretation in the first half of the twentieth century). The problem, of course, was their adherence to economic determinism—the insistence that imperialism was an inevitable consequence of America's capitalist economy. This was the primary point of differentiation between the New Left and the Wisconsin scholars. Whereas determinists like Kolko argued that American foreign policy was based on a set of rigid definitions of what it must do to safeguard its vital national interests, Williams, LaFeber, and McCormick argued that US imperialism wasn't decided by what Americans had to do, but what they thought they must do. The difference was subtle but fundamental. The New Left argued that US foreign policy could not change without root and branch reform of America's socioeconomic structure; until that day, they believed the United States would continue to use its "vast power" to enhance "total world economic integration."[48] The Wisconsin scholars were different because they believed that imperialism could be avoided if Americans reappraised their expansionist Weltanschauung.

Horowitz, Kolko, and Magdoff demonstrated their adherence to Marxist-Leninist dogma by arguing on several occasions that imperialism was an inevitable by-product of capitalism. If the United States were not capitalist, they asserted, there would be no need for an empire. This passage from Horowitz's *Empire and Revolution* (1969), a book that made a far greater attempt to explain the origins of US imperialism than *The Free World Colossus*, was a classic case in point: "As Marx recognized, monopoly and imperialism, i.e. the concentration of power within the domestic political economy, and the expansion of capital (and its forms of domination) beyond national frontiers are inherent in the very process of capitalist development: the constantly required revolutionizing of the forces of production, the continual expansion of their base, the constant extension and internationalization of commerce, and above all, the inexorable struggle between capitalist economic units for domination and control of the expanding markets of the capitalist world." This extract laid bare Horowitz's Marxist-Leninist persuasion. Here was an economic determinist who regarded imperialism as "the phenomenon of capitalist relationships reproduced on an international scale," with the struggle for domination between nations "replacing, overlapping and intersecting" the struggle between economic classes.[49] Since Horowitz believed these were inescapable truths, the United States was following the same course that other industrialized imperial nations had taken in the past.

In a similar vein to Kolko and Magdoff, Horowitz's *Empire and Revolution* attempted to update Marx's theories and apply them to the international environment of the 1960s. The end result was a critique that promoted a Soviet definition of the world. "With the continuing expansion of the forces of production and the process of capitalist competition, the related phenomena of *monopoly* and *imperialism* eventually come to predominate within the national and world economies of the capitalist system. . . . Correctly viewed, therefore, imperialism is simply the phenomenon of capitalist relationships reproduced on an international or rather trans-national scale." Horowitz was convinced that the nature of the world economy after World War II entrenched imperialism. He claimed that US policymakers manipulated the global economy to serve American needs, since they realized that wealthy and powerful nations depended on an imperial relationship with poorer countries to sustain their economic vitality. "As long as the national economic framework remains capitalist, domestic prosperity will be dictated by the nation's place in the hierarchy of the international market; therefore imperial and national interest will appear to coincide."[50] The assertion that imperial powers perpetuated the status quo to safeguard their economic viability was central to all New Left critiques. It was also reminiscent of Nearing's work, which argued that capitalist nations would always resort to imperialism; this was "not peculiar to any nation" but corresponded "to a certain stage in the development of economic surplus."[51]

The similarity between Nearing's critique and those of the New Left scholars was to be expected. After all, the Marxist-Leninist interpretation of US imperialism was less flexible than the progressive critique. Whereas the Wisconsin scholars took from Beard what they wanted, the New Left found it hard to escape determinist logic; as a consequence, they found it difficult to see US imperialism as anything other than aggressive and relentless. Although Magdoff and Kolko moderated the Marxist view of imperialism somewhat because imperialism had survived the end of European colonialism, they still could not alter the theoretical foundation of their critique in the same way that LaFeber and McCormick were able to provide a more restrained and cautious version of Williams's *Tragedy*. Lenin's view that capitalist nations would inexorably expand and monopolize raw materials was so fundamental that the New Left considered it sacrosanct.

The following extract from Lenin's "A Caricature of Marxism and Imperialist Economism" demonstrated the kind of powerful theory that the New Left could not ignore: "In order that monopoly may be complete, competitors must be eliminated not only from the home market (the market of the given country) but also from the foreign market, from the whole world. . . . The means to this end are . . . the cornering of sources of raw materials and the buying out of all the competitors' enterprises."[52] Kolko's claim that US policymakers attempted to monopolize the control of raw materials after the fall of Nazi Germany very much belonged to this Marxist-Leninist tradition. In Kolko's eyes, this was all part of the process of capitalist development; if the United States controlled the supply and price of key raw materials, less advanced nations would ultimately become dependent on the United States. Magdoff also followed this tradition by arguing that this dependency was essential for the survival of the American economy itself, for imperialism was not "a matter of choice" for the United States. This hypothesis was so central to the Marxists' critique that they repudiated all other theories. For instance, Magdoff dismissed Hobson's theory that the domestic market could expand infinitely to absorb American surpluses as "iffy history."[53]

However, economic determinism was not the only way in which New Left critiques adhered to Marxist-Leninist dogma. New Left scholars also frequently interpreted US imperialism within the context of class struggle; therefore, they often suggested that American expansion was a conspiracy by the wealthy against the poor. Horowitz was particularly prone to this, as were the student radicals. All New Left texts bemoaned the influence of the capitalist class over US foreign policy to a certain extent—for example Kolko's penchant for productive force determinism led him to believe that foreign policy was a mechanism by which the elite safeguarded their position in society—but Horowitz's *Empire and Revolution* went further by bluntly describing American history from the nineteenth century to the Vietnam War as a conservative capitalist conspiracy. What is more, Horowitz suggested this was a globally orchestrated conspiracy that transcended national borders. As evidence for this conspiracy was obviously lacking, Horowitz's claim seemed typically speculative.

Horowitz claimed that the dominant theme of world history over the last one hundred years was the suppression of the proletariat by the wealthy; World War II was allegedly an aberration when conservative forces temporarily turned away from the suppression of the political left in order to fight the more immediate threat of Nazi Germany. Consequently, Horowitz depicted the Cold War as a return to the norm in international affairs, as the suppression of the proletariat in Greece and, more recently, Vietnam supposedly proved. The author asserted that the absence of any genuine military threat from the Soviet Union post-1945 proved that the Cold War was perceived by US policymakers as a class struggle from the start; talk of security was simply propaganda to obscure reality, namely, that the Cold War was essentially a struggle between Western capitalists and their puppet dictators against benevolent socialist revolutionaries. Horowitz argued that imperialism was the method used by conservative forces to control the poor, advance the capitalist agenda, and suppress the global left.

Although Kolko did not subscribe to this overtly conspiratorial view of US imperialism, he agreed with Horowitz that American policymakers were not always honest with the public about the goals of US foreign policy. Although Horowitz typically went further than Kolko by quoting the famous Russian revolutionary Leon Trotsky—who claimed that US imperialism was "in essence ruthlessly rude" and "predatory" but, "owing to the special conditions of American development," able to drape itself "in the toga of pacifism"—all the New Left scholars believed that American officials were disingenuous to a certain extent.[54] For example, when discussing what he called the "one-ness" of American political, security, and economic aims, Magdoff believed that US policymakers were "usually quite shy" when it came to "the unity" of security goals and economic interests.[55]

Although Williams argued that American elites favored economic expansion because they believed it would provide enough wealth for all citizens (and therefore make socioeconomic reforms that might challenge their wealth and status unnecessary), he did not portray US imperialism as a conspiracy directed by the wealthy against the poor. This is because he claimed that the majority of the American people actually wanted economic expansion, as they believed ever-expanding frontiers were the only way to prevent stagnation and economic turmoil. It was therefore a national intellectual failure that caused US imperialism—not the government deliberately hoodwinking the working classes. In addition, LaFeber's *New Empire* emphasized how US policymakers were frequently under political pressure to further American economic expansion, as this is what the public wanted. Horowitz, on the other hand, frequently claimed that US imperialism was driven forward by self-interested elites who wanted to suppress the poor and expand their personal wealth.

The difference between Horowitz's critique and that of the Wisconsin scholars was therefore pronounced. Indeed, it could be argued that even though Horowitz and New Left student antiwar protestors attempted to make a break with the past, they were actually influenced by the Old Left's Leninist theory of imperialism, which insisted that "conspiracy was a necessary ingredient to the power structure's recipe of self-preservation and acquisition."[56] Consequently, one might ask whether they actually added anything new to the historiography of US imperialism at all. Kolko also believed that US foreign policy was manipulated by self-interested corporate elites who cared little for public sentiment, but his analysis was not so crude. Although he believed that support for the Vietnam War among the corporate elite proved that American businessmen were not afraid to support unpopular wars—"at no time has the government conceded so little to democratic sentiment, pursuing as it has a policy of escalation that reveals that its policy is formulated not with an eye to democratic sanctions and compromises but rather the attainment of specific interests and goals scarcely shared by the majority of the nation"[57]—Kolko did not insist that US imperialism was a deliberate attempt to suppress the proletariat. In Kolko's eyes, the Vietnam War was simply a means for wealthy men to accumulate more wealth, protect their business interests, and keep Southeast Asia within the US capitalist orbit.

The strength of Kolko's work was his ability to accommodate his economic determinism into a coherent critique of American imperialism that examined the systemic origins of US imperialism without resorting to vague conspiracy theories. Instead, he found a more rational explanation for US expansion: he stated, quite simply, that it all came down to making money. Whereas Horowitz's interpretation seemed somewhat paranoid and cynical, Kolko argued that industrial elites expanded overseas simply because this was the best way to increase their profits. He also explored the link between government and big business and concluded that "the welfare of government and business is, in the largest sense, identical." Kolko claimed that there were numerous "examples of interlocking government-business leadership," including the fact that two-thirds of Foreign Service employees were sons of business executives or other professionals. Kolko also demonstrated a link between government, big business, and law firms, where employees would move seamlessly between the three sectors during their careers. This led him to conclude that US "foreign policy decision-makers are in reality a highly mobile sector of the American corporate structure, a group of men who frequently assume and define high level policy tasks in government . . . and then return to business."[58] This particular analysis was more reminiscent of Mills's *Power Elite* than old Marxist-Leninist clichés.

Although it followed from Kolko's analysis that "American diplomacy has traditionally been the prerogative of the rich and well placed," he did not agree with Horowitz that US imperialism was purely an attempt by conservative forces to suppress the proletariat. Instead, he blamed the functioning of capitalism itself, which consolidated the influence of corporations in American society organically. For example, Kolko explained that the potential leaders of any socialist revolution had been integrated into the existing capitalist system because the best minds attracted the highest wages. This was not because of any conspiracy or grand design; it was simply the natural functioning of the free market. Overall, Kolko believed that US capitalism had created an economic class that was both "the arbiter and beneficiary of the existing structure of American society" and (via an integrated world economy and military power) "the world."[59] This elite class was self-regulating and almost impervious to change for it was institutionalized in America's socioeconomic structure. As Kolko integrated fresh ideas like this into his critique, he made a greater contribution to the historiography of US imperialism than Horowitz and groups such as SDS, who for the most part simply reiterated old Marxist-Leninist axioms that existed long before the 1960s.

Unfortunately, however, for all the extra sophistication of Kolko and Magdoff's work, their critiques were undermined by the fact that they were still based on determinist logic. Therefore, while one could argue that they made a greater contribution to the historiography of American empire, it is also possible to claim that all New Left critiques were equally problematic on a theoretical level; they were, after all, essentially limited by their insistence that imperialism was an inequitable consequence of capitalism. The numerous problems with economic determinism have been well documented by several historians. For example, Wolfgang Mommsen's *Theories of Imperialism* (1977), which dissected various critiques of empire by international scholars from Marx to Mao, contained a detailed repudiation of studies that attributed complex historical events to single theories. More recently, Steven Hurst's *Cold War US Foreign Policy: Key Perspectives* (2005) revisited the topic. Hurst's book, which contained an insightful dissection of Kolko's analysis, reiterated the fundamental truism that "one cannot deduce a country's foreign policy simply from the fact that it is capitalist."[60]

While Hurst praised Kolko for making a serious attempt to unearth the roots of American foreign policy, he found it hard to accept the New Left scholar's insistence that "the structural needs of US capitalism required continued expansion and access to the rest of the world to survive and prosper." This is because Kolko's contention was essentially a leap of faith: it is impossible to demonstrate unequivocally that capitalism actually needs to expand (and that US diplomacy was determined by this fact). Furthermore, Hurst was unconvinced by the logic, implicit in Kolko's analysis, that economics was autonomous. Productive forces, for example, do not determine social relations; therefore, the argument that a country's "superstructure" is entirely shaped by economic factors was erroneous.[61] Hurst also pointed out that while the modes of production basically took the same form in every capitalist nation, different capitalist countries pursued different foreign policies. Therefore the idea that foreign policy was determined purely by a nation's economic system was clearly flawed. Hurst believed determinists were wrong because capitalist superstructures were also shaped by a country's particular culture, politics, and ideology (it was not simply a matter of economics). Furthermore, foreign policy was also driven by the psychology of individual policymakers (their ambitions, fears, and worldviews).

Wolfgang Mommsen reached similar conclusions about economic determinism during the 1970s. Assessing New Left scholarship within the broader context of the international historiography of imperialism, he claimed there was "no foundation" in the old Marxist theory that "expansionist opportunities are necessary to the preservation of capitalism." Instead he argued that "historical analysis shows us that imperialist expansion in the nineteenth and twentieth centuries was not a necessary condition of the development of imperialism," it merely "hastened its growth." He also rejected the New Left's assertion that imperialism was caused by elites desperately clinging on to their social status. Although he conceded that imperialism was "promoted" by social processes within industrialized nations, he denied that elites actually "caused" expansion. This is because "the interplay of interests that contributed to imperialist policy was highly complex and could at no time be clearly associated with particular social groups."[62]

In effect, Mommsen depicted industrialized societies as diverse melting pots; different industries and different corporations often had contrasting goals and sought to influence government policy in contrasting ways. Consequently, the New Left's conception of a united capitalist class manipulating foreign policy to deliberately foil the aspirations of the proletariat was farfetched. Indeed, in a similar manner to Hurst, Mommsen also highlighted that "the imperialist expansion of the western industrial powers over the globe was by no means a unilinear process"; Marxist determinists were therefore wrong to apply universal laws to every single capitalist country. Mommsen also denied that there was anything inevitable about capitalist nations (by their very nature) becoming aggressive and expansionist. Rather than attributing imperialism to the structural needs of industrialized economies, Mommsen believed that the historical phenomenon of imperialism was simply "the overflowing energy of European societies in the economic, military and political fields: it was not necessarily inherent in their socio-economic systems."[63]

The problem for New Left scholars like Kolko and Magdoff, historians who wanted to present a scholarly case rather than just score political points, was that hard evidence supporting their radical perspective was scant. *The Politics of War* occasionally produced statistics to support Kolko's contentions—the book specifically referred to a document titled "the Petroleum Policy of the United States," which allegedly illustrated "the specific nature of American War aims" in World War II (aims that policymakers "labeled internationalist" but really "revealed a classic pursuit of national self-interest")—but this was an isolated case.[64] After all, how was it even possible to find evidence that imperialism was an inevitable consequence of American capitalism? The New Left scholar who searched hardest for this elusive proof was Magdoff, who presented an abundance of statistics to test "the almost universal assumption that [US] foreign economic activities are small, even insignificant."[65] This was a response to contemporary critics who, like Mommsen and Hurst, highlighted that exports were just 1 percent of America's gross domestic product from 1945 to 1974. The critics also emphasized that only about 5 percent of total US investment during this period was foreign.

Magdoff argued that the size of overseas operations was misleading, for when added to the export of goods, "the cumulative effect of the annual flow of investment results in a US economic involvement which [was] much greater." Using a meticulous approach that delved into the structure of American corporations and their foreign enterprises, Magdoff's *Age of Imperialism* stated that the amount of overseas investments might seem "relatively small" compared with the overall turnover of multinational corporations, but the returns from them were essential if companies were to make an overall profit. Magdoff claimed that "if one speaks of the relatively small amount of investments flowing abroad each year, one misses the full meaning of the accumulated impact of such investment activity."[66]

Magdoff also contended that overseas investments had become self-perpetuating, for once profits had been made from foreign activities, this money was then reinvested abroad—thus creating an ever-growing cycle of dependence on overseas projects. After looking at actual statistics of US economic activity, including the pattern of export trade, dollar holdings by foreign countries, the number of American banks abroad, the number of subsidiary corporations in international banking, the US share of stocks held in foreign countries, manufacturing sales abroad, and US imports of raw materials, *The Age of Imperialism* proclaimed a "close parallel between aggressive United States foreign policy aimed at controlling as much of the world as possible, and, on the other hand, an energetic international expansionist policy of US business." Magdoff asserted that it would be impossible for the United States to return to isolationism, for "the spread of US international economic affairs has to be introduced as an important consideration in any hypothesis attempting to explain what goes on in the world today."[67]

Because he provided statistical evidence to support his case, Magdoff's analysis seemed more substantial than that of his New Left contemporaries. For example, he cited data calculated by the US Census Bureau and the US Department of Interior to verify his assertion that America had become a net importer of minerals and raw materials post-1945. This added substance to his claim that American control over the sources of these materials was a priority for US policymakers. Furthermore, he quoted the United Nations' *Statistical Yearbook* to buttress his argument that underdeveloped countries had become totally dependent on the production of raw materials. Cumulatively, these statistics made his allegation that America had distorted the development of poorer nations more convincing. By exploring the role played by the IMF, the International Bank for Reconstruction and Development, and the inner workings of the World Bank, Magdoff's *Age of Imperialism* gave readers an insight into how America's alleged economic empire actually functioned—not just in theory, but in practice.

Yet even if one is impressed with Magdoff's analysis, which was meticulously researched and superficially persuasive, his overall thesis was still undermined by its Marxist determinist limitations. For example, Mommsen argued that economic determinism was simply not valuable "as a scholarly method of analyzing complex imperial processes" because it ignored "the political circumstances in which relations between unequally developed countries" developed. It also neglected the important role played "by impulses from the periphery." Furthermore, the specific economic evidence presented by the New Left and the other neo-Marxists did not convince Mommsen. For example, he claimed that the export sectors of the metropolitan economies were "not weighty enough" to support capitalism, nor were colonial markets "large enough." It was a similar story when it came to investments. Mommsen argued that foreign investments were usually profits from operations that were already located abroad; therefore, they were simply "reinvestments of funds accruing" overseas and so had "little to do with the developments of profit rates on the home market." This was certainly not enough to "significantly alleviate the falling trend in profit rates at home."[68]

Arguably the most convincing aspect of Magdoff and Kolko's interpretation was their contention that imperialism derived from market forces and the natural functioning of capitalism; this was an improvement from Horowitz's tendency to make speculative statements that suggested unlikely conspiracies. However, even the suggestion that capitalism *was* imperialism (in other words, Kolko's implication that the natural functioning of international markets was in itself imperial because it exploited developing nations) hinted at flaws in the Marxist determinist critique. As Mommsen pointed out, this neo-Marxist perspective was initially promoted by Stalin when his prediction that capitalism would die after World War II failed to materialize. Until this point, Stalin had been convinced that capitalism could not exist without colonialism; therefore, he expected the era of capitalism to end when European empires were forced to relinquish their colonies. When the Western powers recovered economically after World War II, Stalin took the expedient decision to shift his definition of capitalism so that imperialism and capitalism were portrayed as one and the same thing. It could be argued, therefore, that the neo-Marxist position was a somewhat artificial and rather convenient perspective. Mommsen certainly believed it was useful for "ideological purposes" only (rather than possessing any analytical value). Moreover, one must ask whether, if imperialism was as malevolent and immoral as the neo-Marxists portrayed, it was appropriate to depict imperialism as the mere functioning of capitalism. Surely the term "imperialism" implied something more deliberate and sinister than simply the organic functioning of international markets?[69]

The New Left Critiqued

Even though New Left scholars often provided highly detailed and, in the case of Magdoff, statistically bolstered arguments, their main problem was their adherence to determinist logic. Consequently, even though New Left critiques offered a valuable contrast to the Wisconsin interpretation, they ultimately failed to convince orthodox critics that their thesis was valid. For example, Robert James Maddox, a onetime student of Williams at UW who had accused the Wisconsin scholars of "proof by lack of evidence," made a similar charge against David Horowitz, labeling *The Free World Colossus* a "polemic with footnotes."[70] Meanwhile, Robert Tucker failed to see how the economic determinism of Kolko and Magdoff could possibly add up; he could see why American corporations needed foreign investments, but he did not believe that the United States was dependent on foreign raw materials other than oil.

Tucker also criticized the New Left scholars for failing to appreciate why it was necessary for America to stand and fight in Vietnam. His explanation lay in the dynamics of imperial systems, which indicated that a defeat in one sphere of influence threatened the security of other spheres. Tucker's *Nation or Empire?* (1968) claimed there was actually a "measure of truth" in the argument that "national security may come to depend upon imperial security. . . . The protection of conventional, yet vital, national interests may come to depend upon the protection of imperial interests."[71] This analysis demonstrated one of the central problems of New Left critiques: writers such as Horowitz and Kolko were always quick to criticize the United States for sustaining its empire and refusing to tolerate revolutions, but if the United States had to protect its imperial interests because capitalism required foreign markets to survive, what other choice did US policymakers have?

Of all the New Left scholars, only Kolko seemed to appreciate this apparent contradiction (he stressed that given the needs of the US economy, "American foreign policy could hardly have been different").[72] This represented something of a saving grace in Kolko's eyes; US imperialism might have been self-interested, but policymakers were simply doing what needed to be done. Magdoff, on the other hand, was not as sympathetic. Although he argued that imperialism was a natural by-product of international capitalism, he refused to exonerate American politicians from moral culpability. The United States' control of raw materials might have been designed to eliminate risk rather than satisfy "the malice of businessmen," but this did not excuse the United States for provoking wars and suppressing the development of poor countries.[73] Unfortunately though, Magdoff did not follow his logic to its natural conclusion: if the United States economy required an empire to sustain its prosperity, American policymakers clearly had no alternative. This contradiction was particularly unfortunate in Magdoff's case, as he admitted the global economy would have been destabilized if the United States abandoned its current course.

However, although it is easy to dissect New Left critiques and highlight their inadequacies, it would be harsh to concentrate purely on their weaknesses. It is important to remember that Cold War revisionism in general was, in the words of Steven Hurst, "the first serious attempt to illuminate the underlying sources of US foreign policy." This was an improvement from the "naivety and simplicity" of traditional orthodox perspectives that offered "a celebratory, even triumphalist interpretation of American foreign policy." Furthermore, New Left critiques did successfully demonstrate that economic factors were indeed significant; as Hurst highlighted, it is harder to argue that economics plays no role whatsoever in US foreign policy than it is to assert that economics determines everything. Likewise, there can be no denying that "big business *is* the most powerful interest group" in the United States; to deny that economic factors played a significant role would be churlish.[74]

New Left critiques, then, made some valuable observations. They were right to assert that capitalist elites controlled the US economy, because corporate leaders clearly controlled wages and production. They were also right to stress that the influence of Washington policymakers was somewhat limited. Politicians needed the support of big business and a healthy economy to get reelected; consequently, they did not have the freedom of action they may have wanted. Furthermore, New Left intellectuals like Kolko made a contribution to the historiography of US imperialism by "drawing attention to the importance of long-term structural elements" when analyzing American foreign policy.[75] Where the New Left went wrong was in overemphasizing the significance of economics while excluding all other factors. Although it cannot be ignored that the United States has a capitalist economy (which has become integrated with the global economy over time), this fact has not necessarily determined the entire course of American foreign policy. Yes, the US government has a responsibility to promote economic vitality (and they have to be aware of the overseas operations of US corporations), but they also have to weigh up political scenarios and the contrasting (and often conflicting) interests of different business groups and various lobbyists; US officials are not simply drones mechanically serving the needs of a monolithic capitalist juggernaut.

Consequently, for all of Kolko's research on the structural roots of American foreign policy, and for all the statistical evidence presented by Magdoff, New Left critiques failed to surpass the Wisconsin interpretation as the most valuable and illuminating critique of US imperialism during the Vietnam War. Although writers like Magdoff attempted to demonstrate the validity of their critique by unearthing what they considered to be hard evidence (whereas Williams's *Tragedy* read like a work of intellectual history with few footnotes), the New Left scholars essentially produced a narrow thesis that simply masqueraded as something more complex owing to the plethora of supporting arguments and statistics. Therefore, even the most nuanced New Left critiques were only superficially more sophisticated, as they were confined by the same Marxist-Leninist determinism that had also restricted the radical students. The

Wisconsin scholars, on the other hand, were prepared to embrace more than economic factors. Because Williams and his friends also embraced the psychological, cultural, and ideological dimensions of US imperialism, their interpretation was more holistic.

There was one area, however, where New Left critiques surpassed the Wisconsin interpretation. While it is debatable whether economic relations between unequally developed countries should be called "imperialist" simply because they conformed to the rules of the capitalist international marketplace, the New Left scholars were better at elucidating how the American empire actually functioned. Williams predominantly provided a psychological analysis of US economic expansion; he did not examine the specific economic apparatus that held the empire together sufficiently enough. For example, *Contours* provided insights into the workings of international capitalism and bemoaned the intrusive role of corporations in American life, but the book did not explain how devices such as foreign aid provided US imperialism with a structure. New Left scholars, by contrast, were determined to do this. In fact, the statistical approach of scholars like Magdoff was well suited to this purpose.

Magdoff's *Age of Imperialism* was arguably the best elucidation of the methods used to solidify the United States' economic empire. For example, the book explained how developing nations were integrated into the world marketplace as "reliable and continuous suppliers of their natural resources"; thus, they became "feeder states," whose only purpose was to provide America (and her strategic partners) with essential raw materials. Magdoff argued that the United States deliberately prevented these nations from escaping this role, since their economic development beyond this stage would upset the delicate balance of the world economy. Fortunately for US policymakers, however, the natural functioning of capitalism prevented developing nations from becoming economic rivals to the United States. This was because "integration into the world capitalist markets" had "uniform effects on the supplying countries" in three different ways: "(1) they depart from, or never enter the paths of development that require independence and self-reliance; (2) they lose their economic self-sufficiency and become dependent on exports for their economic viability; (3) their industrial structure becomes adapted to the needs of supplying specialized exports at prices acceptable to the buyers, reducing thereby such flexibility of productive resources as is needed for a diversified and growing economic productivity." Magdoff therefore argued that once a developing country was integrated into the world capitalist economy as a feeder state, it remained so indefinitely. He claimed this was a classic characteristic of imperialism, for although developing countries were not occupied colonies in the traditional sense, they were still exploited to serve the needs of a greater power; the prime example of this was the economic relationship between the United States and Latin America. Magdoff claimed that "despite industrialization efforts and two World Wars, well over 90 percent of most countries' total exports consisted of agricultural and mineral products."[76] This allegedly provided evidence that global capitalism was not always equitable and benevolent.

Magdoff argued that the "extreme dependence" of developing nations on the export of raw materials also perpetuated the imperial relationship in another way: because poor nations were at the mercy of international prices (which America could manipulate) they frequently needed to borrow money to survive. Because "debt engenders increasing debt," and "the servicing of the debt adds additional balance of payment difficulties," Magdoff claimed this created a cycle of dependency; consequently, feeder nations became entwined in a complex financial world that not only forced them to borrow increasing amounts of financial aid but also prevented the level of economic development required to break the cycle of debt. This is why Magdoff concluded that America's imperial system was caused by the natural functioning of the capitalist system. "The chains of dependence may be manipulated by the political, financial, and military arms of the centers of empire, . . . but the material basis of dependence is an industrial and financial structure which through the so-called normal operations of the market-place reproduces the conditions of economic dependence."[77]

Unlike developed countries that had more flexible economies, Magdoff argued that developing countries had no option but to borrow increasing amounts from US-sponsored financial organizations during times of economic crisis. He claimed the market fluctuations that affected the price of raw materials exacerbated the balance of payments deficits that afflicted poor nations, thus forcing them to borrow greater and greater amounts. This made the need for future loans inevitable, since revenue from exports was frequently used to service rising interest charges rather than reducing the overall level of debt. Meanwhile, underdeveloped countries never had the funds to develop and diversify their economies, a fact that rendered them permanent "satellite nations" or "periphery countries."[78]

Horowitz's *Empire and Revolution* reached similar conclusions to Magdoff's *Age of Imperialism*, although Horowitz's language was typically more extreme; for example, he provided a stinging condemnation of capitalist imperialism, which he described as "parasitic." Like his New Left contemporaries, Horowitz's main gripe was the United States' failure to allow poorer nations to develop. "The monopolistic combines of the metropolitan countries block the formation of domestic industries in the satellite countries which are vital for economic advance but competitive with their own operations; they secure the exploitation of natural forces for raw material export rather than for internal development; they pump out scarce capital not only via retained profits but also through discriminating financial arrangements and the manipulation of commodity markets." Horowitz also believed that the natural functioning of capitalism was responsible for a cycle of imperialism and dependency. He claimed that the dominance of the imperial center was backed up by financial regulations and tariffs that served the interests of rich nations and pumped wealth away from the poor—thus leaving little or no funds for satellites' social and economic development. Horowitz argued that foreign aid programs, which he described as "a primary mode of modern imperialist penetration," solidified this pattern of exploitation. Far from helping the recipients, *Empire and Revolution* stated that foreign aid simply guaranteed conditions for further foreign private investment and forced poor nations to buy goods from donor countries. As a result, financial aid did nothing to help Third World development and actually hindered the chances of natural self-sustaining economic growth. Instead Horowitz claimed that "hybrid" or "mutant" economies emerged in underdeveloped countries—economies that could not break out of an economic "cul-de-sac" of dependency on the West.[79]

Kolko also believed that foreign aid was manipulated to tie underdeveloped nations to the American empire. He claimed that the Export-Import Bank did little to help the development of poor countries, since servicing payments wiped out "the advantages of loans to the developing nations." Meanwhile, he argued that the United States only provided loans "to build the internal infrastructure" that was "a vital prerequisite to the development of resources" required by US private investments. Kolko also argued that loans were used as leverage to secure future raw materials, since developing nations were forced to export these goods to the United States in order to pay back their loans in dollars. Consequently, he concluded that loans were "a species of imperialism" designed to help US businesses penetrate the developing world.[80]

However, although Kolko and Horowitz also blamed the rules of global finance and the international marketplace for US imperialism, it was Magdoff who provided the greatest insight into financial aid. He claimed these programs served five purposes: (1) to spread US military and political influence, (2) to enforce the Open Door, (3) to ensure that poor countries develop along pro-American capitalist lines, (4) to create trade and investment opportunities for US businessmen, and (5) to make underdeveloped nations dependent on American capital. In Magdoff's eyes, foreign aid was therefore designed to extend and solidify America's position as the leader of the imperial capitalist system; it had very little to do with genuine humanitarian goodwill. The author supported this supposition by highlighting that only 30 percent of US foreign aid went to the poorest 70 percent of the world's population, whereas countries like Britain and Japan (nations he depicted as senior partners in the imperialist network) received more than twice as much. Magdoff also quoted figures from the US Agency of International Development to demonstrate that America spent more on military aid than initiatives designed to promote Third World development. The inference was that US policymakers were far more interested in preserving American power than helping the world's poor.

Magdoff concluded that the United States used foreign aid "as a weapon" to obtain treaties that protected American investments abroad and to prohibit the nationalization of industries in those countries. He also claimed that the World Bank would only provide loans to poor nations if they followed America's model for economic development. Under the auspices of the United States, the World Bank would keep the recipients of loans on a tight leash, even to the extent that they would need permission before appointing officials to the utilities sector. Once again, Magdoff claimed that the United States' prime motivation was not the development of Third World countries but the preservation of American power and the creation of a helpful environment for US investment, or in other words, "an unabashed conduit for the movement of private capital."[81]

Magdoff believed that the complex imperial web of foreign aid and loans, bolstered by US military and political influence, made it virtually impossible for underdeveloped nations to escape what he described as the impoverished periphery of America's economic empire. The economic ties were apparently so hard to cut because they were sustained by the natural functioning of the international marketplace—the only way out was to fight bloody nationalist wars of revolution and liberation. However, because these developing nations played an important role in the imperial network, and the United States and its Western partners were dependent on the raw materials they provided, American policymakers were determined to keep these feeder nations/satellites/hybrid economies (whatever one wants to call them) within the pro-US global capitalist orbit. Imperialist wars were therefore inevitable whenever a developing nation attempted to establish its independence.

The problem, as Magdoff and the New Left saw it, was the symbiotic relationship that emerged between the imperial core and the periphery. America's economy needed essential raw materials as much as poor nations needed to export them. However, Kolko went one step further by arguing that "the nations of the third world may be poor, but in the last analysis the industrial world needs their resources more than these nations need the west"—especially as underdeveloped populations were accustomed to poverty and subsistence living standards. He argued, then, that in the event of "a total rupture between the industrial and supplier nations . . . it is the industrial world that proportionately will suffer the most."[82] Kolko believed this was why imperialism was necessary for American prosperity; the United States had to maintain existing economic arrangements and deny poor countries the opportunity of development in order to sustain its own economic vitality.

Although one might disagree with the New Left scholars' ultimate conclusions, and question whether the inequitable economic relationship between the United States and the developing world constituted imperialism, at least their observations about foreign aid (and the symbiotic relationship between different countries within the capitalist orbit) provided an insight into the economic power enjoyed by the United States (and the advantages accrued by US corporations from the natural functioning of the marketplace). In this regard they provided a more comprehensive insight into the workings, if not the origins, of US imperialism than the Wisconsin scholars. What is more, despite the polemical language of scholars like Horowitz, New Left scholars also provided firmer definitions of what they meant by the word "imperialism." Horowitz might have seemed overly eager to use the word because it was an expedient political stick with which to beat US policymakers, but at least he appreciated the need to define the term; he described it as "capitalism which has burst the boundaries of the nation-state."[83]

Horowitz also explained the difference between "classic imperialism" and modern "economic empire" more precisely. He described the former as a type of colonialism whereby "investment was largely in extractive industries, . . . indigenous manufacturing industry was suppressed, . . . while direct control of the state was used to enforce this basic pattern." On the other hand, America's economic empire relied on a "national bourgeoisie . . . to mediate with the local environment and the national state over which the metropolitan power no longer exerts control." This analysis provided a helpful insight into the functioning of the American empire, although *Empire and Revolution* reached the familiar conclusion that "the conflict between the policies of these monopolistic international firms and the requirements of national development" remained "as intense and unresolvable as before."[84]

Overall, however, the weaknesses of New Left critiques outnumbered their strengths. This explains why even fellow Cold War revisionists often disagreed with the New Left's interpretation. A prominent example was Gar Alperovitz, who shunned determinism and dismissed mechanistic theories that claimed US expansion was either inevitable or planned with diabolical foresight. Instead, Alperovitz argued that political factors were ascendant in America's Cold War strategy; he explained that American ideological beliefs forced US policymakers to support right-wing dictators in order to appear tough on communism. Alperovitz claimed that US imperialism was actually a "patterned reflex" that stemmed from America's "democratic political culture" and her ideological legacy. Since the public expected their leaders to confront communism wherever it arose, Vietnam was nothing more than "an application of established policy" rather than part of a grand plan to exert hegemony over the world.[85]

It was perhaps telling that Alperovitz dismissed the New Left's determinism while agreeing with Williams that US policymakers' commitment to the Open Door eventually created imperial policies: "Over time, these quite specific policies were transformed from an economic preference into a diplomatic principle, and acting upon it through direct or indirect intervention to make other nations conform to its biases, the United States became a subtly imperialist power. Not a colonial power, but what is sometimes called 'indirect' or 'neo-imperialist'—a nation which, for reasons it thought good, tried to shape the future of other nations and thereby establish an 'informal,' but powerful, empire of client states that were dependable and controllable."[86] Alperovitz also agreed with Williams that US policymakers' assumption that socialist governments threatened domestic prosperity (because they restricted free trade) played a key role in their decision to pursue an imperialist course during the Cold War. Like the Wisconsin scholars, he argued that the US government saw leftist revolutions as a threat to world peace and economic stability. The New Left intellectuals agreed with this assessment, but they did not focus on the assumptions of policymakers. Instead they argued that indigenous revolutions threatened the US economy regardless of what policymakers thought. After all, they believed that capitalism actually required imperialism to survive; it was not a matter of perception, it was an inescapable historical reality.

Because it is impossible to accept New Left critiques unless one is an economic determinist oneself, historiographers have generally been kinder to the Wisconsin interpretation of US imperialism. It did, after all, require less of a leap of faith. Although the Wisconsin scholars believed economic factors were paramount, their emphasis on psychology and their acceptance that US expansion was also constrained by circumstance and political factors left more room for debate and careful consideration. For example, although Lloyd Gardner's *Architects of Illusion: Men and Ideas in American Foreign Policy, 1941–1949* (1970) stressed that erroneous assumptions were the root cause of US imperialism, the book also claimed that policymakers had to exaggerate the communist threat in order to win political support for expansionist policies; Gardner argued that US policymakers created a "holy pretense" in order to combat the left within America itself. The "illusions" to which Gardner referred in the title of his book therefore had a double meaning: on the one hand, "illusions" could be interpreted as "false assumptions" (i.e., policymakers' mistaken belief that expansion was necessary), but on the other hand, "illusions" could also mean "propaganda" that served a political purpose by masking the real intentions of US diplomacy.[87]

The problem with the New Left's determinist interpretation, of course, was its lack of flexibility. It simply stated alleged historical truths—which readers were expected to accept uncritically—and then contextualized US foreign policy (and world events) within a predetermined framework. Methodically this was profoundly unsound; instead of analyzing events and then reaching conclusions based on the evidence, economic determinists worked backward (establishing the rule and then finding the facts to fit their preconceived ideas). As numerous critics, including Mommsen and Hurst, have pointed out, economic determinism also diminishes the role of the historian. After all, what is there for historians to unearth and ponder if complex events can be explained by a single unifying theory?

This is why, although Kolko and Magoff's attempt to explain expansion as a product of internal structures within the United States was valuable, the Wisconsin critique did more to expand the debate on American imperialism. One might not be enamored with Williams's approach (with its ambiguities and false continuities), but books like *Tragedy* and LaFeber's *New Empire* offered altogether more holistic interpretations—and because they did not attribute all American history to single factors, and instead emphasized the psychology of US policymakers, orthodox scholars were ultimately more prepared to engage with their thesis. For example, Robert Tucker, whose *Nation or Empire?* was arguably the most balanced assessment of Cold War revisionism, tacitly praised Williams's work by agreeing that the best chance for world peace lay in the United States' abandonment of "the conviction that America can only regenerate herself by regenerating the world."[88]

The fact that Tucker was prepared to reiterate one of *Tragedy*'s central assertions demonstrates the respect many orthodox scholars eventually developed for Williams's work. It is hard to imagine the New Left neo-Marxists, with their devotion to economic determinism, being treated similarly. The New Left were far too radical for liberal sensibilities, and as far as many New Left dissidents were concerned, they were happy being intellectual pariahs: it heightened their sense of individuality, nourished their confrontational outlook, and reaffirmed their belief in the bankruptcy of liberal intellectual thought. While the New Left thrived on confrontation, the Wisconsin scholars were committed to intellectual enlightenment. This meant engaging with orthodox contemporaries and trying to convince them that intellectual failures were leading the nation astray.

Conclusion

When Williams composed his critique of American development—an interpretation that emphasized economic expansion and classified this economic aggrandizement as imperialism—orthodox contemporaries regarded his work as non-history because he did not comply with conventions of accepted discourse. The Wisconsin scholar used few footnotes; he sympathized with the Soviet Union; he identified broad trends and contextualized events to fit his framework; most significantly, however, he assaulted conventional wisdom concerning US imperialism. When the Cold War consensus froze out dissenting perspectives, orthodox scholars told "the story of America's rise to power the way Americans themselves preferred to tell it."[1] The imperial turn of the late nineteenth century was portrayed as an aberration, an accident of history, or reframed as a benevolent experiment. By stressing the self-interested dimensions of US expansion, and emphasizing the less savory consequences of the Open Door expansion, Williams therefore became an intellectual pariah. This made him a hero in the eyes of the antiwar movement, but his perceived association with the New Left made it easier for detractors to criticize his work. Because he (superficially) seemed to have much in common with student radicals, the subtleties of his critique were frequently overlooked.

When the New Left turned their back on the study of imperialism after the Vietnam War, the vacuum was filled by neoconservatives, democratic socialists, post-revisionists, and disillusioned liberals: intellectuals whose interpretations of US foreign policy were tantamount to "orthodoxy re-stated."[2] Prevailing critiques of US imperialism therefore reverted to type by emphasizing "Soviet depravity and American virtue."[3] As a result, the New Left squandered the opportunity Vietnam gave them to change perceptions of America's global role. In the 1970s "conservatism grew . . . to an impressive intellectual and mass movement wielding millions of dollars, . . . funding numerous intellectual think tanks, media endeavors, and specific political causes." Meanwhile, because the war had been the glue that "symbiotically held [the radical left] together," the New Left "came quickly undone" and "its death came . . . less with a bang than with a whimper."[4] The Wisconsin scholars, on the other hand, remained persistent. After the fall of Saigon, they remained focused on US imperialism—convinced that American empire was an effective analytical tool to study the causes and manifestations of US foreign policy.

When the emotions aroused by the Vietnam War had subsided, and a new generation of historians reflected on what had been a heated and bitter intellectual debate, they belatedly discovered that the Wisconsin critique of US imperialism, for all its false continuities and perceived ambiguities, had significant merit. For example, orthodox scholars began to concede that economic triggers and the assumptions of US policymakers were indeed significant. Most importantly, however, they began to see the advantages of studying imperialism as a conceptual framework. For example, in her essay "The Empire Strikes Back" (1988), Emily Rosenberg described how historians once "ran for cover" by employing the term "expansion" rather than joining one of the "warring camps" who quarreled over the existence of US imperialism. By the 1980s, however, Rosenberg claimed that the concept of US imperialism had become "increasingly acceptable"; if anything, it had achieved "a nostalgic prominence once unthinkable."[5] This is because the Wisconsin scholars, by developing a critique that repudiated Marxism and crude economic determinism, demonstrated that the study of empire wasn't just for communists and those who sought to inspire revolution. In fact, once its pejorative connotations were removed, the study of imperialism had the potential to breathe new life into the field of American diplomatic history.

Although this change in attitude was not immediate, by the 1980s scholars began to use the word "imperialism" as a descriptive term, rather than a condemnatory one. For example, in an essay titled "The American Struggle with 'Imperialism': How Words Frighten" (1980), Robin Winks argued that it was time for scholars to realize that imperialism simply meant the interaction of technologically advanced nations with less developed societies.[6] Meanwhile, scholars like David Pletcher, who continued to play down the significance of US imperialism, found themselves marginalized for the first time.[7] Edward Crapol, for example, argued that Pletcher's work exhibited "a certain ambivalence and defensiveness about the undeniable success of American imperial expansion." He also claimed that Pletcher identified with the same "apologetic tone" and a "pattern of evasion" that had characterized orthodox interpretations of US foreign policy from the early Cold War period.[8] As a result, Pletcher's views were considered to be an anachronism; the debate had moved on.

Although some New Left scholars played a part in this metamorphosis—Kolko and Magdoff made brave attempts to explain how US expansion was rooted in the domestic economy—it was the Wisconsin scholars who expanded the debate on American empire the most; they moved the discussion into new territory by providing a holistic and nuanced interpretation that embraced psychological, ideological, and political factors as well as exploring economic triggers. The Wisconsin critique also considered the impact of the United States' historical experience and the unique American Weltanschauung. The New Left scholars, on the other hand, remained constrained by the limits of economic determinism—a methodology the historical profession continued to shun. Because the New Left prioritized economic factors at the expense of everything else, and contextualized US expansion as part of the broader international history of imperialism, they were unable to consider the idiosyncrasies of US foreign policy. Furthermore, because this approach derived from Marxism-Leninism, the New Left said little that was new.

Critics' propensity to bracket the Wisconsin scholars and the New Left together has disguised this crucial point. Although previous literature has eloquently explained how Williams "skewered sacred cows" and "conveyed a frisson of bravura and insolence," it has frequently failed to place the Wisconsin scholars in their true intellectual context.[9] For example, Robert Tomes described Williams as an "intellectual hero" of the New Left, and attributed the "formation of the New Left as a cohesive intellectual force" to "the first publication of *Studies on the Left*."[10] He also claimed that Williams was "most attuned to traditional Marxist methodology," and described his critique as "pseudo-Leninistic interpretation of American imperialism."[11] These statements were misleading. The relationship between Williams and the Madison editors of *Studies* on the one hand, and New Left radicals like Tom Hayden on the other, was often strained. Although Williams was transformed from "gadfly to seer" during the Vietnam War, and *Tragedy* was revered by many antiwar protestors, there were fundamental differences between the Wisconsin scholars and the Marxist New Left.[12]

Of course, to say that Williams and the New Left had nothing in common would be wrong. The New Left was inspired by *Tragedy* because the book established a new context for the study of US foreign policy. They also emulated Williams by identifying economic imperialism as a thread that ran throughout American history, regardless of personalities and politics. However, Williams substituted restrictive economic determinism for a more sophisticated critique. His theory that US imperialism was caused by a mistaken conviction that expansion was necessary read like intellectual history; it was based on the psychology of the American people and how a desire to spread liberal values had catastrophic unintended consequences. Furthermore, LaFeber and McCormick enhanced Williams's thesis and made it more specific; they identified instances when economic factors were eclipsed by political or pragmatic concerns and mollified their instructor's penchant for emotive language. Consequently, they enhanced the Wisconsin critique, amplified its most insightful aspects, and made consideration of its core thesis less contentious.

The contrast between the Wisconsin critique and the Marxist determinist alternative was a fascinating one. Indeed, it could be argued that Williams's interpretation was the antithesis of Marxism-Leninism in many ways. Not only did Williams argue that expansion would be unnecessary if the United States reformed its socioeconomic system, but his critique also implied that American policymakers themselves were Marxists of a sort—after all, they were the ones who believed that expansion was actually essential. Furthermore, the accusation that Williams was a Marxist determinist totally ignored one of the Wisconsin scholar's primary books, *The Roots of the Modern American Empire*, which diverted attention away from the industrial origins of US expansion. In fact, Williams should be credited with "disproving, or at the very least seriously challenging, Lenin's theory of imperialism by demonstrating that the roots of America's late-nineteenth century overseas empire were distinctly agrarian."[13]

The Wisconsin scholar's critique also contrasted with Marxism-Leninism because it argued that the United States was unique. Williams did not believe Americans were subject to inescapable historical truths; he refused to accept that an imperial foreign policy was inevitable simply because the United States possessed a capitalist economy. Williams expected, and demanded, better things from his country. In fact, Williams made the concept of American exceptionalism an important component of his interpretation because he himself believed the United States was exceptional. Like the visionaries of the late nineteenth century, Williams thought his country should be a shining example to mankind. This is why he believed American diplomacy was so tragic; it subverted the United States' better nature.

The difference between the Wisconsin and New Left critiques of American empire derived from two contrasting intellectual approaches. This was demonstrated by the confrontational attitude of student radicals who protested against the Vietnam War. Despite being admirers of *Tragedy* and, in the case of SDS in Madison, having the opportunity to hear Williams speak in public, the New Left ultimately rejected the Wisconsin scholars' methods and outlook. The New Left radicals were young and impatient, and the Marxist interpretation of US foreign relations suited their political leanings: their approach was simplistic, but it was easy to digest and convey. Consequently, when historians have argued that Cold War radicals followed "in Beard's footsteps" by arguing that "the exercise of American power throughout the twentieth century could not be fully understood except as a deliberate project aimed at accruing wealth, influence and military might," they were guilty of generalizing.[14] The New Left actually shunned progressivism. Although Beard has been described as "the Moses of the New Left," much of this "homage" was purely "ceremonial."[15] The Wisconsin scholars were the only real exemplars of the progressive interpretation of American diplomacy during the 1960s (and even then, they took Beard's analysis further).

Whereas New Left scholars frequently treated scholarship as "an opportunity for a political harangue," and allowed "the tone and rhetoric of the picket line" to "invade their professional work," Williams used history as "a way of learning."[16] It was therefore misleading to call him "a senior member of the New Left."[17] Furthermore, as Lloyd Gardner has argued, those who formed "the core of Wisconsin's intellectual influence . . . would not have considered themselves to be 'New Leftists,' but rather the bearers of the Wisconsin progressive tradition."[18] When the New Left became disillusioned with peaceful methods, Williams continued to advocate the benefits of educating the public and inspiring reform democratically. When the Vietnam War "moved to the periphery" of American politics (and the New Left diverged into "a variety of struggles, ranging from gay and lesbian rights, to opposition to apartheid in South Africa"), it was the Wisconsin scholars who continued to promote the study of American empire.[19] The enlightened approach to achieving domestic reform and the progressive-style interpretation of US expansion therefore went hand in hand.

Because the Wisconsin critique was more nuanced, and its authors remained dedicated to the field, it enjoyed far greater longevity than the Marxist alternative. While economic determinism remained ostracized, the Cold War postrevisionists of the 1970s assimilated important aspects of Williams's interpretation into their new perspectives of US diplomacy. John Lewis Gaddis's *The United States and the Origins of the Cold War* (1972) was one such example. Although Gaddis appealed to orthodox scholars because he blamed the Soviet Union for causing the Cold War (in many ways his work reaffirmed the "messianic rhetoric" of US global interventionism), he also accepted some of Williams's key assertions: he recognized that the USSR wanted a sphere of influence in Eastern Europe (rather than world domination) and admitted that economic factors were important to US policymakers.[20]

Although Gaddis disagreed with the Wisconsin scholars that American economic expansion was motivated by self-interest—instead he insisted that

US officials hoped the Marshall Plan would "alleviate social and economic unrest" in Europe and "lessen the danger of future war"—the integration of economic factors into his post-revisionist critique was a small victory for Williams, LaFeber, and McCormick. Gaddis also emulated Williams to a certain extent by claiming that events were always "filtered through the perceptions and preconceptions of the men who made American foreign policy."[21] He did not agree with *Tragedy* that Americans were guided by a false conviction that economic expansion was necessary (rather, Gaddis attributed US strategy to policymakers' hypotheses about Soviet intentions), but he at least acknowledged that US policymakers exacerbated international tensions by adhering to inflexible assumptions.

Despite this concession, Gaddis was often extremely critical of the Wisconsin scholars. For example, he claimed revisionists only provided a "narrow" interpretation that ignored "bureaucratic inertia" and "quirks of personality." He also argued that revisionists neglected "the profound impact of the domestic political system on the conduct of American foreign policy." Gaddis argued that US policymakers were forced to take a hard line in dealing with the Soviet Union because of public opinion; therefore, they should not be blamed for creating the Cold War. This argument, which was somewhat incongruous because Gaddis admitted that the US government itself was responsible for whipping the public into an anticommunist frenzy, was diametrically opposed to the Wisconsin critique. Gaddis's stance was also a little eccentric on occasions. For example, he blamed Stalin for the Cold War because the Russian dictator had "a larger selection of alternatives" open to him (because of "the very nature" of Soviet politics).[22] This argument was curious because it seemed to blame international tensions on the democratic nature of America's political system. Yet overall, Gaddis's interpretation emulated revisionists more than he let on. This is because he acknowledged that the United States established a global economic sphere of influence after World War II.

Although Gaddis was reluctant to use the word "imperialism," Melvyn Leffler claimed that *The United States and the Origins of the Cold War* tacitly "acknowledged" that Americans had established their "own empire." This is because Gaddis described American attempts to shape and preserve a "new economic order."[23] Meanwhile, Gaddis discussed Williams's assertion that US policymakers believed the "survival of the capitalist system . . . required the unlimited expansion of American economic influence overseas" without dismissing this argument as preposterous. Instead, Gaddis claimed revisionists were "correct in emphasizing the importance of internal constraints" on Washington officials. Therefore, he did not refute Williams's hypothesis entirely. He simply argued that his critique was defined "too narrowly."[24]

The work of another post-revisionist, Thomas Paterson, indicated the influence of the Wisconsin critique more explicitly. Paterson agreed with Williams that erroneous assumptions influenced American diplomacy to a significant degree. He also claimed it was irrelevant that overseas markets comprised only a small percentage of US trade during the 1890s; policymakers' belief in the necessity of economic expansion was the crucial thing. Because Paterson concurred that "key segments of the economy" saw foreign markets as a solution to overproduction, he interpreted America's rise to global power in the same context as the Wisconsin scholars. Although Paterson used slightly different language, arguing that statistics "tell only part of the story, . . . the rest lies in attitude," the parallels between Paterson's "attitude" and Williams's "assumptions" were obvious.[25]

Paterson's *American Foreign Policy: A History* (1977), a book co-written with J. Garry Clifford and Kenneth Hagan, often discussed the expansionist forces that guided US diplomacy. The book agreed with McCormick and LaFeber (rather than Williams) that American expansion was often spluttering and frequently held back by "self-imposed limitations" but overall concurred that US development had been shaped by imperial impulses. The book also emulated the Wisconsin scholars by claiming that the key to US expansionism lay in the nation's past. Paterson, Clifford, and Hagan argued that it was difficult to isolate the various roots of US expansion, but it was inadequate to claim that American power simply grew organically and without deliberate purpose. They also agreed with *Tragedy* that US policymakers truly believed they had a divine duty to civilize the world, but this should not prevent the United States from being portrayed as imperial because Americans showed "a self-righteous disregard for the rights and sensibilities of small nations."[26]

Although the post-revisionists denied that US policymakers put economics first all the time—Paterson, Clifford, and Hagan also argued that the United States intervened in the world wars to "implant in the Old World the best principles and goods America had to offer"—they agreed with the Wisconsin scholars that the US government was motivated by a desire to shape the peace (and thus facilitate further US economic expansion). Similarly, even though Paterson, Clifford, and Hagan claimed that Americans were sincere in their intention to spread "peace and liberty" and eradicate the "lawlessness" of Nazi Germany, they adhered to the revisionist theory that "the zealous pursuit" of US economic and political goals antagonized the Soviet Union (even if American policymakers were determined to avoid further Munichs).[27]

When it came to the Vietnam War, the post-revisionists were also influenced by revisionists like Williams. Perhaps the most striking example was Paterson,

Clifford, and Hagan's claim that revolutions in the developing world were not in the United States' national interest, because they "challenged an established order that guaranteed" the United States "both a prominent position in international relations" and "an affluent society." At first glance, this interpretation echoed both the Wisconsin scholars and the New Left—after all, Paterson argued that the United States was "deeply entwined in global economic issues" and that America's strategy was to "defend its stakes"[28]—however, the post-revisionists rejected the New Left's theories concerning the inevitability of imperialism. Therefore, the post-revisionists owed a greater debt to the Wisconsin scholars.

Interestingly, Paterson, Clifford, and Hagan used the words "empire" and "imperialism" liberally; therefore, they did not have the same concerns as LaFeber when he was writing *The New Empire* fourteen years earlier. They argued explicitly that US foreign policy "was imperialistic because . . . it prevented citizens from freely making national choices." This analysis was clearly reminiscent of *Tragedy*, which also complained that US expansion violated self-determination. Most important, this language showed that it was no longer so "radical" to write about an American "empire."[29] As the first scholars to discuss US imperialism during the Cold War, and demonstrate that the study of imperialism wasn't just for subversive intellectuals, Marxists, and unruly student radicals, the Wisconsin scholars should receive a great deal of credit.

Since the 1970s, the study of US imperialism has blossomed. It has branched off in a number of fascinating directions—all of which demonstrate that US imperialism is now a vibrant field of historical research. For example, Emily Rosenberg's *Spreading the American Dream* (1982) fused the economic line with a cultural analysis that also examined the role played by propaganda. Rosenberg defined American imperialism as "liberal-developmentalism," because it attempted to advance developing nations by promoting a culture of liberal free-market economics; this was to be accomplished by missionary activity, plus a concerted campaign to convince foreign nations that the free market was best. Rosenberg argued that policymakers justified this strategy by hiding behind "a shield of rhetoric and extolling American individualism and free enterprise."[30] They were aided in this regard by a plethora of state and nongovernmental organizations, such as relief agencies, aid programs, missionaries, and Hollywood films, all of which helped to promote the notion that US values were superior.

While it could be argued that the study of American imperialism within the United States is still afflicted by a "spatial and temporal parochialism" that has blighted American diplomatic history in general, a number of historians have tried to introduce a broader and more objective approach.[31] For example, the

Australian scholar Phillip Darby made a greater effort to compare the United States to previous empires (something the Wisconsin scholars had largely failed to do during the 1960s). Darby's *Three Faces of Imperialism* (1987) argued that Americans emulated the British by talking about distant regions in vague terms without really understanding the local populace; instead, they thought of developing nations as pawns in the game of international power politics. Although Darby believed that economic concerns were significant, he claimed that both British and US policymakers knew little about the specific financial advantages to be accrued from distant lands. Therefore, they thought broadly in terms of establishing an interlocking economic system across the globe.[32]

Like Darby, the British scholar Paul Kennedy also compared the United States to other empires. In *The Rise and Fall of the Great Powers* (1987), Kennedy conducted a broad sweep of international history that traced the evolution of power politics from the sixteenth century to the Cold War. American expansion was therefore analyzed as a recent phenomenon that followed in the footsteps of European, Japanese, and Russian imperialism. Kennedy's central assertion was that all great nations used military force to protect their economic interests overseas. However, this tendency was tempered when the costs of such imperial endeavors outweighed the potential benefits. This enabled Kennedy to speculate whether the American empire had started to decline in power.

Significantly, *The Rise and Fall of the Great Powers* also emphasized the racist dimensions of US policy. For example, Kennedy described how "it was fine to grant self-determination to the peoples of Eastern Europe because they were European and thus regarded as "civilized," yet America did not "extend the same principles to the Middle East, Africa, or Asia."[33] In the new millennium, a number of recent scholars have focused on race almost exclusively. For example, Michael Krenn's *The Color of Empire* (2006) and Paul Kramer's *The Blood of Government* (2006) claimed that late nineteenth-century US expansion was motivated by a powerful elixir of racism, Social Darwinism, and a passionate belief that it was righteous and benevolent to assimilate less developed nations. These powerful psychological triggers not only helped to propel US territorial aggrandizement, but they also provided moral justification for the murder of Native Americans, Mexicans, and Filipinos.

Because these modern critiques often ignored economics, McCormick has argued that some scholars, such as Jeremy Suri and John Cooper, have done "the old aberration theory all over again"; in other words, they argued that "whatever America's sins in the past, they were small sins," and consequently, the United States should still be perceived as "the defender of civilization."[34] Although McCormick's assessment was debatable, interpretations that portray

American expansion in a flattering light have certainly made a comeback. For example, while Darby believed the word "imperialism" was the most appropriate way to describe American foreign policy, he denied that US expansionism was malevolent. Instead, the Australian scholar asserted that "imperialism" existed "on several planes" and showed "a number of faces." For example, while American policymakers undoubtedly sought "economic benefit," their strategy was also "an expression of moral responsibility" for less developed peoples and "an exercise in power politics."[35] This critique, which essentially depicted the United States as a benevolent force, was a new approach for orthodox scholars: rather than simply denying the existence of an American empire, they attempted to rehabilitate the concept of imperialism and free the term from its pejorative connotations. Another example of this was Niall Ferguson's *Colossus* (2005), a book that celebrated the existence of an American empire because US hegemony was infinitely preferable to possible alternatives.

Despite the best efforts of conservatives like Ferguson, however, a consensus on the nature of US imperialism has yet to be reached. Walter LaFeber, for example, still believes that "economic interpretations are attacked not because critics have worked out some sophisticated analysis of causation" but because critics still automatically associate "economic causes" with "attacks on US foreign policies."[36] Therefore, while historians on the right have sung the praises of the American empire, there are still many scholars who follow the economic line established by the Wisconsin scholars. For example, Joseph Fry's essay "Phases of Empire" (2000) promoted an interpretation of late nineteenth-century US expansion that appeared to be an amalgamation of the Wisconsin scholars' work. Fry argued that Americans' "belief in the necessity of enlarging overseas markets in order to sustain national prosperity" was prominent in policymakers' minds, as was a sense of racial supremacy and Manifest Destiny. Although Fry argued that no "grand imperial design" existed (a nod to LaFeber and McCormick), he asserted that US policy in Samoa, Puerto Rico, Cuba, Hawaii, and the Philippines was "grounded solidly on an imperial ideology with roots extending deep into the American past." Fry also repeated the familiar Wisconsin assertions that "formal annexation was not required for military, economic, or cultural domination" and that US policymakers interpreted events within a specific "belief system."[37]

Another book that demonstrates the lingering influence of the Wisconsin scholars is Andrew Bacevich's *American Empire* (2002). Like Williams, Bacevich found "continuity where others see incoherence" and identified "purpose and structure" where contemporaries saw "incoherence." Although *American Empire* accused Cold War radicals of a "stigmatism" (i.e., they were "blind to inconvenient facts"), the book emulated *Tragedy* by arguing that US Cold War diplomacy required "not only containing communism but also taking active measures to open up the world politically . . . and above all, economically." Bacevich also attributed American expansion to the same psychological factors as Williams, arguing that US imperialism "derives from . . . convictions widely held by members of the political elite and the foreign policy establishment," namely, the "conviction that robust and continuing economic growth is an imperative, absolute and unconditional." *American Empire* even reiterated the familiar Beardian theory that "US foreign policy" is "above all an expression of domestically generated imperatives."[38]

Although Bacevich's interesting contribution made a number of new observations about US imperialism since the Cold War, *American Empire* essentially took Williams's perspective and applied it to the new international environment. He argued that "the end of the Cold War left US interests and the Weltanschauung informing those interests intact," therefore the administrations of George H. W. Bush and Bill Clinton relied on the same "received wisdom of American statecraft accumulated across a century or more"—namely, the perceived necessity of advancing "global openness" as "a prerequisite for prosperity at home." Bacevich also imitated *Tragedy* by claiming that expansion via openness had been the priority of US policymakers since the late nineteenth century: "The politicoeconomic concept to which the United States adheres today has not changed in a century: the familiar quest for an open world" designed to "extend and perpetuate American political, economic and cultural hegemony." As for whether this strategy was imperial, Bacevich again emulated Williams by answering in the affirmative: "The strategy of openness implies expansion," because although it is "strongly averse to acquiring territory or colonies," it still "consolidates" and "enlarges" a conception of "a global order."[39] The parallels between *American Empire*'s "openness" and *Tragedy*'s Open Door were therefore evident (although Bacevich also considered the spread of US culture, ideas, and technology).

Consequently, while the debate on US imperialism has clearly moved on since the Vietnam War, the contribution of the Wisconsin scholars was essential in establishing the critical concept of American empire as an invaluable analytical prism for the study of US diplomacy. Their critique, when considered as a whole, was an intellectual catalyst that challenged lingering parochial assumptions and made it easier for subsequent historians to assess Americans' global role with candor and accuracy. Although the paradigm of denial was always likely to unravel eventually—and had it not been for the Wisconsin scholars another group of intellectuals might have shattered orthodox allusions in an equally emphatic manner—it must be stressed that orthodox historians denied the existence of American empire for the majority of the twentieth century; the paradigm was therefore particularly resilient. Furthermore, when presented with the same opportunity as Williams, LaFeber, and McCormick to change perceptions of US imperialism, the New Left largely squandered that opportunity. As a result, the achievement of the Wisconsin scholars was a considerable one.

Whereas the role played by Marxist economic determinism in the historiography of US foreign relations was ephemeral, the Wisconsin critique had an enduring impact on the field. Although Williams was initially reviled by many orthodox scholars, his work slowly became more accepted. For example, Paul Buhle noted that by the 1970s Williams's "once-despised views reverberated through the halls of Congress." Williams's message even became associated with that well-known phrase "Vietnam Syndrome," as the American public turned against US intervention in Central America during the 1980s. Buhle believed this marked the acceptance of the Wisconsin critique into "mainstream political dialogue."[40] Although this might have overstated the case, there is little doubt that Williams, as the historical profession's "leading advocate" of America's "imperial past" during the Cold War, did more than any other scholar to close the ideological gap on the subject that was so "prevalent and virulent" during the 1960s.[41]

Before Williams arrived in Madison, "to speak of American empire was to place oneself outside the boundaries of legitimate scholarly discourse." However, "after Williams, . . . this was not at all the case." The Wisconsin scholars "transformed the terms of the discussion" and wrenched the study of imperialism "away from its previous state as a mere adjunct to the conduct of foreign policy."[42] Although this transformation took time, in the words of Crapol it was necessary for American historians to "accept the concept of empire in a nondefensive, non-condemnatory manner" before the study of US foreign relations could evolve."[43] Consequently, when Gaddis admitted in 1990 that American "expansion in the nineteenth century took place on a scale sufficient to merit the adjective 'imperial' by any standard," it was a belated triumph for the Wisconsin scholars, and a sign that the concept of American empire had not only struck back, but was here to stay.[44]

Notes

Introduction

1. Madison Students for a Democratic Society, "The War Is Coming Home," unpublished flyer, November 1968, University of Wisconsin (UW) Steenbock Library Archives, Student Unrest Subject Files.

2. "The Dow Protest: A Narrative," *Connections*, The Dow War Edition, November 1967, 5–7.

3. Carl Oglesby, "Notes on a Decade Ready for the Dustbin," *Kaleidoscope*, June 1969, 10.

4. Edward Crapol, "Coming to Terms with Empire: The Historiography of Late Nineteenth-Century American Foreign Relations," in *Paths to Power: The Historiography of American Foreign Relations to 1941*, ed. Michael J. Hogan (Cambridge: Cambridge University Press, 2000), 95, 98–99, 95, 115.

5. See Hugo DeSantis, "The Imperial Impulse and American Innocence, 1965–1990," in *American Foreign Relations: A Historiographical Review*, ed. Gerald K. Hainer and J. Samuel Walker (Westpoint, CT: Greenwood Press, 1981).

6. E-mail correspondence with Walter LaFeber, 30 October 2012.

7. Emily S. Rosenberg, "The 'Empire' Strikes Back," *Reviews in American History* 16, no. 4 (December 1988): 585.

8. Henry Luce, "The American Century," in *America in Vietnam: A Documentary History*, ed. William Appleman Williams, Thomas McCormick, Lloyd Gardner, and Walter LaFeber (New York: W. W. Norton, 1985), 22–23.

9. "President Bush Delivers Graduation Speech at West Point," Office of the Press Secretary, 1 June 2002, http://georgewbush-whitehouse.archives.gov/news/releases/2002/06/20020601-3.

10. David Cannadine, "Big Tent Historiography: Transatlantic Obstacles and Opportunities in Writing the History of Empire," *Common Knowledge* 11, no. 3 (Fall 2005): 384.

11. Samuel Flagg Bemis, *A Diplomatic History of the United States* (London: Jonathan Cape, 1936), 475; Ernest R. May, *Imperial Democracy: The Emergence of America as a Great Power* (New York: Harcourt Brace and World, 1961), 27.

12. Cannadine, "Big Tent Historiography," 383.

13. David Cannadine, *Ornamentalism: How the British Saw Their Empire* (Oxford: Oxford University Press, 2001), xiii.

14. Amy Kaplan, "'Left Alone with America': The Absence of Empire in the Study of American Culture," in *Cultures of United States Imperialism*, ed. Amy Kaplan and Donald Pease (Durham, NC: Duke University Press, 1993), 13.

15. E-mail correspondence with LaFeber.

16. Maurice Isserman and Michael Kazin, *America Divided: The Civil War of the 1960s* (Oxford: Oxford University Press, 2004), 174.

17. Crapol, "Coming to Terms with Empire," 103.

18. John Lewis Gaddis, "The Emerging Post-Revisionist Synthesis on the Origins of the Cold War," *Diplomatic History* 7, no. 3 (July 1983): 173n.

19. "Dynamic Duo," *Daily Cardinal*, opinion page, 7 March 1969, 8.

Chapter 1
The Paradigm of Denial

1. Alan Brinkley, *The End of Reform: New Deal Liberalism in Recession and War* (New York: Vintage Books, 1996), 4, 7.

2. Beard wrote a number of books and articles pleading with Franklin Roosevelt to stay out of a European war. When America finally entered World War II, Beard attacked the president for allegedly misleading the American public. The best examples of this are Charles Beard, *The Devil Theory of War: An Inquiry into the Nature of History and the Possibility of Keeping Out of the War* (New York: Vanguard Press, 1936), and Charles Beard, *President Roosevelt and the Coming of War: A Study in Appearances and Realities* (New Haven, CT: Yale University Press, 1948).

3. Brinkley, *End of Reform*, 267–68.

4. Peter Novick, *That Noble Dream: The "Objectivity Question" and the American Historical Profession* (1988; reprint, Cambridge: Cambridge University Press, 1999), 281.

5. Ibid., 304–5.

6. Robert Tomes, *Apocalypse Then: American Intellectuals and the Vietnam War* (New York: New York University Press, 1998), 54.

7. Interview with Thomas McCormick, recorded at the University of Wisconsin, 29 July 2009.

8. Irwin Unger, "The 'New Left' and American History: Some Recent Trends in United States Historiography," *American Historical Review* 72, no. 4 (July 1967): 1239.

9. Jonathan M. Wiener, "Radical Historians and the Crisis in American History, 1959–1980," *Journal of American History* 76, no. 2 (September 1989): 402.

10. E-mail correspondence with LaFeber.

11. Clyde Barrow, *More Than a Historian: The Political and Economic Thought of Charles A. Beard* (New Brunswick, NJ: Transaction Publishers, 2000), 241.

12. Novick, *That Noble Dream*, 416, 332.

13. Ellen Schrecker, *Many Are the Crimes: McCarthyism in America* (Princeton, NJ: Princeton University Press, 1988), 404.

14. Ibid., 404–5.

15. *The Rights and Responsibilities of Universities and Their Faculties: A Statement by the Association of American Universities* (Princeton, NJ: Dept. of Public Relations, Princeton University, 1953), 9–12.

16. Jonathan Bell, *The Liberal State on Trial: The Cold War and American Politics in the Truman Years* (New York: Columbia University Press, 2004), xiv, 96.

17. "The Talk of the Town," *New Yorker*, 26 February 1949.

18. Alexander Meiklejohn, "Should Communists Be Allowed to Teach?," *New York Times Magazine*, 27 March 1949, 64.

19. Broadus Mitchell, "Rutgers: A Warning—Lessons of a Lost Fight," *Nation*, 14 March 1953, 228.

20. Alan Barth, "Congress on Campus—A Warning to Universities," *Nation*, 18 April 1953, 322–24.

21. I. F. Stone, "Zero Hour in the Fight to Keep America Free," *Daily Compass*, 12 April 1950.

22. Tomes, *Apocalypse Then*, 25.

23. Mark Hamilton Lytle, *America's Uncivil Wars: The Sixties Era from Elvis to the Fall of Richard Nixon* (Oxford: Oxford University Press, 2006), 51–52.

24. Ibid., 32, 2.

25. Seymour Martin Lipset, "American Exceptionalism Reaffirmed," in *Is America Different? A New Look at American Exceptionalism*, ed. Byron E. Shafer (Oxford: Oxford University Press, 1991), 22.

26. Rosenberg, "The 'Empire' Strikes Back," 585.

27. "The Truman Doctrine Calls for Aid to Greece and Turkey to Contain Totalitarianism, 1947," in *Major Problems in American Foreign Relations*, vol. 2, *Since 1914*, ed. Thomas G. Paterson and Dennis Merrill (Boston: Houghton Mifflin, 2005), 201.

28. Cannadine, "Big Tent Historiography," 384.

29. Bemis, *Diplomatic History of the United States*, 475.

30. Ibid.

31. Julius W. Pratt, *America's Colonial Experiment: How the United States Gained, Governed, and in Part Gave Away a Colonial Empire* (New York: Prentice Hall, 1951), 3.

32. Robert Osgood, *Ideals and Self-Interest in America's Foreign Relations* (Chicago: University of Chicago Press, 1953), 27.

33. Ibid., 27, 44, 49.

34. Richard Hofstadter, "Cuba, the Philippines, and Manifest Destiny," in *The Paranoid Style in American Politics* (London: Jonathan Cape, 1966), 148.

35. Allen Swerdlowe and Amy Tankoos, "History Faculty Loses Williams," *Daily Cardinal*, 8 March 1969, 1, 5.

36. William Appleman Williams, *The Tragedy of American Diplomacy* (New York: World Publishing, 1959), 24, 26, 29.

37. Ibid., 150–51, 153.

38. Ibid., 154, 150–51.

39. A prime example of the orthodox perspective on the origins of the Cold War is Thomas A. Bailey, *America Faces Russia* (Ithaca, NY: Cornell University Press, 1950).

40. Williams, *Tragedy*, 1st ed. (1959), 208–9, 212.

41. O. T. Barck Jr., "Review of *American-Russian Relations*," *American Historical Review* 59, no. 1 (October 1953): 84.

42. Keith B. Berwick, "Review of *The Contours of American History*," *William and Mary Quarterly* 20, no. 1 (January 1963): 144.

43. See Lloyd Gardner's foreword to the 50th Anniversary Edition of Williams, *The Tragedy of American Diplomacy* (New York: W. W. Norton, 2009), ix.

44. James P. Warburg, "Review of *The Tragedy of American Diplomacy*," *Political Science Quarterly* 74, no. 2 (June 1959): 273.

45. Paul M. Buhle and Edward Rice-Maximin, *William Appleman Williams: The Tragedy of Empire* (New York: Routledge, 1995), xi.

46. Before the Vietnam War, the civil rights struggle was SDS's primary concern. The students believed that the plight of African Americans represented a larger malaise in US society.

47. Lytle, *America's Uncivil Wars*, 73.

48. Ibid., 66–67.

49. Tomes, *Apocalypse Then*, 113.

50. Lytle, *America's Uncivil Wars*, 109, 140.

51. Tomes, *Apocalypse Then*, 117, 166–67.

52. Wilfred Burchett, *Vietnam Will Win!* (New York: Monthly Review Press, 1968), xvii.

53. Buhle and Rice-Maximin, *William Appleman Williams*, 162.

54. Thomas McCormick, "What Would William Appleman Williams Think Now?," *Passport—The Official Newsletter of SHAFR* 38 (August 2007): 1.

55. Bradford Perkins, "*The Tragedy of American Diplomacy*: 25 Years After," in William Appleman Williams, *The Tragedy of American Diplomacy*, 3rd ed. (New York: W. W. Norton, 1972), 313.

56. Unger, "The 'New Left' and American History," 1246; Robert Maddox, *The New Left and the Origins of the Cold War* (Princeton, NJ: Princeton University Press, 1973), 35, 37.

57. John Higham, "Review of *The Contours of American History*," *Studies on the Left* 2, no. 1 (1961): 73.

58. See Buhle and Rice-Maximin, *William Appleman Williams*.

59. Ibid., xi.

60. Willard L. Hogeboom, "The New Left and the Revision of American History," *The History Teacher* 2, no. 1 (November 1968): 54.

61. Tomes, *Apocalypse Then*, 27; Doug Rossinow, "Restless Natives," *Reviews in American History* 25, no. 1 (1997): 170.

Chapter 2
Pushing the Boundaries

1. Tomes, *Apocalypse Then*, 37–38.

2. Barrow, *More Than a Historian*, 47.

3. Richard Hofstadter, *The Progressive Historians* (1968; reprint, London: Jonathan Cape, 1969), 42–43.

4. Novick, *That Noble Dream*, 39.

5. Ibid., 49–50.

6. Hofstadter, *Progressive Historians*, 41.

7. Novick, *That Noble Dream*, 63.

8. Robert David Johnson, *The Peace Progressives* (Cambridge, MA: Harvard University Press, 1995), 4, 88.

9. Frederick Jackson Turner, *The Frontier in American History* (1920; reprint, Mineola, NY: Dover, 2010), 1–2, 37, 30.

10. Ibid., 37–38.

11. Ibid., 246–47.

12. Ibid., 315.

13. Hofstadter, *Progressive Historians*, 120, 123.

14. Robert L. Beisner, *Twelve Against Empire* (New York: McGraw-Hill, 1968), iv, 216.

15. Ibid., iv, vii.

16. Ibid., 222.

17. Barrow, *More Than a Historian*, 5.

18. Hofstadter, *Progressive Historians*, 41.

19. Novick, *That Noble Dream*, 307, 320.

20. Richard Hofstadter argued that the Nye Committee "laid the impulse toward American intervention at the door of international bankers and munitions makers." See Hofstadter, *Progressive Historians*, 329.

21. Harry Elmer Barnes argued that President Franklin Roosevelt deliberately provoked the attack on Pearl Harbor. See *Perpetual War for Perpetual Peace: A Critical Examination of the Foreign Policy of Franklin Delano Roosevelt and Its Aftermath* (Caldwell, ID: Caxton Printers, 1953). Barnes believed that Roosevelt subsequently misled the public over the attacks to rally support for America's entry into World War II.

22. John A. Hobson, *Imperialism: A Study* (1902; reprint, Ann Arbor: University of Michigan Press, 1965), 74, 77.

23. Ibid., 61, 160.

24. Ibid., 361.

25. Ibid., 85, 368.

26. Andrew J. Bacevich, *American Empire: The Realities and Consequences of US Diplomacy* (Cambridge, MA: Harvard University Press, 2002), 31.

27. Hofstadter, *Progressive Historians*, 182, 345.

28. Charles Beard, *The Economic Basis of Politics* (1922; reprint, New York: Alfred A. Knopf, 1945), 29, 107, 108, 112–13.

29. Barrow, *More Than a Historian*, 195.

30. Charles Beard, *The Idea of National Interest: An Analytical Study in American Foreign Policy* (New York: MacMillan, 1934), 48.

31. Charles Beard and William Beard, *The American Leviathan: The Republic in the Machine Age* (New York: MacMillan, 1930), 4.

32. Beard, *Idea of National Interest*, 49.

33. Beard and Beard, *American Leviathan*, 474, 452.

34. Ibid., 474.

35. Charles Beard, *The Open Door at Home: A Trial Philosophy of National Interest* (New York: MacMillan, 1934), 38.

36. Ibid., vii.

37. Beard, *Idea of National Interest*, 103.

38. Beard, *Open Door at Home*, 38–40.

39. Ibid., 55.

40. Pratt, *America's Colonial Experiment*, 3.

41. Bemis, *Diplomatic History of the United States*, 488.

42. Beard, *Open Door at Home*, 123, 78, 80.

43. Charles Griffin, "Review of *President Roosevelt and the Coming of War*," *American Historical Review* 54, no. 2 (January 1949): 382.

44. Beard, *Idea of National Interest*, 70.

45. Charles Beard, *A Foreign Policy for America* (New York: Alfred A. Knopf, 1940), 74.

46. Beard, *Idea of National Interest*, 102, 116.

47. John Patrick Diggins, *The Rise and Fall of the American Left* (New York: W. W. Norton, 1992), 307–8.

48. William Appleman Williams, *The Contours of American History* (Chicago: Quadrangle, 1966), 490.

49. Thomas McCormick, *China Market: America's Quest for Informal Empire, 1893–1901* (1967; reprint, Chicago: Ivan R. Dee, 1990), 10.

50. Williams, *Contours*, 490.

51. Beard, *Open Door at Home*, 1, 2, 37.

52. Ibid., 1, 90–91, 68.

53. William Appleman Williams, *The Roots of the Modern American Empire* (New York: Vintage Books, 1969), 5.

54. Diggins, *Rise and Fall of the American Left*, 307.

55. Hofstadter, *Progressive Historians*, 318, 177.

56. Robert Tucker, *The Radical Left and American Foreign Policy* (Baltimore: Johns Hopkins University Press, 1971), 29, 60–61.

57. Walter LaFeber, *The New Empire: An Interpretation of American Expansion, 1860–1898* (Ithaca, NY: Cornell University Press, 1963), 1.

58. Beard and Beard, *American Leviathan*, 679–80.

59. Beard, *Foreign Policy for America*, 103.

60. Scott Nearing, draft of autobiography, quoted in John Saltmarsh, *Scott Nearing: The Making of a Homesteader* (White River Junction, VT: Chelsea Green Publishing, 1991), 178.

61. Ibid., 178.

62. Nearing quoted Hobson on many occasions. See the introduction to Scott Nearing and Joseph Freeman, *Dollar Diplomacy: A Study in American Imperialism* (1925; reprint, New York: ARNO Press, 1970), xii, xiv.

63. Scott Nearing, *The American Empire* (New York: Rand School, 1921), 24.

64. Nearing and Freeman, *Dollar Diplomacy*, 186, xxii, xiv, 246.

65. Ibid., 246.

66. Ibid., 18.

67. Saltmarsh, *Scott Nearing*, 214.

68. Ibid., 209, 205.

69. Beard, *Economic Basis of Politics*, 95.

70. Beard and Beard, *American Leviathan*, 250.

71. Beard, *Idea of National Interest*, 118.

72. Beard, *Open Door at Home*, 140.

73. Beard, *Idea of National Interest*, 405–6.

74. Beard, *Foreign Policy for America*, 40–45.

75. Chester W. Wright, "Review of *An Economic Interpretation of the Constitution of the United States*," *Journal of Political Economy* 22, no. 5 (May 1914): 494; O. G. Libby, "Review of *An Economic Interpretation of the Constitution of the United States*," *Mississippi Valley Historical Review* 1, no. 1 (June 1914): 114, 116–17.

76. Jesse S. Reeves, "Review of *The Idea of National Interest*," *The American Political Science Review* 28, no. 3 (June 1934): 506.

77. Hofstadter, *Progressive Historians*, 324, 325.

78. Campbell Craig, "The Not So Strange Career of Charles Beard," *Diplomatic History* 25, no. 2 (2001): 253.

79. Barrow, *More Than a Historian*, 240.

80. Charles Beard, *An Economic Interpretation of the Constitution of the United States* (1913; reprint, New York: MacMillan, 1948), xii, xvii.

81. Beard, *Open Door at Home*, 213.

Chapter 3
Madison as a Melting Pot

1. E-mail correspondence from LaFeber.

2. William Appleman Williams, "My Life in Madison," in *History and the New Left: Madison, Wisconsin, 1950–1970*, ed. Paul Buhle (Philadelphia: Temple University Press, 1990), 266.

3. Interview with McCormick.

4. E-mail correspondence from LaFeber.

5. David Brown, *Beyond the Frontier: The Midwestern Voice in American Historical Writing* (Chicago: University of Chicago Press, 2009), xx, 50.

6. "Why We Protest, Why You Should Join Us," unpublished student protest flyer, 1966, UW Steenbock Library Archives, Student Unrest Subject Files, Box Reference 501030.

7. Stephen Lieberstein, "Intramural Tedium," *Connections*, 17 July 1968, n.p.

8. David Maraniss, *They Marched into Sunlight: War and Peace, Vietnam and America, October 1967* (New York: Simon & Schuster, 2003), 487.

9. Paul Buhle, ed., *History and the New Left: Madison, Wisconsin, 1950–1970* (Philadelphia: Temple University Press, 1990), 33, 4–5.

10. See Paul Berman, "The Spirit of 67," *Village Voice Literary Supplement*, September 1983.

11. Interview with McCormick.

12. Buhle, *History and the New Left*, 8, 30.

13. Brown, *Beyond the Frontier*, xiv, xxi.

14. Maraniss, *They Marched into Sunlight*, 80.

15. Ibid., 98.

16. Interview of Fred Harvey Harrington by Laura Smail, recorded in 1985, University of Wisconsin Oral History Project, Transcript 135, Part 2, 123.

17. Buhle, *History and the New Left*, 8–9.

18. The University of Wisconsin *Calendar*, Academic Year 1904–05 Special Notice, 27, UW Steenbock Library Archives, Frederick Jackson Turner Papers.

19. Buhle, *History and the New Left*, 11.

20. Interview with Merle Curti and Vernon Carstensen by Barry Teicher, University of Wisconsin Oral History Project, Transcript 333, 36.

21. Buhle, *History and the New Left*, 9.

22. David P. Thelen, *Robert M. La Follette and the Insurgent Spirit* (Boston: Little, Brown and Company, 1976), vii, 128, 78.

23. Ibid., vii, 150.

24. Buhle and Rice-Maximin, *William Appleman Williams*, 100.

25. Buhle, *History and the New Left*, 1.

26. Novick, *That Noble Dream*, 346.

27. Buhle, *History and the New Left*, 3.

28. Williams, "My Life in Madison," 269.

29. Interview of Harrington by Smail, 119, 95, 118, 67.

30. Ibid., 38.

31. Ibid., 118.

32. Ibid., 99.

33. Interview of Merle Curti by Smail, recorded on 23 January 1981, UW Oral History Project, Transcript 27, 16.

34. Interview of Harrington by Smail, 45.
35. Williams, "My Life in Madison," 268.
36. Interview of Harrington by Smail, 127, 53.
37. Jami Moss, introduction to Harrington's interview by Smail, ii.
38. Maraniss, *They Marched into Sunlight*, 98.
39. Buhle, *History and the New Left*, 22.
40. Ibid., 21.
41. Maraniss, *They Marched into Sunlight*, 99.
42. Interview of Harrington by Smail, 100, 47.
43. Interview with McCormick.
44. E-mail correspondence from LaFeber.
45. Words of Thomas McCormick, cited from the introduction of Harrington's interview with Smail, ii.
46. Interview of Harrington by Smail, 6.
47. Ibid., 113, 116.
48. Interview with McCormick.
49. "Announcement of Courses 1956–58," *Bulletin of the University of Wisconsin Catalog*, August 1957, 160, UW Steenbock Library Archives, Printed History Course Materials.
50. See Williams's letter to Harrington, 7 November 1961, and Harrington's reply, 9 November 1961, William B. Hesseltine Papers, Wisconsin Historical Society, Box 24, Mss 345.
51. Interview of Harrington by Smail, 110, 107.
52. Williams, "My Life in Madison," 268.
53. Ibid., 268.
54. Buhle, *History and the New Left*, 3.
55. Williams, "My Life in Madison," 268–69.
56. Interview of Harrington by Smail, 119.
57. See Turner, *Frontier in American History*, 37.
58. Ibid., 315, 38.
59. William Appleman Williams, "The Frontier Thesis and American Foreign Policy," in *A William Appleman Williams Reader*, ed. Henry W. Berger (Chicago: Ivan R. Dee, 1992), 90–93.
60. Interview of Harrington by Smail, 70.
61. Interview with McCormick.
62. Ibid.
63. Interview of Harrington by Smail, 124.
64. Ibid., 124–25.
65. Interview with McCormick.
66. The Editors, "United States History: The Crisis of the 1890s and Developing Imperialism," *Studies on the Left* 1, no. 1 (1959): 59, 65.
67. Frederick L. Schuman, "The Dilemma of Foreign Policy," *Studies on the Left* 1, no. 1 (1959): 93, 94.

68. The Editors, "The Ultra-Right and Cold War Liberalism," *Studies on the Left* 3, no. 1 (1962): 8.

69. Kevin Mattson, "Between Despair and Hope: Revisiting Studies on the Left," in *The New Left Revisited*, ed. John McMillian and Paul Buhle (Philadelphia: Temple University Press, 2003), 29–31.

70. Interview with McCormick.

71. Robert Gabriner, "The Capital Times Confounded," *Connections*, 27 November 1967, n.p.

72. Stephen Lieberstein, "Intramural Tedium," *Connections*, 17 July 1968.

73. William Appleman Williams, "Focus: Protests and Placement," *Daily Cardinal*, 29 November 1967, 3; interview with McCormick.

Chapter 4
Williams and the Wisconsin Critique

1. Brown, *Beyond the Frontier*, 134.
2. Osgood, *Ideals and Self-Interest in America's Foreign Relations*, 363.
3. May, *Imperial Democracy*, 269.
4. Brown, *Beyond the Frontier*, 135–37.
5. Ibid., 135.
6. Williams, "My Life in Madison," 264–65, 256.
7. Ibid., 265.
8. Ibid., 265–66.
9. Ibid., 266.
10. "Speakers at Madison, Arrests in Washington," *Daily Cardinal*, 10 August 1965, 1.
11. William Appleman Williams, "Focus: Protests and Placement—Views Clarified," *Daily Cardinal*, 29 November 1967, 2.
12. David Leeman, "Prof Williams Stresses the Right to Question," *Daily Cardinal*, 25 June 1965, 1.
13. Brown, *Beyond the Frontier*, 137.
14. Interview with McCormick.
15. Williams, "My Life in Madison," 267.
16. Interview with McCormick.
17. Ibid.
18. William Appleman Williams, "American History 1865—Present," University of Wisconsin Course Literature, circa 1963, UW Steenbock Library Archives, William Appleman Williams Biographical File.
19. Ibid., no page numbers available.
20. Ibid.; interview with McCormick.
21. Interview with McCormick.
22. Interview of Harrington by Smail, 124–25.
23. Interview with McCormick.

24. Allen Swerdlowe and Amy Tankoos, "History Faculty Loses Williams," *Daily Cardinal*, 8 March 1969, 1.

25. William Appleman Williams, "A Second Look at Mr. X," in *A William Appleman Williams Reader*, ed. Henry W. Berger (Chicago: Ivan R. Dee, 1992), 69–71.

26. William Appleman Williams, "The Legend of Isolationism in the 1920s," in *A William Appleman Williams Reader*, ed. Henry W. Berger (Chicago: Ivan R. Dee, 1992), 84.

27. Williams, "The Frontier Thesis and American Foreign Policy," 89, 93.

28. Perkins, "*The Tragedy of American Diplomacy*," 1; Michael J. Hogan, "Review of *Redefining the Past: Essays in Honor of William Appleman Williams*, ed. Lloyd C. Gardner," *Journal of American History* 74, no. 3 (December 1987): 1035.

29. Maddox, *The New Left and the Origins of the Cold War*, 34, 35.

30. Williams, *Tragedy*, 1st ed., 25, 26.

31. Pratt, *America's Colonial Experiment*, 1.

32. Williams, *Tragedy*, 1st ed., 26.

33. Ibid., 29.

34. Tomes, *Apocalypse Then*, 28.

35. Williams, *Tragedy*, 1st ed., 31.

36. "Fair field and no favor" was the term used by Secretary Hay in the original Open Door Notes.

37. Williams, *Tragedy*, 1st ed., 45; William Appleman Williams, *The Tragedy of American Diplomacy*, 3rd ed. (New York: Norton, 1972), 45–46.

38. Williams, *Tragedy*, 3rd ed., 86.

39. Williams, *Tragedy*, 1st ed., 82–83.

40. Williams, *Tragedy*, 3rd ed., 167.

41. Williams, *Tragedy*, 1st ed., 143, 145.

42. Ibid., 146.

43. Interview of Harrington by Smail, 125.

44. Williams, *Tragedy*, 1st ed., 174, 175, 177.

45. Ibid., 150.

46. Williams, *Tragedy*, 3rd ed., 309–12.

47. John Vaughan, "Williams Criticises Far Eastern Policies," *Daily Cardinal*, 4 May 1966, 1.

48. Williams, *Tragedy*, 3rd ed., 293.

49. Ibid., 55, 56, 57, emphasis added.

50. Williams, *Tragedy*, 1st ed., 64.

51. Ibid., 134.

52. See Williams, *Tragedy*, 3rd ed., 293.

53. "William A. Williams Discusses His View of American Imperialism," *Daily Cardinal*, 9 April 1970, 1.

54. Williams, *Tragedy*, 3rd ed., 37.

55. Ibid., 37–38.

56. Ibid., 38.

57. Ibid., 45.

58. Williams, *Tragedy*, 1st ed., 28, 29.

59. Williams, *Tragedy*, 3rd ed., 15.

60. Tucker, *The Radical Left and American Foreign Policy*, 56, 57.

61. Williams, *Tragedy*, 1st ed., 41.

62. *Tragedy*, 3rd ed., 327.

63. Richard Melanson, "The Social and Political Thought of William Appleman Williams," *Western Political Quarterly* 31, no. 3 (September 1978): 396, 404.

64. Alfred E. Eckes Jr., "Open Door Expansion Reconsidered: The World War II Experience," *Journal of American History* 59, no. 4 (March 1973): 911, see also 923.

65. Williams, *Tragedy*, 1st ed., 35, 36.

66. J. A. Thompson, "William Appleman Williams and the American Empire," *Journal of American Studies* 7, no. 1 (April 1973): 103.

67. Perkins, "*The Tragedy of American Diplomacy*," 2.

68. Tucker, *The Radical Left and American Foreign Policy*, 81, 88.

69. John Gallagher and Ronald Robinson, "The Imperialism of Free-Trade," *Economic History Review* 6, New Series, no. 1 (1953): 1.

70. Interview with McCormick.

71. Williams, *Contours*, 63.

72. Ibid., 329.

73. Ibid., 285.

74. Ibid., 215.

75. Ibid., 319; May, *Imperial Democracy*, 27.

76. Williams, *Contours*, 350, 358.

77. Ibid., 223, 183.

78. Ibid., 462. On the eve of World War II, Assistant Secretary of State Francis Bowes Sayre observed how "the economic world became a battlefield"; Williams believed this remark offered "an insight of considerable value," especially considering the progressive movement's half-century commitment to the frontier thesis of prosperity and democracy. He believed these remarks helped to prove his supposition that World War II was a war for the Open Door; see Williams, *Contours*, 462.

79. Williams, *Contours*, 418.

80. Ibid., 485.

81. Harrington interview with Smail, 126.

82. Ted G. Goertzel, "*The Causes of World War Three*: Thirty Years Later," *Sociological Forum* 4, no. 2 (June 1989): 241.

83. C. Wright Mills, *The Power Elite* (New York: Oxford University Press, 1956), 3–4.

84. Ibid., 4, 18, 26.

85. Ibid., 166, 211–12.

86. Ibid., 131.

87. Ibid., 212, 213.

88. Ibid., 212, 215.

89. C. Wright Mills, *The Causes of World War Three* (New York: Ballantine Books, 1958), 66.

90. Ibid., 73.

91. Ibid., 81.

92. Mills, *Power Elite*, 361.

93. Mills, *Causes of World War Three*, 26, 21.

94. Mills, *Power Elite*, 360–61.

95. Mills, *Causes of World War Three*, 127–29.

96. Leonard Reissman, "Review of *The Power Elite*," *American Sociological Review* 21, no. 4 (August 1956): 513.

97. Robert Agger, "Review of *The Power Elite*," *Social Forces* 35, no. 3 (March 1957): 287–88.

98. Goertzel, "*The Causes of World War Three*," 242.

99. Tom Hayden, "Who Are the Student Boatrockers?," *Mademoiselle*, August 1961, 334–35.

100. See Harry Magdoff, *The Age of Imperialism* (New York: Monthly Review Press, 1969), 134, 137.

101. R. W. Van Alstyne, *The Rising American Empire* (New York: Oxford University Press, 1960), 195, i. Van Alstyne's thesis was a simple one, which largely ignored economic factors; he essentially attributed US expansion to the greed and personal ambition of US policymakers.

102. Interview of Harrington by Smail, 126.

103. May, *Imperial Democracy*, 18, 159, 255, 247, 243.

104. Ibid., 258.

105. Warburg, "Review of *The Tragedy of American Diplomacy*," 273.

106. Brown, *Beyond the Frontier*, 137.

107. Williams, "Some Thoughts on Revolution," *Daily Cardinal*, 10 April 1970, 3.

108. Interview with McCormick.

109. Brown, *Beyond the Frontier*, 145, 133.

110. Interview with McCormick.

111. Perkins, "*The Tragedy of American Diplomacy*," 1.

112. Graham Stuart, "Review of *The Tragedy of American Diplomacy*," *American Journal of International Law* 54, no. 2 (April 1960): 455.

113. Warburg, "Review of *The Tragedy of American Diplomacy*," 274.

Chapter 5
The Wisconsin Interpretation Expanded

1. Tomes, *Apocalypse Then*, 4.
2. Interview of Harrington by Smail, 126.
3. Tomes, *Apocalypse Then*, 7–8.

4. Novick, *That Noble Dream*, 445.

5. Ibid., 459.

6. Interview with McCormick.

7. E-mail correspondence from LaFeber.

8. Interview of Harrington by Smail, 126–27.

9. Interview with McCormick.

10. E-mail correspondence from LaFeber.

11. Ibid.

12. E-mail correspondence from LaFeber.

13. Ibid. LaFeber revealed, "My ideas about my dissertation and then *The New Empire* came out of Fred's seminars"; this was the last teaching Harrington did before taking up his new role in the administrative side of UW life.

14. LaFeber, *New Empire*, xxxi.

15. Osgood, *Ideals and Self-Interest in America's Foreign Relations*, 27.

16. May, *Imperial Democracy*, 269–70.

17. LaFeber, *New Empire*, xviii.

18. Ibid., xvi.

19. Ibid., 60, 6.

20. Ibid., 61, 24, 25.

21. Ibid., 105–6.

22. Ibid., 301.

23. Ibid., 400.

24. Ibid., 143, 268.

25. Ibid., 410.

26. Ibid., 62.

27. Ibid., 72, 73.

28. Ibid., 92.

29. Ibid., 98.

30. Osgood, *Ideals and Self-Interest in America's Foreign Relations*, 27, 28.

31. LaFeber, *New Empire*, 417, 416.

32. Ibid., xxxii.

33. Pratt, *America's Colonial Experiment*, 241–42.

34. LaFeber, *New Empire*, xxxii.

35. E-mail correspondence from LaFeber.

36. LaFeber, *New Empire*, 417.

37. Ibid., 416.

38. E-mail correspondence from LaFeber. Williams frequently used to tease LaFeber about his relative caution. LaFeber recalled in an e-mail to me how Williams once gave him a copy of *Tragedy* inscribed with the message "Don't frown so, Walt. It doesn't say that the answer has to be socialism."

39. See Lloyd Gardner, *Economic Aspects of New Deal Diplomacy* (Madison: University of Wisconsin Press, 1964).

40. LaFeber, *New Empire*, 410, 411.
41. McCormick, *China Market*, 7–9.
42. Interview with McCormick.
43. McCormick, *China Market*, 106–7.
44. Ibid., 60, 54, 62.
45. Ibid., 106–7.
46. Ibid., 10.
47. Ibid., 9.
48. Williams, *Contours*, 366.
49. McCormick, *China Market*, 10, 24.
50. Ibid., 7.
51. Williams, *Tragedy*, 3rd ed., 56.
52. McCormick, *China Market*, 128.
53. Williams, *Tragedy*, 1st ed., 37; McCormick, *China Market*, 128.
54. Williams, *Tragedy*, 1st ed., 39, 43.
55. McCormick, *China Market*, 145, 155, 186, 184, 185.
56. Williams, *Tragedy*, 1st ed., 34, 53.
57. McCormick, *China Market*, 137.
58. Ibid., 154.
59. Ibid.
60. Ibid., 125.
61. Interview with McCormick.
62. McCormick, *China Market*, 34, 123.
63. Although Williams's analysis implied that a consensus existed on the desire to annex Hawaii in 1893, he did not explain why the island was not annexed until 1898. This is why LaFeber's *New Empire* provided a more convincing interpretation of the Hawaiian issue.
64. Williams, *Roots of the Modern American Empire*, 60.
65. Ibid., 41, 420–21.
66. Carl N. Degler, "Review of *The Roots of the Modern American Empire*," *American Historical Review* 75, no. 6 (1970): 1781.
67. McCormick, *China Market*, 10.
68. Edmund Ions, "Review of *The Roots of the Modern American Empire*," *English Historical Review* 87, no. 344 (1972): 647.
69. David M. Pletcher, "Review of *The Roots of the Modern American Empire*," *Journal of American History* 57, no. 1 (1970): 173.
70. Williams, *Tragedy*, 3rd ed., 206–9.
71. See Hogeboom, "The New Left and the Revision of American History," 54; Unger, "The 'New Left' and American History," 1242, 1244.
72. Interview of Harrington by Smail, 125–27.
73. Walter LaFeber, *America, Russia and the Cold War, 1945–1966* (New York: John Wiley and Sons, 1967), 2.

74. Ibid., 30, 31.

75. Ibid., 52.

76. Ibid., 12, 20.

77. Lloyd Gardner, *Architects of Illusion: Men and Ideas in American Foreign Policy, 1941–1949* (Chicago: Quadrangle Books, 1970), x.

78. LaFeber, *America, Russia and the Cold War*, 90, 91.

79. Ibid., 173.

80. Ibid., 57, 11.

81. Ibid., 78.

82. Ibid., 212.

83. Ibid., 167, 256.

84. E-mail correspondence from LaFeber.

85. James A. Field, "American Imperialism: The Worst Chapter in Almost Any Book," *American Historical Review* 83, no. 3 (1978): 645, 650.

86. Ibid., 650–51.

87. LaFeber, *New Empire*, 415.

88. Field, "American Imperialism," 665–66.

89. E-mail correspondence from LaFeber.

Chapter 6
The Student Radicals

1. Andrew Hunt, "How New Was the New Left?," in McMillian and Buhle, *New Left Revisited*, 141–42.

2. David Caute, *The Year of the Barricades: A Journey through 1968* (New York: Harper and Row, 1988), 37–39.

3. See Staughton Lynd, *Living Inside Our Hope* (Ithaca, NY: Cornell University Press, 1997).

4. Hunt, "How New Was the New Left?," 141.

5. John McMillian, "Introduction," in McMillian and Buhle, *New Left Revisited*.

6. Hunt, "How New Was the New Left?," 141–42.

7. Barbara Ehrenreich, "Legacies of the 1960s: New Rights and New Lefts," in *Sights on the Sixties*, ed. Barbara L. Tischler (New Brunswick, NJ: Rutgers University Press, 1992), 233.

8. Madison Students for a Democratic Society, "What Is SDS?," unpublished flyer, 1969, UW Steenbock Library Archives, Student Unrest Subject Files.

9. "Twenty Years of Counter-Revolution: The United States in Greece," *Connections*, May 1967, 1–4.

10. SDS, "There Is No Moratorium on the Struggle against US Imperialism," unpublished event flyer, November 1966, UW Steenbock Library Archives, Student Unrest Subject Files.

11. "Twenty Years of Counter-Revolution," *Connections*, May 1967, 4–5.

12. Ibid.

13. UW Committee to End the War in Vietnam, "Hiroshima and Hanoi," unpublished event flyer, circa 1966, UW Steenbock Library Archives, Student Unrest Subject Files.

14. Che Guevara, "Cuba: Exceptional Case?," in *History as It Happened: Selected Articles from "Monthly Review," 1949–1989*, ed. Bobbye S. Ortiz (New York: Monthly Review Press, 1990), 63, 62, 64.

15. University of Wisconsin SDS Anti-Imperial Research and Action Project, *Stability and Progress*, unpublished pamphlet, circa 1967, 7, 4, 5, 7, UW Steenbock Library Archives, Student Unrest Subject Files.

16. Young Socialist Alliance, "Repression, Rights and Resistance," unpublished flyer, 28 February 1968, UW Steenbock Library Archives, Student Unrest Subject Files.

17. Paul Buhle, "SDS Split in Chicago," *Kaleidoscope*, 7 July 1969, 18.

18. SDS, "The Moratorium Is a Cover, Not a Solution," *New Left Notes*, October 1969, 1–2.

19. Buhle and Rice-Maximin, *William Appleman Williams*, 146.

20. Interview with McCormick.

21. Gaddis, "The Emerging Post-Revisionist Synthesis on the Origins of the Cold War," 173.

22. Interview of Harrington by Smail, 126–27.

23. Maraniss, *They Marched into Sunlight*, 105.

24. Interview with McCormick.

25. Interview of Harrington by Smail, 130.

26. Interview with McCormick.

27. "Nuremberg," *Connections*, 23 March 1968.

28. "Terrorism Lives," *Connections*, September 1967, 12.

29. The *Daily Cardinal* warned against violent revolution, but often criticized the university in the late 1960s, as well as condemning US foreign policy in Vietnam.

30. "War in Vietnam: Continuing Crisis," *Daily Cardinal*, Fall Registration Issue, 1967, 1.

31. The Editors, "Big Deal," *Daily Cardinal*, 17 October 1967, 2.

32. Buhle, *History and the New Left*, 34.

33. The Editors, "The Radicalism of Disclosure," *Studies on the Left* 1, no. 1 (Fall 1959): 4.

34. Williams, "My Life in Madison," 271.

35. Mattson, "Between Despair and Hope," 36–37.

36. Maraniss, *They Marched into Sunlight*, 98.

37. Young Socialist Alliance, "Repression, Rights and Resistance."

38. "The Dow Protest: A Narrative," *Connections*, The Dow War Edition, November 1967, 3.

39. Maraniss, *They Marched into Sunlight*, 387.

40. "Connectorial," *Connections*, October 1967, 7.

41. "Terrorism Lives," *Connections*, September 1967, 12.

42. "The Dow Protest: A Narrative," *Connections*, The Dow War Edition, November 1967, 3.

43. SDS, *The Call*, 1 March 1968, 3–4.

44. Walter Draude Jr., "House of Ill-Repute," *Connections*, 22 October 1967, 14.

45. "No Confidence," *Daily Cardinal*, 20 October 1967, 2.

46. University Community Action Party, unpublished flyer distributed at UW, 10 November 1967, UW Steenbock Library Archives, Student Unrest Subject Files.

47. SDS Positioning Paper, unpublished flyer, 23 October 1968, UW Steenbock Library Archives, Student Unrest Subject Files.

48. University of Wisconsin SDS Anti-Imperial Research and Action Project, *Stability and Progress*, unpublished pamphlet, circa 1967.

49. UW Students for a Democratic Society, *In the Firing Line*, unpublished pamphlet, August 1968, UW Steenbock Library Archives, Student Unrest Subject Files.

50. "On the Western Front," *Connections*, February 1968, 4.

51. UW Committee to End the War in Vietnam, "Crisis Newsletter," unpublished literature, November 1968, UW Steenbock Library Archives, Student Unrest Subject Files.

52. SDS, *The Call*, vol. 2, April 1968.

53. Allen Swerdlowe and Amy Tankoos, "History Faculty Loses Williams," *Daily Cardinal*, 8 March 1969, 1. Williams's departure was not officially announced until March 1969, although he spent much time in Oregon beforehand.

54. "Statement by History Students," *Daily Cardinal*, 7 March 1969, 9.

55. Interview with McCormick; "William Williams: Some Thoughts on Revolution," *Daily Cardinal*, 10 April 1970, 3.

56. Williams, "Some Thoughts on Revolution," *Daily Cardinal*, 10 April 1970, 10.

57. Ibid., 3, 19.

58. William Appleman Williams, "Faculty Focus: Protests and Placement," *Daily Cardinal*, 29 November 1967, 2.

59. Carl Oglesby, "Notes on a Decade Ready for the Dustbin," *Kaleidoscope*, June 1969, 10.

60. See Maraniss, *They Marched into Sunlight*, 396, 324.

61. Young Socialist Alliance, "Repression, Rights and Resistance."

62. "Manifesto," *Kaleidoscope*, 23 June 1967, 2.

63. Unpublished SDS pamphlet distributed on UW campus, 31 October 1968, UW Steenbock Library Archives, Student Unrest Subject Files.

64. "Manifesto," *Kaleidoscope*, 23 June 1967, 2.

65. Interview of Harrington by Smail, 128–30.

66. Interview with McCormick.

67. Hunt, "How New Was the New Left," 144.

68. Williams, "My Life in Madison," 271.

69. Interview with McCormick.
70. Ibid.
71. Ibid.

Chapter 7
The New Left Intellectuals

1. Arthur Schlesinger Jr., "The Origins of the Cold War," *Foreign Affairs* 46, no.1 (October 1967): 52.

2. David Horowitz, *The Free World Colossus: A Critique of American Foreign Policy in the Cold War*, rev. ed. (New York: Hill and Wang, 1971), 3.

3. Tomes, *Apocalypse Then*, 113, 117.

4. Ibid., 183, 179.

5. Norman Mailer, *Armies of the Night* (Harmondsworth: Penguin Books, 1968), 169.

6. Norman Mailer, *Why Are We in Vietnam?* (1967; reprint, New York: Picador, 2000), 3.

7. Unger, "The 'New Left' and American History," 1244.

8. Ibid., 1245–46.

9. Foster Rhea Dulles, "Review of *The Tragedy of American Diplomacy*," *American Historical Review* 64 (July 1959): 1022–23.

10. Wiener, "Radical Historians and the Crisis in American History," 400.

11. Tomes, *Apocalypse Then*, 118.

12. LaFeber, *New Empire*, xxxiii.

13. Gaddis, "The Emerging Post-Revisionist Synthesis on the Origins of the Cold War," 173.

14. Unger, "The 'New Left' and American History," 1246, 1251.

15. Rossinow, "Restless Natives," 164.

16. Horowitz's *Free World Colossus* quoted Williams on many occasions; the book's preface even began with a Williams quote about the idea of history. The quote here refers to Williams's take on US-Cuban relations; see *The Free World Colossus*, 196.

17. Gabriel Kolko, *The Politics of War: The World and United States Foreign Policy, 1943–1945* (1968; reprint, New York: Pantheon Books, 1990), 346.

18. Ibid., 4, 5, 7, 40.

19. Ibid., 624–25.

20. Gabriel Kolko, *The Roots of American Foreign Policy* (Boston: Beacon Press, 1969), 88.

21. Magdoff, *Age of Imperialism*, 13–14.

22. Kolko, *Politics of War*, 347.

23. Wolfgang J. Mommsen, *Theories of Imperialism* (1977; reprint, Chicago: University of Chicago Press, 1980), 17, 47.

24. See Kwame Nkrumah, *Neo-Colonialism: The Last Stage of Imperialism* (London: Thomas Nelson and Sons, 1965).

25. Mommsen, *Theories of Imperialism*, 82.

26. David Horowitz, *Empire and Revolution* (New York: Vintage Books, 1969), 54.
27. Ibid., 231.
28. Magdoff, *Age of Imperialism*, 34.
29. Ibid., 88.
30. Williams, *Contours*, 450; Horowitz, *Empire and Revolution*, 249, 250, 254, 255.
31. Horowitz, *Empire and Revolution*, 233.
32. Kolko, *Politics of War*, 445, 165.
33. Horowitz, *Free World Colossus*, 403.
34. Ibid., 69, 68, 72.
35. Ibid., 341, 142, 127, 84.
36. Ibid., 84, 229, 182–85, 211.
37. Ibid., 423.
38. Ibid., 81.
39. Ibid., 425.
40. H. G. Nicholas, "Review of *Free World Colossus*," *International Affairs* 42, no. 4 (October 1966): 769.
41. Horowitz, *Free World Colossus*, 222.
42. Mommsen, *Theories of Imperialism*, 122–23.
43. Kolko, *Roots of American Foreign Policy*, 48.
44. Steven Hurst, *Cold War US Foreign Policy: Key Perspectives* (Edinburgh: Edinburgh University Press, 2005), 30.
45. Magdoff, *Age of Imperialism*, 166.
46. Kolko, *Politics of War*, 624, 263, 293–94.
47. Nearing and Freeman, *Dollar Diplomacy*, 17.
48. Kolko, *Roots of American Foreign Policy*, 85–87.
49. Horowitz, *Empire and Revolution*, 31–32.
50. Ibid., 31, 33.
51. Nearing and Freeman, *Dollar Diplomacy*, xii.
52. Vladimir Lenin, "A Caricature of Marxism and Imperialist Economism," quoted in *The New Economics*, ed. Evgeny Preobrazhensky (Oxford: Clarendon Press, 1965), 154.
53. Magdoff, *Age of Imperialism*, 21–26.
54. Leon Trotsky, *The Age of Permanent Revolution* (New York: Dell Publishing, 1964), 210. Horowitz quoted these words himself; see Horowitz, *Empire and Revolution*, 230.
55. Magdoff, *Age of Imperialism*, 175. Magdoff argued that because "political freedom" was "equated with Western-style democracy," and the economic basis of this democracy was free enterprise, "the political aim of the defense of the free world must also involve the defense of free trade."
56. Tomes, *Apocalypse Then*, 79.
57. Kolko, *Roots of American Foreign Policy*, 88, 89.
58. Ibid., 24, 25, 17.
59. Ibid., 14, 26.
60. Hurst, *Cold War US Foreign Policy*, 50.

61. Ibid., 48.
62. Mommsen, *Theories of Imperialism*, 146, 147, 149.
63. Ibid., 147–149.
64. Kolko, *Politics of War*, 302–3.
65. Magdoff, *Age of Imperialism*, 11.
66. Ibid., 9, 10.
67. Ibid., 12.
68. Mommsen, *Theories of Imperialism*, 144–48.
69. Ibid., 144–45.
70. Maddox, *The New Left and the Origins of the Cold War*, 16, 19, 101.
71. Robert W. Tucker, *Nation or Empire? The Debate over American Foreign Policy* (Baltimore: Johns Hopkins University Press, 1968), 81–82.
72. Kolko, *Politics of War*, 625.
73. Magdoff, *Age of Imperialism*, 38.
74. Hurst, *Cold War US Foreign Policy*, 6, 10, 53, emphasis added.
75. Ibid., 55.
76. Magdoff, *Age of Imperialism*, 197.
77. Ibid., 197, 198.
78. Ibid., 88, 99.
79. Horowitz, *Empire and Revolution*, 112, 111, 112, 113.
80. Kolko, *Roots of American Foreign Policy*, 72, 71.
81. Magdoff, *Age of Imperialism*, 127, 143.
82. Kolko, *Roots of American Foreign Policy*, 50.
83. Horowitz, *Empire and Revolution*, 38.
84. Ibid., 243–44.
85. Gar Alperovitz, "The United States, the Revolutions, and the Cold War: Perspective and Prospect," in *Cold War Essays*, ed. Gar Alperovitz (New York: Anchor Books, 1970), 76–78.
86. Ibid., 87.
87. Gardner, *Architects of Illusion*, 208.
88. Tucker, *Nation or Empire?*, 157.

Conclusion

1. Bacevich, *American Empire*, 7.
2. Barton Bernstein, "Cold War Orthodoxy Restated," *Reviews in American History* 1 (1973): 460.
3. Novick, *That Noble Dream*, 454.
4. Tomes, *Apocalypse Then*, 232–33.
5. Rosenberg, "The 'Empire' Strikes Back," 585–86.
6. See Robin Winks, "The American Struggle with 'Imperialism': How Words Frighten," in *The American Identity: Fusion and Fragmentation*, ed. Rob Kroes (Amsterdam: Amsterdam University, 1980), 143–77.

7. See David M. Pletcher, "Rhetoric and Results: A Pragmatic View of American Economic Expansion, 1865–1898," *Diplomatic History* 5 (Spring 1981): 103.

8. Crapol, "Coming to Terms with Empire," 98–99.

9. Bacevich, *American Empire*, 3.

10. Tomes, *Apocalypse Then*, 77, 29.

11. Ibid., 27–28.

12. Bacevich, *American Empire*, 28.

13. Crapol, "Coming to Terms with Empire," 103.

14. Bacevich, *American Empire*, 243.

15. Unger, "The 'New Left' and American History," 1242.

16. Ibid., 1262; see also William Appleman Williams, *History as a Way of Learning; Articles, Excerpts, and Essays* (New York: New Viewpoints, 1973).

17. Hogeboom, "The New Left and the Revision of American History," 54.

18. Lloyd Gardner, "Review of Paul Buhle, ed., *History and the New Left: Madison, Wisconsin 1950–1970*," *History of Education Quarterly* 32, no. 2 (Summer 1992): 243.

19. Tomes, *Apocalypse Then*, 222, 233.

20. Novick, *That Noble Dream*, 457; although New Left scholars like Kolko made similar assertions, Williams made them first. Furthermore, it is important to stress that post-revisionists rejected economic determinism outright.

21. John Lewis Gaddis, *The United States and the Origins of the Cold War* (New York: Colombia University Press, 1972), 317, 21, 353.

22. Ibid., viii, 357, 360–61. Gaddis claimed that US policymakers exaggerated somewhat the threat of Soviet communism to drum up support for the Truman Doctrine. Therefore, his argument that US policymakers should be absolved from blame, because they were at the mercy of public opinion, was hard to accept.

23. Melvyn Leffler, "The Cold War: What Do 'We Now Know'?" *American Historical Review* 104, no. 2 (April 1999): 503.

24. Gaddis, *The United States and the Origins of the Cold War*, 23, 357.

25. Thomas G. Paterson, J. Garry Clifford, and Kenneth Hagan, *American Foreign Policy: A History* (Toronto: D.C. Heath and Company, 1977), 163–64.

26. Ibid., 182, 192.

27. Ibid., 274, 329.

28. Ibid., 505, 594.

29. Ibid., 251.

30. Emily Rosenberg, *Spreading the American Dream* (New York: Hill and Wang, 1982), 232–33.

31. John Lewis Gaddis, "New Conceptual Approaches to the Study of US Foreign Relations: Interdisciplinary Perspectives," *Diplomatic History* 14, no. 3 (July 1990): 419.

32. See Philip Darby, *Three Faces of Imperialism: British and American Approaches to Asia and Africa, 1870–1970* (New Haven, CT: Yale University Press, 1987).

33. Paul Kennedy, *The Rise and Fall of the Great Powers* (New York: Random House, 1987), 392–93.

34. Interview with McCormick.

35. Darby, *Three Faces of Imperialism*, 1.

36. E-mail correspondence from LaFeber.

37. Joseph Fry, "Phases of Empire," in *The Gilded Age: Essays on the Origins of Modern America*, ed. Charles W. Calhoun (Wilmington, DE: Scholarly Resources, 2000), 264, 267, 280, 282–83.

38. Bacevich, *American Empire*, 3, 4, 79, 77.

39. Ibid., 6, 85, 77, 72–73.

40. Buhle, *History and the New Left*, 3.

41. Crapol, "Coming to Terms with Empire," 103, 98–99.

42. Rossinow, "Restless Natives," 171.

43. Crapol, "Coming to Terms with Empire," 98.

44. Gaddis, "New Conceptual Approaches," 416.

Bibliography

Archival Research

UNIVERSITY OF WISCONSIN–MADISON STEENBOCK LIBRARY ARCHIVES

Frederick Jackson Turner Papers
History Department Correspondence and Clippings
History Students Association File
Merle Curti Papers, 1943–67
Printed History Course Materials
Student Unrest Subject Files (Protest flyers, radical pamphlets, newsletters, Madison Students for a Democratic Society literature)
William Appleman Williams biographical file

UNIVERSITY OF WISCONSIN–MADISON MEMORIAL LIBRARY

Studies on the Left

WISCONSIN HISTORICAL SOCIETY

Articles from *The Nation*, *I. F. Stone's Weekly*, *New York Review of Books*, *New Yorker*, *New York Times*, *Village Voice*, *Daily Compass*, *New Left Notes*, *Capital Times*, *Vietnam Courier*
Newsletter of the Radical Caucus of the American Historical Association
Radical America: Correspondence with readers and contributors
The Rights and Responsibilities of Universities and Their Faculties: A Statement by the Association of American Universities (Princeton, NJ: Princeton University Press, 1953)
Staughton Lynd Papers
Students for a Democratic Society Records, 1958–1970
Studies on the Left Papers
William B. Hesseltine Papers

UNIVERSITY OF WISCONSIN ORAL HISTORY PROGRAM

Interview of Merle Curti by Laura Smail, 1981, Transcript 27
Interview of Merle Curti and Vernon Carstensen by Barry Teicher, 1986, Transcript 333

Interview of Fred Harvey Harrington by Laura Smail, 1985, Transcript 135
Interview of Thomas McCormick by Earl Mulderink, 1982, Transcript 266
Interview of George Mosse by Laura Smail, 1982, Transcript 227
Interview of William Sewell by Laura Smail, 1977, Transcript 101

INTERVIEWS AND CORRESPONDENCE

E-mail correspondence with Walter LaFeber, 30 October 2012
Interview with Thomas McCormick, recorded at the University of Wisconsin, 28 July 2009

JOURNALS, MAGAZINES, NEWSPAPERS

American Historical Review
Connections
Daily Cardinal
Diplomatic History
International Affairs
Journal of American History
Journal of Political Economy
Kaleidoscope
Monthly Review
Nation
New Left Notes
New York Review of Books
Political Science Quarterly
Ramparts
Reviews in American History
Studies on the Left
Village Voice
William and Mary Quarterly

Books and Journal Articles

Alperovitz, Gar. *Atomic Diplomacy: Hiroshima and Potsdam*. New York: Vintage Books, 1965.

———, ed. *Cold War Essays*. New York: Anchor Books, 1970.

———. "The United States, the Revolutions, and the Cold War: Perspective and Prospect." In *Cold War Essays*, edited by Gar Alperovitz, 75–121. New York: Anchor Books, 1970.

Bacevich, Andrew J. *American Empire: The Realities and Consequences of U.S. Diplomacy*. Cambridge, MA: Harvard University Press, 2002.

Bailey, Thomas A. *America Faces Russia*. Ithaca, NY: Cornell University Press, 1950.

Barnes, Harry Elmer. *Perpetual War for Perpetual Peace: A Critical Examination of the Foreign Policy of Franklin Delano Roosevelt and Its Aftermath*. Caldwell, ID: Caxton Printers, 1953.

Barrow, Clyde W. *More Than a Historian: The Political and Economic Thought of Charles A. Beard.* New Brunswick, NJ: Transaction Publishers, 2000.

Beard, Charles. *The Devil Theory of War: An Inquiry into the Nature of History and the Possibility of Keeping Out of the War.* New York: Vanguard Press, 1936.

———. *The Economic Basis of Politics.* 1922. Reprint, New York: Alfred A. Knopf, 1945.

———. *An Economic Interpretation of the Constitution of the United States.* 1913. Reprint, New York: MacMillan, 1948.

———. *A Foreign Policy for America.* New York: Alfred A. Knopf, 1940.

———. *The Idea of National Interest: An Analytical Study in American Foreign Policy.* New York: MacMillan, 1934.

———. *The Open Door at Home: A Trial Philosophy of National Interest.* New York: MacMillan, 1934.

———. *President Roosevelt and the Coming of War: A Study in Appearances and Realities.* New Haven, CT: Yale University Press, 1948.

Beard, Charles, and William Beard. *The American Leviathan: The Republic in the Machine Age.* New York: MacMillan, 1930.

Beisner, Robert. *From the Old Diplomacy to the New, 1865–1900.* New York: Thomas Y. Cromwell, 1975.

———. *Twelve Against Empire.* New York: McGraw-Hill, 1968.

Bell, Jonathan. *The Liberal State on Trial: The Cold War and American Politics in the Truman Years.* New York: Columbia University Press, 2004.

Bemis, Samuel Flagg. *A Diplomatic History of the United States.* London: Jonathan Cape, 1936.

Benson, Lee. *Turner and Beard: American Historical Writing Reconsidered.* New York: Free Press, 1966.

Berger, Henry W., ed. *A William Appleman Williams Reader.* Chicago: Ivan R. Dee, 1992.

Bernstein, Barton. "Cold War Orthodoxy Restated." *Reviews in American History* 1 (1973): 453–62.

Brinkley, Alan. *The End of Reform: New Deal Liberalism in Recession and War.* New York: Vintage Books, 1996.

Brown, David S. *Beyond the Frontier: The Midwestern Voice in American Historical Writing.* Chicago: University of Chicago Press, 2009.

Buhle, Paul, ed. *History and the New Left: Madison, Wisconsin, 1950–1970.* Philadelphia: Temple University Press, 1990.

Buhle, Paul M., and Edward Rice-Maximin. *William Appleman Williams: The Tragedy of Empire.* New York: Routledge, 1995.

Burchett, Wilfred G. *Vietnam Will Win!* New York: Monthly Review Press, 1968.

Calhoun, Charles W., ed. *The Gilded Age: Essays on the Origins of Modern America.* Wilmington, DE: Scholarly Resources, 2000.

Cannadine, David. "Big Tent Historiography: Transatlantic Obstacles and Opportunities in Writing the History of Empire." *Common Knowledge* 11, no. 3 (Fall 2005): 375–92.

———. *Ornamentalism: How the British Saw Their Empire.* Oxford: Oxford University Press, 2001.

Caute, David. *The Year of the Barricades: A Journey Through 1968*. New York: Harper and Row, 1988.

Chomsky, Noam. *American Power and the New Mandarins*. Middlesex: Penguin Books, 1969.

———. *For Reasons of State*. Suffolk: Fontana, 1973.

Cohen, Warren I. *Empire without Tears: America's Foreign Relations, 1921–1933*. New York: Alfred A. Knopf, 1987.

Craig, Campbell. "The Not So Strange Career of Charles Beard." *Diplomatic History* 25, no. 2 (2001): 251–74.

Crapol, Edward. "Coming to Terms with Empire: The Historiography of Late Nineteenth-Century American Foreign Relations." In *Paths to Power: The Historiography of American Foreign Relations to 1941*, edited by Michael J. Hogan, 79–116. Cambridge: Cambridge University Press, 2000.

Darby, Philip. *Three Faces of Imperialism: British and American Approaches to Asia and Africa, 1870–1970*. New Haven, CT: Yale University Press, 1987.

DeSantis, Hugo. "The Imperial Impulse and American Innocence, 1965–1990." In *American Foreign Relations: A Historiographical Review*, edited by Gerald K. Hainer and J. Samuel Walker, 63–90. Westpoint, CT: Greenwood Press, 1981.

Diggins, John Patrick. *The Rise and Fall of the American Left*. New York: W. W. Norton, 1992.

Doyle, Michael W. *Empires*. Ithaca, NY: Cornell University Press, 1986.

Eckes, Alfred E., Jr. "Open Door Expansion Reconsidered: The World War II Experience." *Journal of American History* 59, no. 4 (March 1973): 909–24.

Ehrenreich, Barbara. "Legacies of the 1960s: New Rights and New Lefts." In *Sights on the Sixties*, edited by Barbara L. Tischler, 227–34. New Brunswick, NJ: Rutgers University Press, 1992.

Feis, Herbert. *From Trust to Terror: The Onset of the Cold War*. New York: W. W. Norton, 1970.

Ferguson, Niall. *Colossus: The Rise and Fall of the American Empire*. London: Penguin Books, 2005.

Field, James A. "American Imperialism: The Worst Chapter in Almost Any Book." *American Historical Review* 83, no. 3 (1978): 644–68.

Fry, Joseph. "Phases of Empire." In *The Gilded Age: Essays on the Origins of Modern America*, edited by Charles W. Calhoun, 307–32. Wilmington, DE: Scholarly Resources, 2000.

Fulbright, William. *The Arrogance of Power*. New York: Random House, 1966.

Gaddis, John Lewis. "The Emerging Post-Revisionist Synthesis on the Origins of the Cold War." *Diplomatic History* 7, no. 3 (July 1983): 171–90.

———. "New Conceptual Approaches to the Study of US Foreign Relations: Interdisciplinary Perspectives." *Diplomatic History* 14, no. 3 (July 1990): 405–24.

———. *The United States and the Origins of the Cold War*. New York: Columbia University Press, 1972.

Galbraith, John Kenneth. *The Affluent Society*. Boston: Houghton Mifflin, 1958.

Gallagher, John, and Ronald Robinson. "The Imperialism of Free-Trade." *Economic History Review* 6, no. 1 (1953): 1–15.

Gardner, Lloyd. *Architects of Illusion: Men and Ideas in American Foreign Policy, 1941–1949*. Chicago: Quadrangle Books, 1970.

———. *Economic Aspects of New Deal Diplomacy*. Madison: University of Wisconsin Press, 1964.

———. "Foreword." In *The Tragedy of American Diplomacy*, by William Appleman Williams, ix–xvii. 50th Anniversary Ed. New York: W. W. Norton, 2009.

———. *Imperial America: American Foreign Policy since 1898*. New York: Harcourt Brace, 1976.

———, ed. *Redefining the Past: Essays in Diplomatic History in Honor of William Appleman Williams*. Corvallis: Oregon State University Press, 1986.

Gardner, Lloyd, Walter LaFeber, and Thomas McCormick. *Creation of the American Empire*, vol. 1. Chicago: Rand McNally, 1976.

Gardner, Lloyd, and Thomas McCormick. "Walter LaFeber: The Making of a Wisconsin School Revisionist." *Diplomatic History* 28, no. 5 (November 2004): 613–24.

Gardner, Lloyd, and Marilyn Blatt Young. *The New American Empire: A 21st Century Teach-In on U.S. Foreign Policy*. New York: New Press, 2005.

Goertzel, Ted. "*The Causes of World War Three*: Thirty Years Later." *Sociological Forum* 4, no. 2 (June 1989): 241–46.

Guevara, Che. "Cuba: Exceptional Case?" In *History as It Happened: Selected Articles from "Monthly Review," 1949–1989*, edited by Bobbye S. Ortiz, 59–71. New York: Monthly Review Press, 1990.

Hainer, Gerald K., and J. Samuel Walker, eds. *American Foreign Relations: A Historiographical Review*. Westpoint, CT: Greenwood Press, 1981.

Herring, George C. *America's Longest War: The United States and Vietnam, 1950–1975*. New York: McGraw-Hill, 1986.

Hobson, John A. *Imperialism: A Study*. 1902. Reprint, Ann Arbor: University of Michigan Press, 1965.

Hofstadter, Richard. *The Age of Reform*. New York: Vintage Books, 1955.

———. "Cuba, the Philippines, and Manifest Destiny." In *The Paranoid Style in American Politics*, edited by Richard Hofstadter, 145–87. London: Jonathan Cape, 1966.

———. *The Paranoid Style in American Politics*. London: Jonathan Cape, 1966.

———. *The Progressive Historians*. 1968. Reprint, London: Jonathan Cape, 1969.

Hogan, Michael J. *Paths to Power: The Historiography of American Foreign Relations to 1941*. Cambridge: Cambridge University Press, 2000.

Hogan, Michael J., and Thomas G. Paterson, eds. *Explaining the History of American Foreign Relations*. Cambridge: Cambridge University Press, 1991.

Hoganson, Kristin. *Fighting for American Manhood: How Gender Politics Provoked the Spanish-American and Philippine-American Wars*. New Haven, CT: Yale University Press, 1998.

Hogeboom, Willard. "The New Left and the Revision of American History." *The History Teacher* 2, no. 1 (November 1968): 51–55.

Horowitz, David. *Empire and Revolution*. New York: Vintage Books, 1969.

———. *The Free World Colossus: A Critique of American Foreign Policy in the Cold War*. 1965. Rev. ed., New York: Hill and Wang, 1971.

Hunt, Andrew. "How New Was the New Left?" In *The New Left Revisited*, edited by John McMillian and Paul Buhle, 139–55. Philadelphia: Temple University Press, 2013.

Hurst, Steven. *Cold War US Foreign Policy: Key Perspectives*. Edinburgh: Edinburgh University Press, 2005.

Isserman, Maurice, and Michael Kazin. *American Divided: The Civil War of the 1960s*. Oxford: Oxford University Press, 2004.

Johnson, Chalmers. *Blowback: The Costs and Consequences of American Empire*. London: Time Warner, 2003.

———. *The Sorrows of Empire*. New York: Verso, 2004.

Johnson, Robert David. *The Peace Progressives*. Cambridge, MA: Harvard University Press, 1995.

Kaplan, Amy. "'Left Alone with America': The Absence of Empire in the Study of American Culture." In *Cultures of United States Imperialism*, edited by Amy Kaplan and Donald Pease, 3–21. Durham, NC: Duke University Press, 1993.

Kaplan, Amy, and Donald Pease, eds. *Cultures of United States Imperialism*. Durham, NC: Duke University Press, 1993.

Karnow, Stanley. *Vietnam: A History*. London: Penguin Books, 1991.

Kennedy, Paul. *The Rise and Fall of the Great Powers*. New York: Random House, 1987.

Kimball, Roger. *The Long March: How the Cultural Revolution of the 1960s Changed America*. San Francisco: Encounter Books, 2001.

Kolko, Gabriel. *The Politics of War: The World and United States Foreign Policy, 1943–1945*. 1968. Reprint, New York: Pantheon Books, 1990.

———. *The Roots of American Foreign Policy*. Boston: Beacon Press, 1969.

———. *Vietnam: Anatomy of a War, 1940–1975*. London: Unwin Paperbacks, 1986.

Kramer, Paul. *The Blood of Government: Race, Empire, the United States, and the Philippines*. Chapel Hill: University of North Carolina Press, 2006.

———. "Empires, Exceptions, and Anglo-Saxons: Race and Rule Between the British and United States Empires, 1880–1910." *Journal of American History* 88, no. 4 (March 2002): 1315–53.

Krenn, Michael. *The Color of Empire: Race and American Foreign Relations*. Washington, DC: Potomac Books, 2006.

Kroes, Rob, ed. *The American Identity: Fusion and Fragmentation*. Amsterdam: Amsterdam University, 1980.

LaFeber, Walter. *The American Age: United States Foreign Policy at Home and Abroad Since 1750*. New York: W. W. Norton, 1989.

———. *The American Search for Opportunity, 1865–1913*. Cambridge: Cambridge University Press, 1993.

———. *America, Russia and the Cold War, 1945–1966.* New York: John Wiley and Sons, 1967.

———. *Inevitable Revolutions.* New York: W. W. Norton, 1983.

———. *Michael Jordan and the New Global Capitalism.* New York: W. W. Norton, 2002.

———. *The New Empire: An Interpretation of American Expansion, 1860–1898.* Ithaca, NY: Cornell University Press, 1963.

LaFeber, Walter, and Richard Polenberg. *The American Century: A History of the United States since the 1890s.* New York: John Wiley and Sons, 1975.

Leffler, Melvyn. "The Cold War: What Do 'We Now Know'?" *American Historical Review* 104, no. 2 (April 1999): 501–24.

Lenin, Vladimir. *Imperialism, the Highest Stage of Capitalism: A Popular Outline.* New York: International Publishers, 1933.

Levin, Gordon N., Jr. "The Open Door Thesis Reconsidered." *Reviews in American History* 2, no. 4 (December 1974): 598–605.

Levin, Matthew. *Cold War University: Madison and the New Left in the Sixties.* Madison: University of Wisconsin Press, 2013.

Lipset, Seymour Martin. "American Exceptionalism Reaffirmed." In *Is America Different? A New Look at American Exceptionalism*, edited by Byron E. Shafer, 1–45. Oxford: Oxford University Press, 1991.

Luce, Henry. "The American Century." In *America in Vietnam: A Documentary History*, edited by William Appleman Williams, Thomas McCormick, Lloyd Gardner, and Walter LaFeber, 22–27. New York: W. W. Norton, 1985.

Lynd, Staughton. *Living Inside Our Hope.* Ithaca, NY: Cornell University Press, 1997.

Lytle, Mark Hamilton. *America's Uncivil Wars: The Sixties Era from Elvis to the Fall of Richard Nixon.* Oxford: Oxford University Press, 2006.

Maddox, Robert James. *The New Left and the Origins of the Cold War.* Princeton, NJ: Princeton University Press, 1973.

Magdoff, Harry. *The Age of Imperialism.* New York: Monthly Review Press, 1969.

Mailer, Norman. *Armies of the Night.* Harmondsworth: Penguin Books, 1968.

———. *Why Are We in Vietnam?* 1967. Reprint, New York: Picador, 2000.

Maraniss, David. *They Marched into Sunlight: War and Peace, Vietnam and America, October 1967.* New York: Simon & Schuster, 2003.

Martel, Gordon, ed. *American Foreign Relations Reconsidered, 1890–1993.* London: Routledge, 1998.

Mattson, Kevin. "Between Despair and Hope: Revisiting Studies on the Left." In *The New Left Revisited*, edited by John McMillian and Paul Buhle, 28–47. Philadelphia: Temple University Press, 2003.

May, Ernest R. *Imperial Democracy: The Emergence of America as a Great Power.* New York: Harcourt Brace and World, 1961.

McCormick, Thomas. *America's Half-Century: United States Foreign Policy in the Cold War.* Baltimore: Johns Hopkins University Press, 1989.

———. *China Market: America's Quest for Informal Empire, 1893–1901.* 1967. Reprint, Chicago: Ivan R. Dee, 1990.

———. "Drift or Mastery? A Corporatist Synthesis for American Diplomatic History." *Reviews in American History* 10, no. 4 (December 1982): 318–30.

———. "What Would William Appleman Williams Think Now?" *Passport—The Official Newsletter of SHAFR* 38 (August 2007): 1–11.

McMillian, John, and Paul Buhle, eds. *The New Left Revisited.* Philadelphia: Temple University Press, 2003.

Melanson, Richard. "The Social and Political Thought of William Appleman Williams." *Western Political Quarterly* 31, no. 3 (September 1978): 392–409.

Mills, C. Wright. *The Causes of World War Three.* New York: Ballantine Books, 1958.

———. *The Power Elite.* New York: Oxford University Press, 1956.

Mommsen, Wolfgang J. *Theories of Imperialism.* 1977. Reprint, Chicago: University of Chicago Press, 1980.

Nearing, Scott. *The American Empire.* New York: Rand School, 1921.

Nearing, Scott, and Joseph Freeman. *Dollar Diplomacy: A Study in American Imperialism.* 1925. Reprint, New York: ARNO Press, 1970.

Nkrumah, Kwame. *Neo-Colonialism: The Last Stage of Imperialism.* London: Thomas Nelson and Sons, 1965.

Novick, Peter. *That Noble Dream: The "Objectivity Question" and the American Historical Profession.* 1988. Reprint, Cambridge, MA: Cambridge University Press, 1999.

Ortiz, Bobbye S., ed. *History as It Happened: Selected Articles from "Monthly Review," 1949–1989.* New York: Monthly Review Press, 1990.

Osgood, Robert. *Ideals and Self-Interest in America's Foreign Relations.* Chicago: University of Chicago Press, 1953.

Parenti, Michael. *Dirty Truths.* San Francisco: City Lights Books, 1996.

Paterson, Thomas G., ed. *American Imperialism and Anti-Imperialism.* New York: Thomas Y. Cromwell, 1973.

———, ed. *Containment and the Cold War: American Foreign Policy since 1945.* Reading, MA: Addison-Wesley Publishing, 1973.

———. *On Every Front: The Making of the Cold War.* New York: W. W. Norton, 1979.

———. *Soviet-American Confrontation.* Baltimore: Johns Hopkins University Press, 1973.

Paterson, Thomas G., J. Garry Clifford, and Kenneth Hagan. *American Foreign Policy: A History.* Toronto: D.C. Heath and Company, 1977.

Paterson, Thomas G., and Dennis Merrill, eds. *Major Problems in American Foreign Relations.* Vol. 1, *To 1920.* Boston: Houghton Mifflin, 2005.

———, eds. *Major Problems in American Foreign Relations.* Vol. 2, *Since 1914.* Boston: Houghton Mifflin, 2005.

Perkins, Bradford. "*The Tragedy of American Diplomacy*: 25 Years After." In *The Tragedy of American Diplomacy*, 3rd. ed., by William Appleman Williams, 313–34. New York: W. W. Norton, 1972.

Pletcher, David M. "Rhetoric and Results: A Pragmatic View of American Economic Expansion, 1865–1898." *Diplomatic History* 5 (Spring 1981): 93–106.

Pratt, Julius W. *America's Colonial Experiment: How the United States Gained, Governed, and in Part Gave Away a Colonial Empire.* New York: Prentice-Hall, 1950.

———. *Expansionists of 1898: The Acquisition of Hawaii and the Spanish Islands.* Baltimore: Johns Hopkins University Press, 1936.

———. *A History of United States Foreign Policy.* New York: Prentice-Hall, 1955.

Preobrazhensky, Evgeny, ed. *The New Economics.* Oxford: Clarendon Press, 1965.

Rogin, Michael Paul. *The Intellectuals and McCarthy: The Radical Specter.* Cambridge, MA: M.I.T. Press, 1967.

Rosenberg, Emily. *Spreading the American Dream.* New York: Hill and Wang, 1982.

———. "The 'Empire' Strikes Back." *Reviews in American History* 16, no. 4 (December 1988): 585–90.

Rossinow, Doug. "Restless Natives." *Reviews in American History* 25, no. 1 (1997): 163–73.

Said, Edward S. *Orientalism.* New York: Vintage Books, 2003.

Saltmarsh, John. *Scott Nearing: The Making of a Homesteader.* White River Junction, VT: Chelsea Green Publishing, 1991.

Schlesinger, Arthur, Jr. *The Bitter Heritage: Vietnam and American Democracy, 1941–1966.* Boston: Houghton Mifflin, 1966.

———. "The Origins of the Cold War." *Foreign Affairs* 46, no.1 (October 1967): 22–52.

———. *The Vital Center.* Boston: Houghton Mifflin, 1949.

Schrecker, Ellen. *Many Are the Crimes: McCarthyism in America.* Princeton, NJ: Princeton University Press, 1988.

Shafer, Byron E., ed. *A New Look at American Exceptionalism.* Oxford: Oxford University Press, 1991.

Smith, Adam. *An Inquiry into the Nature and Causes of the Wealth of Nations.* 1776. Reprint, Chicago: University of Chicago Press, 2012.

Stampp, Kenneth. *The Peculiar Institution: Slavery in the Ante-bellum South.* New York: Knopf, 1956.

Stone, I. F. *Hidden History of the Korean War.* New York: Monthly Review Press, 1952.

Strong, Josiah. *Our Country: Its Possible Future and Its Present Crisis.* New York: American Home Missionary Society, 1885.

Thelen, David P. *Robert M. La Follette and the Insurgent Spirit.* Boston: Little, Brown and Company, 1976.

Tischler, Barbara L., ed. *Sights on the Sixties.* New Brunswick, NJ: Rutgers University Press, 1992.

Tomes, Robert. *Apocalypse Then: American Intellectuals and the Vietnam War.* New York: New York University Press, 1998.

Thompson, J. A. "William Appleman Williams and the American Empire." *Journal of American Studies* 7, no.1 (April 1973): 91–104.

Trotsky, Leon. *The Age of Permanent Revolution.* New York: Dell Publishing, 1964.

"The Truman Doctrine Calls for Aid to Greece and Turkey to Contain Totalitarianism, 1947." In *Major Problems in American Foreign Relations*, vol. 2, *Since 1914*, edited by Thomas G. Paterson and Dennis Merrill, 200–201. Boston: Houghton Mifflin, 2005.

Tucker, Robert W. *Nation or Empire? The Debate over American Foreign Policy.* Baltimore: Johns Hopkins University Press, 1968.

———. *The Radical Left and American Foreign Policy*. Baltimore: Johns Hopkins University Press, 1971.

Turner, Frederick Jackson. *The Frontier in American History*. 1920. Reprint, Mineola, NY: Dover, 2010.

Unger, Irwin. "The 'New Left' and American History: Some Recent Trends in United States Historiography." *American Historical Review* 72, no. 4 (July 1967): 1237–63.

Van Alstyne, R. W. *The Rising American Empire*. New York: Oxford University Press, 1960.

Vidal, Gore. *Imperial America: Reflections on the United States of Amnesia*. New York: Nation Books, 2004.

Webber, Karl, ed. *The Best of I. F. Stone*. New York: Public Affairs, 2006.

Wiener, Jonathan M. "Radical Historians and the Crisis in American History, 1959–1980." *Journal of American History* 76, no. 2 (September 1989): 399–434.

Williams, Walter L. "United States Indian Policy and the Debate over Philippine Annexation: Implications for the Origins of American Imperialism." *Journal of American History* 66, no. 4 (March 1980): 810–31.

Williams, William Appleman. *American-Russian Relations, 1781–1947*. New York: Rinehart, 1952.

———. *Americans in a Changing World: A History of the United States in the Twentieth Century*. New York: Harper and Row, 1978.

———. *The Contours of American History*. 1961. Reprint, Chicago: Quadrangle, 1966.

———. *Empire as a Way of Life*. New York: Oxford University Press, 1980.

———, ed. *From Colony to Empire: Essays in the History of American Foreign Relations*. New York: John Wiley and Sons, 1972.

———. "The Frontier Thesis and American Foreign Policy." In *A William Appleman Williams Reader*, edited by Henry W. Berger, 89–104. Chicago: Ivan R. Dee, 1992.

———. *History as a Way of Learning: Articles, Excerpts, and Essays*. New York: New Viewpoints, 1973.

———. "The Legend of Isolationism in the 1920s." In *A William Appleman Williams Reader*, edited by Henry W. Berger, 75–88. Chicago: Ivan R. Dee, 1992.

———. "My Life in Madison." In *History and the New Left: Madison, Wisconsin, 1950–1970*, edited by Paul Buhle, 264–71. Philadelphia: Temple University Press, 1990.

———. *The Roots of the Modern American Empire: A Study of the Growth and Shaping of Social Consciousness in a Marketplace Society*. New York: Vintage Books, 1969.

———. "A Second Look at Mr. X." In *A William Appleman Williams Reader*, edited by Henry W. Berger, 68–74. Chicago: Ivan R. Dee, 1992.

———. *Some Presidents*. New York: Vintage Books, 1972.

———. *The Tragedy of American Diplomacy*. New York: World Publishing, 1959.

———. *The Tragedy of American Diplomacy*. 3rd ed. New York: W. W. Norton, 1972.

Williams, William Appleman, Thomas McCormick, Lloyd Gardner, and Walter LaFeber. *America in Vietnam: A Documentary History*. New York: W. W. Norton, 1985.

Winks, Robin. "The American Struggle with 'Imperialism': How Words Frighten." In *The American Identity: Fusion and Fragmentation*, edited by Rob Kroes, 143–77. Amsterdam: Amsterdam University, 1980.

Young, Marilyn Blatt. *The Rhetoric of Empire*. Cambridge, MA: Harvard University Press, 1968.

Films

The War at Home. Directed by Glenn Silber. New Frost Films, 1979.

Index

STUDIES IN AMERICAN THOUGHT AND CULTURE

The American Jeremiad
Sacvan Bercovitch

Back to the Land: The Enduring Dream of Self-Sufficiency in Modern America
Dona Brown

Margaret Fuller: Transatlantic Crossings in a Revolutionary Age
Edited by Charles Capper and Cristina Giorcelli

Channeling the Past: Politicizing History in Postwar America
Erik Christiansen

Ernest Hemingway: Thought in Action
Mark Cirino

Creating the College Man: American Mass Magazines and Middle-Class Manhood, 1890–1915
Daniel A. Clark

Robert Koehler's "The Strike": The Improbable Story of an Iconic 1886 Painting of Labor Protest
James M. Dennis

The Education of an Anti-Imperialist: Robert La Follette and U.S. Expansion
Richard Drake

Emerson's Liberalism
Neal Dolan

Observing America: The Commentary of British Visitors to the United States, 1890–1950
Robert P. Frankel

The University and the People: Envisioning American Higher Education in an Era of Populist Protest
Scott M. Gelber

Picturing Indians: Photographic Encounters and Tourist Fantasies in H. H. Bennett's Wisconsin Dells
Steven D. Hoelscher

Cosmopolitanism and Solidarity: Studies in Ethnoracial, Religious, and Professional Affiliation in the United States
David A. Hollinger

Cold War University: Madison and the New Left in the Sixties
Matthew Levin

Thoreau's Democratic Withdrawal: Alienation, Participation, and Modernity
Shannon L. Mariotti

The Cross of War: Christian Nationalism and U.S. Expansion in the Spanish-American War
Matthew McCullough

Seaway to the Future: American Social Visions and the Construction of the Panama Canal
Alexander Missal

Into New Territory: American Historians and the Concept of US Imperialism
James G. Morgan

Faithful Passages: American Catholicism in Literary Culture, 1844–1931
James Emmett Ryan

Imaginary Friends: Representing Quakers in American Culture, 1650–1950
James Emmett Ryan

American Evangelicals and the 1960s
Edited by Axel R. Schäfer

Countercultural Conservatives: American Evangelicalism from the Postwar Revival to the New Christian Right
Axel R. Schäfer

The Trashing of Margaret Mead: Anatomy of an Anthropological Controversy
Paul Shankman

The Presidents We Imagine: Two Centuries of White House Fictions on the Page, on the Stage, Onscreen, and Online
Jeff Smith

Unsafe for Democracy: World War I and the U.S. Justice Department's Covert Campaign to Suppress Dissent
William H. Thomas Jr.